In Ma's Footsteps

Footsteps

KATHLEEN DOYLE

POOLBEG

Published 2010
by Poolbeg Books Ltd
123 Grange Hill, Baldoyle
Dublin 13, Ireland
E-mail: poolbeg@poolbeg.com

13 5 7 9 10 8 6 4 2

A catalogue record for this book is available from the British Library.

ISBN 978-1-84223-427-3

Cover design by Glen McArdle
Typeset by Patricia Hope in Sabon 10.75/14.5

Printed by CPI Cox & Wyman, UK

www.poolbeg.com

About the author

Kathleen McGrath was born Kathleen Doyle in 1948. She is married to Alan, and they have three children – Martina, Alan Junior and Amanda – three granddaughters – Danielle, Jessica and Robin – and one great-grandson, Conor. Kathleen set up her own hairdressing business, running three salons. She has now retired and lives in Tallaght. In 2009, her first memoir, *What Would Ma Say?* was published. This is how the story continued.

Acknowledgements

I would like to thank Poolbeg Press for giving me the opportunity to write this book, following the success of *What Would Ma Say?* Special thanks to Brian for all your patience, encouragement, and hard work. Many thanks to Jean and all the staff at Eason's, The Square, Tallaght, for putting on a great launch for the first book. To my neighbour and friend Bernie, thank you so much for taking on the typing of my second book. We made a great team.

A big thank you to my sisters and brothers for encouraging me along the way. To my children and grandchildren – thanks for all your praise, which means so much to me. To everyone in the family: thank you so much for letting me tell your stories.

And finally, to my husband Alan: I couldn't have done it without you. Thank you for all your love and support.

For My Family

Prologue

I've been enjoying every minute of my retirement. Our family are all grown up, each of them doing well for themselves. Both Alan and I have our health. What more could I ask for?

We were lucky enough to be able to buy a little apartment in Portugal about five years ago and I have to say it was one of the best things we ever did. We always loved Portugal and the people there. Our apartment has become a home from home.

As I lay back in the heat of the Portuguese sun, I thought about all the hard work that Alan and myself had done over the years. Looking around me now at what we have today, it was worth every hour we put in. We've been married now for over forty years and love each other as much as we did when we first met.

Not that things came easy for us – far from it. We had some very tough times, but between us we always came through it in the end. I've always been good at counting the pennies – I got that from Ma – and would make sure that I would save every which way I could. No matter how small it was, there was always some money put by.

'All the same,' I said to Alan, who was lying beside me on the beach, 'did yeh ever think tha' yeh'd see us havin' our own little place in the sun, bein' able to come away on holidays like this? I mean, when yeh think back to when we lived with yer Grandad Pop, we didn't even have a bath to wash ourselves in. If we were lucky, we'd just about enough money to get by from week to week.'

'We've come a long way since then, Kathleen, but tha' was sheer determination and hard grafting from the pair of us. So tha's wha' has us sittin' here today – enjoyin' ourselves like this.'

'Yeh're so righ', Alan. I get tired just thinkin' about all the hours we put in between us. I must ask yeh, Alan, if yeh had yer time over again, would yeh have done anythin' different with yer life?'

'Yeh mean as regards you and me, is tha' wha' yeh're tryin' to say, Kathleen?'

'Well, actually, tha's not wha' I mean. I was thinkin' more about yeh givin' up yer job in Gallaghers and buyin' the ice-cream van. But seein' tha' yeh brought up you and me, wha' would yeh change?'

'Well now, let me see Kathleen . . . If I'd known yeh were goin' to be the biggest chatterbox tha' stood on this earth, I'd have traded yeh in years ago, and tha's for sure.'

I looked at him with half a smile. 'Jaysus, Alan, are yeh serious?'

He was laughing his head off as he spoke. 'Would yeh stop it, Kathleen! Yeh know I wouldn't change a hair on yer head for anythin' or anyone.'

'Tha's alrigh', Alan, 'cause I wouldn't change you either, so now.'

'As far as the ice-cream van is concerned, I think I would've thought it through a bit more, Kathleen, instead of jumpin' straight in the way I did. I mean, look at the way yeh had to start doin' the markets on Sundays after doin' a week's work because I wasn't bringin' in enough money in the winter. And when the van would break down and I'd be off work – it was times like tha' I was sorry.'

'Ah, would yeh get away with yerself, Alan. Yeh love bein' yer own boss and I never minded any of the extra work. Anyway, I used to enjoy headin' off for the day to spend a bit of time with me sisters. I had some craic with them over the years.'

'Wha' about yerself, Kathleen? Would you have done anythin' different?'

'There is one thing tha' I definitely wouldn't do again, and tha's live with Pop. Ma tried to warn me about livin' on somebody else's floor, as yer Da did with you, but I suppose yeh can't put an old head on young shoulders. We had to make our own mistakes. Now, havin' said tha', I was very happy livin' there and it did break me heart when we had to leave tha' little house. You know tha' more than anybody.'

'We never should've moved there in the first place, Kathleen. Tha' was all my fault.'

'It was meant to be, Alan, because so many doors opened up for us after we moved. I went out and started mixin' with people a lot more, somethin' I never did, which helped me become more outgoin', and tha's how I was able to go on and follow me dream to become a hairdresser. I really do believe everythin' happens for a reason.'

'Ah, maybe yeh're righ', Kathleen. Who knows? All I know is tha' we're at a very happy place at this time in our lives and tha's all tha' matters at the minute. Now, are yeh comin' down for a swim or are yeh goin' to keep rammagin' on all day?'

'You go ahead, Alan. I think I'll stay here for a while and get a bit of heat into me bones.'

As I lay back on the chair and closed my eyes, I listened to the sound of the waves on the beach – it was so relaxing. I thought of Ma and how tough her life had been. Between having us twelve kids, it took her all her time to keep her head above water. I'd love nothing better than to have her here with me now. I would spoil her so much. I know it's a bit of a cliché to say that we were poor but in our way we were happy, but that's the truth for my family. Anyway, I've told that story already.[1] This one's for us – for Alan and me.

[1] See *What Would Ma Say?*

1

The Geyser

I was ready to settle down to married life at last. I was so happy being married and living with Alan; he was everything I had ever wished for and more. We were still lodging with Alan's granddad, 'Pop', in Kimmage, but hopefully that wouldn't be for too long. Alan was working really hard to get enough money together for a deposit for our own house, just as he'd promised.

'Alan,' I said as we sat there drinking a cup of tea one morning, 'I'm goin' to see if I can get meself a job at the hairdressin'. It's wha' I always wanted to do and then I'll be able to help with the savin's. It's not fair on you havin' to look after everythin'.'

'Kathleen, didn't I tell yeh I'd take care of all tha'? Now, don't be worryin' yer pretty little head, will yeh? Anyway, I was just lookin' at yer Ma the other evenin' and by the looks of her she needs yeh more.'

'I have to agree with yeh, Alan, she looks so tired and worn out. Maybe I will leave it for another while. She's not able for the last two babies.' These were my little brothers, Paul, who was only two years old, and Mano, barely twelve

5

months. Mano was the last of Ma's kids – number twelve. I was the second, after young Phil.

'Come on, Kathleen, get yerself ready and I'll drop yeh off before I head off to work,' he said, giving me a nice big kiss.

'De yeh know somethin', Alan? Yeh're so good. Tha's why I love yeh so much.'

* * *

And that was it. Every morning, as soon as I had the place tidied and my washing done, I'd make my way up to Ma's house in Crumlin every day, helping her clean up and look after the kids. Phil and Carmel were working away and Noel hadn't been too long out there in the workforce, starting to fend for himself. Da had got a couple of rises in his pay packet and Ma made sure each time that he handed them over to her. Life was starting to get a little bit easier at last.

We were heading down towards Old County Road one day, making our way to the clinic to get Mano one of his needles, when Ma turned around to me and said, 'Kathleen, I have a bit of news for yeh.'

I stopped dead in my tracks, stood and looked her straight in the face 'Jaysus, Ma, don't tell me yeh're havin' a baby – please don't say yeh're havin' another baby!'

'Ah, for fuck sake, Kathleen, will yeh give it over. Didn't I tell yeh tha' door was long closed after little Mano was born? Didn't I say tha' to yeh?'

'I know, Ma. I know yeh did, but –'

'There's no buts about it, Kathleen. Now yeh're after gettin' me all annoyed and ruinin' me bit of news.'

'Sorry, Ma. Go on, tell us wha' it is.'

'Well. Well . . .' She pushed the pram through the doors of the clinic, still holding on to the words, but you could see she was bursting to tell me. 'Kathleen, I have enough money to buy the geyser for the hot water. Everybody will be able to have a proper bath from now on.'

'Jaysus, Ma, tha's great news. How did yeh manage to put the few bob by?'

'Well, Kathleen, when Noel started work I said to meself, "I don't care, I'm puttin' some of his wages by. No matter wha', come rain or shine, I'm not touchin' it." And I didn't. So will yeh come in to the gas company with me and help me pick one out?'

That's exactly what we did the very next day.

* * *

So the day finally came when there was hot water in Crumlin. No more running up and down the stairs for any of the kids the way us older ones had to, with your pot of water, getting ready to wash all your bits.

There was great excitement among the younger kids the day the geyser was installed. Even Da made his way home early that day. Ma was as proud as Punch, standing there waiting on the men to finish. They were only out the door when she was over to the taps to test the water. When that hot water came pouring out of the tap, the look on her face was priceless. She had waited so long for that day to come.

All the kids were pushing, shoving, screaming and shouting to see who'd be the first to have a splash in the bath. Ma wasn't long quietening them all down with one of her famous looks. She then turned around to me.

'Kathleen,' she said, 'I know yeh don't live here anymore, but yeh waited so long to have tha' bubble bath of yers in this house, I think you should be the first.' She handed me a bottle of bubbles. I couldn't believe Ma had remembered the way I had always gone on about that.

I got such a lump in my throat it took me all my time to hold back the tears.

'Oh, and another thing, Kathleen – when yeh're finished don't let the water out. Tha'll do a few of the younger ones to have a good wash and keep the bill down at the one time. Just because I have a few of them older ones workin' now doesn't mean I still don't have to watch me few pennies around here.'

She was still rammaging on as she gathered all the kids and made her way downstairs.

'Yer mother is righ',' Da said. 'You should be the first to hansel the bath.' He gave me a little wink as he closed the door behind him.

I thought to myself as I slipped into the water, *Things are really startin' to look up around here and it feels good.*

* * *

The months seemed to go by very quickly. I was so happy and in love that I didn't realise at first how quiet Alan had become – probably because I never stopped talking and he didn't get much of a chance to get a word in anyway. But he was extra quiet and seemed to be a million miles away, thinking to himself all the time.

'Wha's wrong with yeh, Alan?' I asked as we drove away from Ma's one evening. 'Yeh're not yerself. Is it me? Are yeh fed up? Wha' is it? Tell me.'

'Jaysus, it's nothin' like tha', Kathleen. It's me job. Me Da has to let me go. He barely has enough work for himself.'

'Oh my God, Alan, why didn't yeh tell me?'

'I was tryin' to hang out as long as I could, hopin' things might pick up.'

'How did this happen? Yer Da is always busy.'

'Ah, there's this fella after settin' himself up in business. He's goin' around the doors collectin' and deliverin' the shoes for repair. Sure, we're only gettin' half the work now. I've been sittin' on me arse for the past couple of weeks, doin' nothin'. I can't expect me Da to keep payin' me wages, so I said I'd finish up this week. I'll go around the factories, see if I can get some work. But I'll tell yeh one thing for nothin', Kathleen, I won't be gettin' anythin' like the money me Da was payin' me.'

'Tha's it, Alan, I'm definitely gettin' meself some work, I don't care wha' yeh say.'

* * *

Sure enough, a few days later, Alan had a job working in a handbag factory called Freedex, and into the bargain he got me a job there as well. Although it was only part-time, it paid more than I would have got from hairdressing, which suited me down to the ground at the time. I was bringing in a few shillings to help out with the bills and I was still able to go up to Ma when I was finished. But the money we were making between us was nothing like what Alan used to make and we were finding it a bit hard to manage. That's when Alan hit me with the bombshell.

'Kathleen, I want to talk to yeh about maybe us stayin' on here – livin' with Pop. There's no way I'm able to save any more money and we're just about gettin' by at the moment. So wha' I was thinkin', yeh know, the money tha' we have saved, we could put it into this house, and by the time I'm finished doin' it up, I promise yeh, yeh'll be well pleased with the results. It's either tha' or we try and get a flat. And believe me, they're not cheap.'

'Does tha' mean we'll never ever get our own house, Alan?'

'Who knows wha' lies ahead, love? All I know is, I'm tryin' to do the best for us for now. And stayin' here to me would be the best option.'

'Okay, if yeh think it's the righ' thing to do. But wha' if he says no?'

'By the time I'm finished suckin' up to him, tha' won't be a problem.'

* * *

Now on top of all that I had just found out I was pregnant, which wasn't supposed to be in the plans. Not at that moment in time anyway. Everything went arse about face. To top it off, Ma went crazy mad when I told her my bit of news.

'In the name of Jaysus, Kathleen,' she roared – I think half the road must have heard her that day – 'Have yeh learnt nothin' over the years, lookin' at me and rearin' most of them kids for me. Was tha' not enough to put yeh off, at least for a few years anyway? And now yeh say yeh're not goin' to have yer own house. Yeh'll be stuck down there with tha' oul' fella.'

'Ah, he's not tha' bad, Ma. Sure yeh wouldn't even know he was there half the time. Anyway I'm hardly ever there meself. If I'm not in work I do be up here with you.'

'Tha'll all change when yeh have yer own child. Mark my words, Kathleen.' Her voice was getting louder and louder.

Jaysus, I thought, *she's sayin' 'child' not 'baby'. She's really pissed off with me. I'd better try and change the subject before she has a fit altogether'.*

'Ma, Phil tells me he's goin' steady; did yeh ask him when we're goin' to meet her?'

She looked over at me, giving me one of her dagger looks, knowing full well what I was up to. 'Hmm! So I believe. He calls her Joan. She's a nurse.'

'Tha's right, Ma, he said she's real nice.'

That was it; I knew once I got her talking about Phil she'd be on a roll and that would take the suss off me, for a little while anyway.

* * *

Alan spoke to Pop about us staying on and everything was okay there.

'Yiz can stay for as long as yiz want,' he said. 'Sure I'm only too glad of the bit of company.'

'Tha's great, Pop. So is it okay if I paint and wallpaper the house? Maybe stick a bit of new furniture in. Would yeh mind us doin' tha'?'

'The place hasn't been touched in years, Alan, and I know it could do with a good overhaul, so yeh have me permission to do wha'ever yeh want. Just don't ask me to help!' I was so happy when I heard him say that.

'Yeh're all righ' there, Pop. Once I get meself goin' I'll have the place done up in no time at all.'

So we went and put every penny that we had saved into doing the house up. We already had our furniture for the bedroom, so we started there first, working our way down, painting all the woodwork white, with matching blinds for all the windows and fresh new wallpaper throughout the house. The carpet in both rooms and on the stairs was to match, a lovely chocolate brown and cream, with a wood-type lino, which was only coming into fashion at the time, in the sitting room and running on into the kitchen.

The kitchen was so small it was more like a little scullery and – can you believe this? – the bath was actually behind the kitchen door along with the sink! Not that Pop used it for washing himself in, no way; he had it filled up with turf. So that was the first thing to go, making room for a small table and chairs.

The toilet was outside the house, just off the kitchen, and it needed a right going-over, which I left for Alan to do. By the time he was finished it was spick and span. The last thing to buy was our black leather suite. (It was plastic really, but I didn't care.) I thought it was massive; with a few orange cushions here and there it really looked the part.

It took us a good few months to do but it was worth the wait and looked very well by the time we were finished. With everything so bright and fresh-looking, and with the new furniture and our bits and bobs, I was happy enough to stay living there. It felt like a proper little home now, ready to welcome our baby – which, by the way, was due any day now.

2

Dick the Cock

I'll never forget the day I went into labour. I'd finished up working two weeks earlier and as usual was heading up to Ma. I was just going into the kitchen when half the kids came charging at me, screaming their heads off. 'Quick, Kathleen, run!' they roared. 'It's Dick – he's on the table and gettin' ready to charge. Run!'

Before I go any further, I have to tell the story about Dick. Ma came home one day with a wooden box. I thought there was food in it. I suppose it was food, but in a different way – fresh eggs every day.

'Gather around, everybody,' she said as she slowly lifted the lid off the box. 'Look wha' I bought.'

There they were, twelve tiny little chickens. One of them turned out to be a cock, which we named Dick, who was mad from day one. Every time you looked at him he'd be up on the hens, tearing the backs off them. He was a randy little bastard. We were always throwing stones at him so he would leave them alone.

He never forgot that – us disturbing him in his hour of passion. Because of that, he hated every one of us. Except for Clare, of course – she wouldn't hurt a fly. He'd sit there and let her rub him. As for the rest of us, whenever he got the chance, you would see him getting himself ready. First the wings would spread; then he'd tilt his head, screaming out his chorus of 'cock-a-doodle-do'. The two legs would start pushing out the soil beneath him. Then the charge would come.

If you weren't quick enough, the ankles would be pecked off you, and if he was really wound up and got a good run at you, he'd latch on to your back and start pecking away.

Now you know why the kids were all running past me, and I was right behind them, holding onto my bump and struggling to get up the stairs after them. We just about made it into the bathroom, locking the door behind us. I sat down on the toilet seat, gasping for breath. You could hear Dick scratching away like mad at the door.

'Where the hell is Ma?' I asked. 'And how did he get into the kitchen?'

'We were sittin' there eatin' our breakfast while Ma went down to the shops for her Woodbines,' Jacinta answered, with the lip trembling, 'when he came flyin' through the window on top of us. It wasn't our fault, Kathleen.'

'I know, I know. Don't be gettin' upset. We'll have to wait here until Ma comes back.'

I only had the words out of my mouth when a big gush of water came pouring out of me. My waters had broken. *Holy Jaysus*, I thought to myself, *I don't believe this is happenin'*.

'Kathleen, why are yeh pissin' on yerself?' asked Jacinta.

'Will yeh stay quiet and let me think for a minute. Throw a few of them towels on the floor to soak up the water, and then give the door a good kick. Patricia, don't just stand there

– help her.' At this stage little Paul was crying and frightened out of his wits. 'Come over here to me, love. Don't mind the bold birdie. Ma will be back in a minute and she'll sort him out. Where the hell are Clare and Marion?' I was starting to scream myself at this stage.

'They're up gettin' the milk,' said Patricia. Back then, if you had a big family you could get free milk from the local clinic.

'It's always the bloody same; when you need one of them, they're never around.' I could feel the pains starting to come and panic was setting in.

There was no moving Dick; he was still scratching away and it felt like forever before we heard Ma opening the front door. She didn't know what hit her with the screams from all of us.

'Ma, Ma, is tha' you? It's Kathleen. I'm up here in the toilet with the kids. Dick's up here. He's gone mad trying to get in at us.'

'In the name of Jaysus, who let tha' bloody cock into the house? Can I not move for five minutes without all hell breaking loose around me?' Ma being Ma and afraid of nothing gave Dick such a kick up the hole, beat him down the stairs and out into the back garden that he didn't 'cock-a-doodle-do' for a few days after. 'I'm tellin' yiz, one of these days I'll ring his fuckin' neck, so I will.'

'Ma, will yeh calm down. It wasn't the kids' fault; he jumped in the window.'

'Is tha' wha' happened, Kathleen? Quick, Jacinta, Patricia, get down them stairs. Make sure the back door is closed and lock the kitchen window or he'll be back in again.'

It was only when all the shouting was over that Ma realised I was in labour.

'For Jaysus' sake, Kathleen, I thought yeh said yeh had another week or two to go?'

'So did I, Ma, but I think the fright I got trying to get away from Dick must have started me off.'

'Come on now, give Paul to me, and let's get yeh downstairs and make a nice cup of tea. We'll keep an eye on them pains. Yeh might as well be sittin' here with me for a while as be on yer own in the hospital. I've helped deliver a good few babies around here over the years, so yeh've nothin' to worry about. I'll know when to make a move.'

She sat there rammaging on about everything and anything that came into her head, all the while keeping her eye on the clock as my pains grew stronger. I wanted to hang on until Alan arrived to collect me, but Ma wasn't having any of it and, once she was sure I was ready, didn't waste any time in getting me into the hospital, with help from one of the neighbours.

Ma kicked up such a racket when I was being brought down to the labour ward. Back then there was no way anyone outside the doctors and nurses were allowed past those labour room doors. At this stage I was doing somersaults in the bed with the pain as Ma held on tight to my hand.

'We'll take over now, Mrs Doyle,' said the nurse.

'I'm not leavin'. I'm goin' in with her.'

'You know that's not allowed. Rules are rules.'

'I don't care wha' yeh say. Me child needs me.'

'Come on now, Mrs Doyle. Don't be makin' a fuss. We have to get Kathleen ready and I promise we will take good care of her.'

'I don't doubt tha' for one minute, nurse, it's just tha' I'm worried. I hate the thought of her goin' in there on her own.'

'I know that, and I'll make sure to keep you informed. Now, we really must go.'

I was scared as hell and wished Ma could come in with me, but I couldn't let her know that, or she would have kicked up more ructions.

'I'll be okay, Ma, don't be worryin'.'

'Our Lady will mind yeh, Kathleen, and I'll be here, standin' in this very spot, when they bring yeh back out.' She gave my hand a little squeeze.

* * *

First I was taken into a small cubicle.

'Right, Kathleen, get yourself up there on the couch. I have to take a look and see how many centimetres you are.'

'Nurse, de yeh have to look when yeh're doin' it?'

'Don't be shy, Kathleen, I'm doing this every day of the week. All you should be worrying about is baby. Now relax there while I give you a quick check. Yes, everything seems fine. Now, roll over on your side for me.' She stood there beside me with a plastic hose, a funnel and a bucket.

'Wha's tha' for?'

'Your enema, of course.'

'Ah, yeh're all righ', nurse, I don't need tha'. I went this mornin'.'

'Come, come now, Kathleen, this has to be done before baby is delivered. I'll have it done in no time at all.'

Talk about holding onto any bit of dignity I had – that went out the door as soon as she stuck that tube up my arse. Between the moans and groans out of me with the labour pains, if that wasn't bad enough, now on top of it I was farting and shitting to beat the band. I didn't know which end of me was up. Then I was finally brought into a small ward. There were two other girls there.

'Nurse, is this where it happens?'

'No, not at all, Kathleen. You have a fair bit to go yet, so we'll be keeping an eye on you for the next couple of hours in here. Then, at the next stage, just before baby comes into the world, we'll bring you down to the delivery room, which is down there at the end of the corridor. Now, try and have a little doze in between, and when the pains come, remember now, big deep breaths.'

One of the girls was asleep. The other girl started talking over to me. 'Howyeh, I'm Frances. Is this yer first?'

'Yeah, tha's right. I'm Kathleen.'

'Don't be nervous, yeh'll be grand! Sure look at me, this is me sixth time to be in here.'

We chatted for a good while and then suddenly she let out such a roar that I nearly shit a brick – not that there was anything left in me to do that!

'Holy Jaysus, these pains are gettin' really strong. Nurse, nurse! I need a bit of gas.'

Then the other girl sat up in the bed and started rocking up and down, up and down. 'Oh please, oh please, nurse. Oh please.' They were the only words she spoke the whole time I was there. You could see it in their faces; they were cringing with the pain. The nurse was in straight away.

'That's right, Lulu, big deep breaths. In and out, in and out. Frances, you're coming along fine, it shouldn't be too long before we're bringing you down. Kathleen, how are you doing over there? Will you have some gas now?'

'Oh, I don't know, nurse. I hate anythin' gettin' put over me face. Maybe I'll leave it.'

'Yeh won't be sayin' tha' in a little while,' said Frances. 'Yeh'll be screamin' for the fuckin' stuff.'

And she was so right. When it came to it, I was eating the mask. I held onto it so tight that I had the imprint of it on my face for hours after. It wasn't too long after that when both girls were brought down to deliver their babies. I seemed to be on my own forever. All the while I kept thinking of Ma and how strong she was to have done this so many times.

'Right, Kathleen,' I could hear the nurse saying as I came back from my thoughts. 'Baby is ready.' I was so happy to hear those words at last.

I was only in the delivery room when I had to push like mad. The nurse was standing beside me, holding my hand. She knew how nervous I was.

'Come on, Kathleen, you're doing great.'

The midwife was at the other end and, believe me, at this stage I didn't care who was looking at what.

'Right, I can see the head. One more hard push and we're there.' I squeezed the nurse's hand so tight I don't know how I didn't break her fingers. I thought my brains were going to burst, never mind down below.

'That's it, Kathleen. The head's out. Now, take it easy. Hold on. Hold on, easy now.'

Then I heard a little cry.

'It's a girl, Kathleen. You have a beautiful baby girl.' The midwife put her across my chest for a few seconds. All I could see were these big blue eyes looking straight at me. It was the most wonderful, magical feeling ever. The tears rolled down my face as I held her close to me.

'We have to check her over, Kathleen, so the nurse will finish here with you and then we'll bring her straight back over. And well done again.'

As I was wheeled out through the doors with my baby, Ma was there with Alan, just as she'd promised. The first thing she did before Alan could even get near me was to bless me and the baby with I don't know how many medals and relics she had in her purse.

'Kathleen, didn't I tell yeh the Holy Mother herself would look after yeh? And she did, thank God.' She blessed herself a half-dozen times.

19

I was soon settled on the ward and I could see Ma was dying to get her hands on the baby. 'There yeh are, Ma,' I said. 'Hold her for me while I talk to Alan for a minute.'

'I thought yeh'd never ask me, Kathleen.'

Alan sat on the side of the bed with his two arms around me, like he was never going to let me go.

'Kathleen, are yeh okay?'

'I'm a bit tired, Alan, tha's all. Isn't she gorgeous?'

'I can't believe it, a little girl; she's lovely.'

'I like the name Martina. Wha' de yeh think?'

'Wha'ever makes yeh happy, love. I'm just so proud of yeh.'

I was so overwhelmed with happiness that day I thought I would burst. Alan had just become a Da, and what a great one he was going to be. Ma was sitting there with her first grandchild in her arms and by the look on her face she was well pleased. As for myself, well, I felt I was ready now to be a real Ma at last.

3

Knickers

Alan wasn't too long gone to work and I was pottering about getting Martina ready and doing my bit of housework when I remembered that I had left my washing out on the line the night before. It was lashing rain out, so I just grabbed everything quickly off the line and made my way back inside.

I was hanging everything on the clothes-horse when I picked up a pair of my knickers. I thought I was seeing things. The whole middle was cut out of them. I thought to myself, *Wha' the fuck is after happenin' to these?* I checked the other three pairs and they were all the same – big holes in all of them. I stood there trying to get my head around it. Just as well Pop wasn't there because at that stage I was talking out loud to myself: 'Now why the fuck would somebody cut me knickers up?'

Then I started getting really annoyed. Martina was only a few weeks old and I'd just got out of my big white cotton tea-strainers, which I'd been wearing over the months when I was pregnant. I had bought a few fancy pairs of knickers – which took me a couple of weeks to save for – and some gobshite goes and does this!

I got ready and made my way up to Ma, taking the knickers with me. I showed them to her as soon as I walked in the door.

'So wha' de yeh think, Ma?'

'Wha' do I think, Kathleen?! I'll tell yeh wha' I think: tha's some dirty bastard tha' can't get himself a woman and is gettin' his bit of enjoyment outta doin' the likes of this, and God only knows wha' else. I'm tellin' yeh, there's some disturbed fuckers out there, Kathleen. Yeh want to make sure tha' when yeh're on yer own down there in tha' house, yeh keep the back door locked.'

'Jaysus, Ma, will yeh not be sayin' the likes of tha' to me? Yeh'll have me a nervous wreck.'

'Well, tha's wha' I think!' She made her way out to the door. 'I'm headin' up to ten o'clock mass. Make yerself a cup of tea. I won't be too long.'

My brother Phil was sitting over beside the fire, laughing his head off, having taken in all of what Ma was saying.

'I don't know wha' yeh think is so funny, Phil. I'm goin' to be shittin' meself down in tha' house after wha' Ma just said.'

'For Jaysus' sake, Kathleen, will yeh ever give it over. Yeh know the way she gets carried away at times, especially if she thinks it's anythin' to do with a man. Anyway, never mind Ma. Yeh know wha's after happenin' here? There was probably one or two young fellas got a glimpse of yer bits of knickers and thought tha' it would be very funny to do the likes of tha'.'

'De yeh really think tha's wha' happened, Phil?'

'I'm tellin' yeh, Kathleen, young fellas are gobshites at times. They dare one another to do all sorts of stupid things. Believe me, yeh want to see some of the things I used to get up to. Mental, so they were. So don't be gettin' yer knickers in a knot. De yeh get it? Knickers in a knot!'

He was nearly falling off the chair laughing. I suppose it was funny and I had to turn my head so he wouldn't see me smile – or I'd never hear the end of it.

Later that day, Alan was only in the door to collect me from Ma's when I launched into telling him the ins and outs of what had happened and what Ma and Phil had said. He wasn't able to keep his face straight as he broke his heart laughing along with Phil. I stood there all serious, with a face on me like I don't know what.

'I'm sorry, Kathleen, but he's makin' me laugh.' He pointed over at Phil, who had a pair of my knickers on his head with his nose sticking out through the hole. The tears were rolling down Alan's face at this stage and, I have to admit, I was laughing along with them. That's when Ma got her spoke in again.

'Yeh're worse, Kathleen, encouraging the pair of them. The smile won't be long gettin' put on the other side of yer face if tha' maniac comes back.'

'Christ, Ma! Will yeh not be sayin' tha'? Yeh'll have me tha' I won't want to go home.'

'Come on now,' said Alan. 'Let's not get all serious about this. It's just like wha' Phil said. Young fellas messin' and actin' the eejit. There yeh are, Lil, yer few smokes as always, and where's tha' famous cup of tea yeh always have ready for me?' He was trying to whisper but I could hear every word they were saying.

'Yeh're a cute hoor, yeh know tha', Alan McGrath?' said Ma. 'Gettin' in there and changin' the subject on me.'

'It's best tha' way, Lil. Yeh know wha' Kathleen's like for worryin'. She'll have me and herself awake all night, thinkin' and talkin' about this.'

'Well, Alan, I suppose when yeh put it like tha' . . .' She took the smokes and put them in her pocket. 'I'll say no more.'

So that was me, having to get back into my white cotton tea-strainers or, as they were sometimes called, 'passion-killers'. I was only glad that I didn't throw them out or I would have had to go bare-arsed until I got a few bob to buy my little fancy ones again.

* * *

A couple of weeks went by and there wasn't a problem with the washing. That was until I hung my new knickers on the line – and the same thing happened again. Big holes in all the middles. But this time it happened during the day and that really scared me, thinking that there was someone in the back garden when I was there.

'Tha's it!' said Ma when I showed them to her. 'We're goin' to the guards.'

'I'm not going down to the police station, Ma, no way.'

'Yeh either walk down with me, Kathleen, or I'll drag yeh down – yer choice, because if yeh think I'm goin' to wait around until somethin' happens to you, yeh have another thing comin'. Now, get yer coat on and hand them knickers over here to me.' Once Ma got like this, there was no going against her and she never said anything that she wouldn't back up, so it was easier to go along.

I was mortified sitting there as we waited to be seen. As soon as the guard came out to speak to us, Ma was up like a light.

'Good afternoon, ladies,' he said. 'How can I help you?'

'I want to report a crime,' said Ma. 'There's a maniac goin' around. Look, he attacked me daughter's knickers.' She slapped them down on the counter.

He looked at them and then at me. You could see he was trying very hard not to laugh. He gave a little cough, clearing his throat.

'Now, what I would need to know is, where exactly were these garments when this happened?' And that was it, he started grinning and I didn't blame him one bit. I was blushing so much I couldn't answer. Ma stepped in again.

'Well, they weren't on her, if tha's wha' yeh mean! And yeh can wipe tha' grin off yer face and take wha' I'm sayin' serious.' You could see he was taken aback when Ma came out with that. She went on, 'Well, if yeh really want to know, guard, they were on the clothes-line, and this is the second time it's after happenin'. And in broad daylight too! Which means tha' dirty bastard is watchin' my Kathleen goin' in and out. She'll end up being a nervous wreck if this keeps up. So now, wha' are yeh goin' to do about it?'

After Ma lashing him out of it, he kept a straight face this time while he spoke. 'I'll take your name and address first. We'll then send out a garda car to check around the area and if it is somebody nearby, when they see the guards that will probably frighten them off and that will be the end of it. Other than that, unless you catch somebody in the act or you have a name for me, I can do no more.'

We gave him all the details. 'Will I take the knickers with me,' asked Ma as we were going, 'or de yeh need them as evidence?'

'Hmm . . . no, that will be fine. You can take them on home with you.' I'd say by this stage the guard had his legs crossed trying to stop wetting himself.

'Ma, are yeh righ'? Come on, will yeh.' I just wanted the ground to open up and swallow me, I was so embarrassed. I didn't say anything to Ma; she was just worried and was doing what she thought was best for me.

The guards knocked on the door that evening and spent a bit of time in the back garden, letting their presence be known, which I was happy enough about. I hoped it would put an end to all this carry-on.

But no, it didn't. It happened again and again. So I stopped hanging the washing out.

* * *

'This is terrible, Alan,' I said one morning. 'I know it's a bit cold out but the weather is lovely and crisp and I can't hang me clothes out.'

'Leave it to me, Kathleen. I'll sort this out once and for all.'

So Alan had a talk with Phil and they decided they were going to catch whoever was doing it in the act, and sort it out themselves.

It was the middle of November so the nights were starting to get very cold. A couple of nights in, Alan got himself good and ready for the big watch. 'Righ', tha's me sorted,' he said as he put the lid on his flask. 'In the name of Jaysus, Phil, wha's keepin' yeh? They'll be here and gone yeh're takin' tha' long.'

'I'm comin', I'm comin',' roared Phil as he came out of the toilet. 'I hope the fuckers turn up tonight, Kathleen.'

'Jaysus, Phil, yeh're in a righ' mood.'

'So would you be. I was on a promise last night and tonight and, believe me, tha' probably won't come around again for God knows how long.'

'Would yeh ever give it over, Phil; de yeh ever have anythin' else on yer mind?'

Alan stood there with his woolly cap and his flask in his hand. You would think Phil was going to the North Pole with his big winter coat, gloves, scarf and, of course, the all-essential torch. The two of them were ready and rearing to pounce on whoever came over the back wall.

'Righ', Kathleen, now remember, turn off the lights here in the kitchen and go into the sitting-room and watch the telly. With a bit of luck, we'll catch whoever is doin' this tonight,' said Alan.

'I certainly hope so,' I said, 'or else you won't be on a promise for a very long time, 'cause I'll be back in me oul' tea-strainers again if the last few pairs of me fancy knickers get destroyed like the others.'

Off they went with a bit of a giggle. I turned the lights off just as I'd done the night before and went in to watch the telly. I wasn't five minutes sitting down when I heard all hell breaking loose in the back garden. I ran out and there were Phil and Alan, dragging two young fellas into the kitchen.

'Get in there, yeh little fucker,' said Phil. He gave one of them a right clatter in the head. 'Well, Kathleen, here's the "Knicker Rippers". Now, wha' have yeh got to say to her?'

'Sorry, Missus, we were just havin' a bit of craic. I promise we won't do it again.'

'And you!' said Alan, as he pushed the younger fella in front of me, who was starting to cry at this stage.

'Sorry, Missus. We thought it was funny. Sorry. Sorry.'

'Righ',' said Alan, 'Now get the fuck outta here, the pair of yiz, before I call the guards, and if I catch yiz around here again yeh'll get worse the next time.' He gave one of them a good kick up the arse.

I never saw anybody run and jump a fence as quick as they did, never to be seen again. I was happy enough the way things went and that it wasn't a dirty maniac, like Ma thought. Not only was I able to get a good night's sleep again, but it was also great to see my knickers blowing in the wind once more.

4

The Diggin' Match

There was no way I could go back to work after I had Martina. Ma had enough of her own kids without me asking her to mind mine, so the pressure was on Alan once more to take on the full load of being the breadwinner.

Alan's Da tried to give him a bit of work one or two evenings a week, finishing off some of the repairs on the shoes. We knew he wasn't all that busy and didn't really need him, but he was always so good to us, helping out every way he could.

Alan wasn't happy just living from week to week. Nor was I, barely getting by, never having money over to buy the little extras, maybe even having a holiday some day, which we both dreamed of. There was no way that was going to happen with the wages he was bringing in. So off he went back out into the workforce looking for a job with better money, which he got with the help of his uncle Joe, who knew somebody that knew somebody that put a good word in for him. He was so excited the day he found out he'd got the job.

'Kathleen, I can't believe it. A job in Gallagher's on the port docks; it's so hard to get in there. De yeh realise how great this is? Wha' this means for us? Me wages will more than double, and they tell me jobs come up every now and then in the main cigarette factory in Tallaght. If I can get meself in there, we'll be laughing all the way to the bank.'

I sat there listening to him going on and on. I really didn't want to burst his bubble but thought to myself, *Now's as good a time as any*.

'I have a bit of news meself, Alan, and I hope yeh'll be pleased with wha' I have to say.'

'Go on, Kathleen. Spit it out.'

Well, me being me, who never shuts up and launches into the ins and outs of everything, instead of just coming out with what I wanted to say, went on a bit that day. Alan had to stop me in my tracks.

'Tha's it, Kathleen. Stop talkin'. Now, just tell me wha' it is yeh're tryin' to say.'

'I'm afraid yeh might be annoyed, Alan.'

'Kathleen –'

'Righ'. I'm pregnant.'

His jaw dropped and I could see he was taken aback a bit, just as I had been. We both thought we had been so careful. He was quiet for a second or two, then came out with the words I needed to hear.

'Well now, Kathleen, aren't we lucky I got meself this job, now tha' we're goin' to have another little mouth to feed.'

* * *

Ma wasn't too bad the second time around when I told her my news. She never said a word but still managed to give me one of her dagger looks, which I suppose wasn't too bad, knowing Ma.

Our son Alan was born six months later, when Martina was barely two years old. There was definitely no way I would be getting myself a job and my dream of becoming a hairdresser seemed to be gone forever.

Alan was as happy as anything working in his new job, getting in as much overtime as he could get his hands on, which was great for the extra money. There's no doubt that we needed it, but I did miss him terribly and would hate going home when he wasn't there. So I would stay on a bit later in the evenings with Ma and Da.

If the truth be known, I loved all the hustle and bustle that went on, with the older ones coming in from work, fighting over who was going to get their dinner first, checking out whose chop was the biggest and giving out if anyone got more chips than they did. Chip days were a classic. Ma would be cooking for hours by the time she got around the whole gang. She would start with the smallest ones and work her way up. The rest would be starving, waiting their turn, borrowing a chip off each other as they were fed, with the promise that they would give back two in return. There was no way anyone would let you off, so by the time the older ones got their dinners, there would be very little left on their plates. I would sit there laughing to myself, listening to the wheeling and dealing going on, with some of them trying to get off paying back what they owed, and Ma in the background shouting her head off.

'Wha' do I keep tellin' yiz? Wait yer turn! But de yiz listen? No. Now yeh have to pay the price, so hand over the chips and be done with it, or yeh'll have me to answer to.'

* * *

There was never a dull moment, with plenty of scraps and digging matches going on. One particular night saw one of the biggest fights ever, or at least the biggest that I was there for.

I was sitting with young Alan in my arms, and Martina was out in the back garden playing with the younger kids. I was talking away to Da, while Ma was cooking as usual. Phil and Noel were sitting at the table with a couple of the older kids when all hell broke loose. Phil, being the messer that he is, and always getting up everyone's back, started on Noel, who had just turned seventeen and wasn't too far off as big as himself. Noel had this terrible habit of tapping his fingers on the table and it really got Phil's back up.

'Noel, stop tha' tappin'. Yeh're annoyin' me,' said Phil.

Noel stopped and then started again. I could hear all this going on in the background as I tried to listen to Da tell me about his day.

'Did yeh hear me, Noel? I told yeh to stop!'

'Yeah, and yeh're goin' to make me stop, righ'? As if I'd let yeh.'

The tapping turned into a hard banging at that stage, and Phil gave Noel a right clatter in the back of the head. Noel was so fast, he was up on his feet in no time, giving Phil a dig, straight into the face. The blood pumped out of his nose and the kids all scattered, leaving just the two of them standing there, face to face. Phil rubbed some of the blood away with his hand, laughing as he spoke.

'So, yeh're puttin' it up to me, Noel, is tha' wha' yer doin'?'

'Tha's righ', Phil. If tha's wha' it takes, yeh won't be hittin' me again.'

'Well then, may the best man win.'

With that, he went in at Noel with a left hook, right into the stomach, knocking him on top of the kitchen table, smashing it to pieces. The kids were screaming and shouting, egging on whichever of them they wanted to win. Ma was fucking and blinding out of her about the house being broken up and who was going to pay for it. I was shouting my head off for them to stop, not realising I was frightening the life out of young Alan.

Because both of them were boxers, it was like looking at a boxing match in the National Stadium. Da made sure that all the boys joined the local boxing club as soon as they were old enough. He used to make his own boxing ring in the house, making sure they all got plenty of practice in on the side. He'd use Ma's old tights, tying them around four of the kitchen chairs. He always wanted them to be the best. I think it was something he would have loved to have done himself but never got around to. So he was living his dream through the boys and, believe me, they were well able to fight.

Between the clinches, the right and left hooks were flying. At one stage I looked over at Da. He was doing a bit of shadow-boxing himself, living the part with them. That's when Ma stepped in.

'Phil Doyle,' she roared in Da's face, 'enough's enough. Now get yerself over there and stop them pair. It's gone on long enough. Look at them – neither of them will give in. They're wreckin' the fuckin' house on me.'

Poor Da got caught up between the pair of them, getting one of their fists in the face which knocked him out cold. That soon brought the fight to a halt, calming the pair of them down. They weren't long getting Da up off the floor and onto a chair. Noel splashed water on Da's face to bring him around, while the other gobshite, Phil, was at the other end tickling his feet, breaking his heart laughing as he looked up at Noel.

'De yeh know somethin'? Tha' was the best scrap I've had in I don't know how long. We should do this more often, Noel. But I tell yeh one thing, I'll be ready the next time, now tha' I know yeh're a sly fucker. The way yeh came in at me with the left hook – caught me right off me guard, so yeh did.'

'I have to say, Phil, it was a beaut.'

And, as Da finally came to, on they went with their cut lips, bloody noses and raw knuckles, talking about who got more digs in at who. At the same time they were promising Ma that they would fix her up with a new table, which kept her happy.

There were many punch-ups and digging matches over the years, some maybe a little more serious than others, but never any that wasn't sorted out at the end with a handshake and a laugh.

* * *

Phil was the only one who kept the boxing up. The rest of the boys slowly gave it up as they got older. Not a week went by that Phil wasn't fighting in the National Stadium or travelling around the country to boxing tournaments. His name became well known, which led to him boxing for the national team. He travelled to many countries in Europe, representing Ireland.

Ma and Da were so proud of him; they never missed any of his fights. I even went along with Alan a few times and, I have to say, he was some boxer, afraid of no-one. It didn't matter if his eyes were cut to bits, blood pumping from his nose, he was like a bulldog, charging in. He would just keep going until he won the fight.

I even found myself jumping up and down one night, screaming, 'Knock him out, kill him!' God, when I think back, that was a terrible thing to say, but you really got so worked up, especially when it was your own brother and his fight was the last one on the night, the one that would decide if Ireland won the title. After the match was over, we waited for the judges' decision. We were all standing there, not a sound to be heard. You could hear a pin drop. I thought Da was going to have a heart attack.

Well, when the referee lifted Phil's fist up in the air, the whole place erupted. Phil lifted the referee up, swinging him around the ring. Everybody was shaking Ma's and Da's hands, saying how proud they should be – not that they needed anybody to say that to them. They were proud as Punch. I even saw Da wipe away a tear or two when he thought nobody was looking. There were write-ups in all the papers and television interviews. In all our eyes, Phil was a star.

* * *

I really thought Phil would have settled down here, but that wasn't meant to be. He had moved to Canada but had returned around the time I got married and was here for about three years afterwards. The two of us were having a chat one day, when I turned around and asked him, 'Well, wha's the story with yerself and Joan? Yeh seem to be hittin' it off really well.'

'Well, now tha' yer after bringin' it up, Kathleen, we're thinkin' of gettin' married. Nothin' fancy, just a small weddin'.'

'Yeh sly fucker, Phil Doyle, and when were yeh goin' to tell me this? Or were yeh even goin' to bother?'

'Don't be gettin' yer knickers in a knot, Kathleen. I was hangin' on for a while just to make sure before I said anythin'. Yeh know the way it is; sometimes yeh have a few scraps, and then I'd be thinkin' to meself, for fuck's sake – is this wha' I really want – to be tied down and all tha'? I mean, Kathleen, surely yeh must've felt a little bit iffy at times before yeh tied the knot with Alan?'

'I have to say, Phil, I never felt like tha'. So yeh'd want to be really clear in yer mind wha' yeh want; otherwise, don't go ahead.'

'I'll be grand. I suppose me feet's just gettin' a bit cold, now tha' I'm actually plannin' things. Anyway, say nothin'. I'll drop the bombshell meself when I'm ready.'

And that's what he did after a few months. He not only announced that he was getting married, but that he was also going back to Canada. He'd been dropping hints here and there for a good while, so it wasn't too much of a shock for any of us.

* * *

It was a small wedding. There was just Ma, Da and a couple of us older brothers and sisters, and the same on Joan's side of the family, along with a few friends from the boxing. Phil was a cute hoor and always had a back-up plan; he had the dinner booked out in the airport hotel and their flights a couple of hours after. That left very little time between for him or any of us to get too upset. We'd all been very upset the first time Phil left for Canada. It didn't seem to be as hard the second time around as we all said our goodbyes. Even Ma held herself together a bit better this time. It helped that Phil promised that as soon as he got settled and got money behind him, he would send for both of them for the holiday of a lifetime. He was still following his dream, and who could blame him for that? Emigration had got into his blood; there was no turning back.

He seemed to settle down really well this time, so much so that they decided to start a family over there. Ma was so excited one day when a letter arrived from Phil with a ticket in it, asking her if she would be able to come over to Canada, as Joan was about to have their first baby any day, and he would love nothing better than to have her there for the arrival. It would be Ma's first holiday.

'Kathleen,' said Ma, 'yer father says he'll take care of things here, tha' he has a few weeks' holidays due to him. Would yeh drop down in between just to make sure everythin's okay? And maybe Alan might slip down the odd evenin' for a smoke and a cup of tea, keep yer Da company for an hour or two? So wha' de yeh think about me goin'?'

'Jaysus, Ma, it's the best bit of news I've heard in I don't know how long. Of course yeh should go. Yeh're after waitin' all this time to go over to Phil. Don't be worryin', Da and the kids will be fine. I promise I'll keep an eye on things.'

'Phil said tha' I don't have to worry about money. I just have to bring meself. But yeh know me, Kathleen, I like to have me own few shillin's in me pocket, especially for me smokes.'

'Yeh'll be fine, Ma, yeh won't be short. We'll all throw yeh a few bob. Anyway, never mind all tha'. Imagine, yer first holiday and all the way to Canada! I wouldn't be able for yeh.'

'I have to say, Kathleen, I have meself a bit worked up and excited at the same time. And yer Father was just sayin' to me, wouldn't it be great if it's a boy? Yeh know, to carry on the Doyle name and all tha'. Once the baby is okay, tha's all should matter, but he takes all tha' stuff serious, with him being the only boy in his family.'

Ma headed off within the next couple of days, making it just in time for the arrival of her new grandson, Philip, which Da was delighted about. Ma stayed on for a few weeks, helping out every which way she could and enjoying every minute.

She talked and talked about it for months on end afterwards, so much so that Da thought he'd never get over to see Phil and Canada. So, the following year, he took out his first credit union loan and the two of them went out. I was so happy to see them take off together. They were starting to have a bit of a life at last.

Phil went on to have two more sons, J.J. and Andrew, and ended up making his life in Canada, bringing Ma and Da over many times down the years, just like he promised.

5

Messers and Pancakes

When Ma was away in Canada with my brother Phil I would drop down to the house to check on the kids, just like I promised. It was late one afternoon when I arrived. Carmel was hanging out the washing while Paul and Mano were playing around.

I tipped Carmel on the shoulder and she jumped. 'It's very quiet around here, Carmel,' I said. 'Where's everyone?'

'Jaysus, Kathleen, yeh're after givin' me an awful fright. Why didn't yeh knock on the front door?'

'Don't be such a wimp, Carmel. The side gate was open so I just came on in. Is Da in the house? Alan gave me a few smokes for him.'

'He slipped out there about ten minutes ago to back a horse. He shouldn't be too long. Come on and I'll make yeh a cup of tea. Did yeh not bring the kids with yeh, Kathleen?'

I followed her into the kitchen and put the teapot on. The two of us sat at the table talking away about one thing and another.

'Ah, they were playin' around in the garden with a couple of their friends. Alan said he'd keep an eye to them until I got

37

back. Anyway, I never leave them; they're always with me, everywhere I go. It'll do me good to get a break for a little while. How's Da doin' with Ma not around? Is he stayin' off the drink? And no lies, de yeh hear me?'

'I swear, Kathleen, he's home every day as soon as he's finished work, with not a drop on him.'

'Tha's good. Ma will be well pleased when we tell her. All the same, Carmel, isn't the house very quiet? It's not the same without Ma. Yeh get so used to her roarin' and shoutin', fuckin' and blindin' about one thing or another.'

I only had the words out of my mouth when I heard some weird sounds coming from upstairs.

'Did yeh hear tha', Carmel? Who's up there?'

'I'm not too sure. I think Thomas is with a couple of the kids.'

'There it is again – listen, Carmel.'

As we made our way into the hall, the sounds came out, louder and clearer: *hee-haw, hee-haw*, like a donkey; *moo, moo, moo*, like a herd of cows; and the noisiest of all was grunting like a pig. That one was so real, and it went on and on. Then we could hear Thomas's voice: 'Faster, faster; louder, louder, or I'll tickle yiz to death.' He was laughing his head off.

'Holy Jaysus, Carmel, wha's tha' Thomas fella up to? Come on upstairs and let's see wha' he's doin'.'

We didn't make a sound as we sneaked up the stairs and had the door open before he knew it. There was Thomas, standing on the bed with a fishing rod in his hand and a big feather attached to the end of it. He had Jacinta and Patricia tied to the bars at the head of the bed. He had taken off their socks and was running the feather across their feet and faces, tickling the life out of them.

'Kathleen, Carmel, save us!' both of them cried. 'He's been torturin' us here for ages.'

I was trying really hard not to laugh when I gave out to him. 'Thomas, yeh stupid thick, would yeh have a look at the pair of them? Can yeh not see how worked up they are? Yeh're drivin' them mad.'

'Ah, would yeh give it over Kathleen,' he laughed. 'I'm just havin' a bit of craic with them, tha's all.'

'We know tha', Thomas, but yeh keep the jokes up too long. Yeh never know when to stop. Now, help me get these knots open. Da will be back soon and there'll be blue murder if he finds out wha' yeh were up to. Yeh're just lucky tha' Ma is not here. She wouldn't be long kickin' the shite out of yeh.'

Jacinta was around thirteen at this time, with Patricia going on eleven. As soon as I had them untied, they were on top of Thomas before I knew it.

'Yeh fuckin' pig, Thomas Doyle,' Jacinta roared, as she tried to put the boot in, which of course was no good, since she had no shoes on. So the pair of them ended up trying to pull every blade of hair out of his head, until myself and Carmel dragged them off him. Of course, we gave them just enough time to get their own back, which he well deserved.

'Yiz are all a shower of mad bitches,' shouted Thomas as he struggled to get himself up off the floor. 'I'll get yiz back for this when yeh least expect. Are yeh listenin', Jacinta? I mean it. Patricia, just you wait and see.'

'Don't be such a spoil-sport, Thomas,' I said. 'If yeh're able to dish it out, then yeh have to be able to take it. Now, tha's the end of it, or I'll be tellin' Da on yeh.' He was still mumbling and giving out to himself as we left the room.

'Jacinta, take Patricia with yeh,' I said, 'and go down to the shops and get a couple of ice pops for yerselves. And bring back two for Mano and Paul. I suppose yeh'd better throw one in for Thomas or he'll only end up gettin' jealous.'

'Can we get a packet of crisps as well, Kathleen?' the pair of them chimed in.

'Go on then, seein' tha' yeh've been through the mill with the Thomas fella. But tha's all. Bring the rest of me change home. Tha'll do me for the bus fare. Carmel, make us a hot cup of tea, will yeh? This one's gone stone cold over the carry-on of them.'

'Yeh know Thomas won't let tha' go, Kathleen. First chance he gets, he'll pounce on them, and God only knows wha' antics he'll put them through the next time.'

'Well, he didn't exactly lick it off a stone, did he? Watchin' Phil over the years gettin' up to all sorts – I swear, he was one mad bastard. Carmel, de yeh remember the day when Thomas was around eight or nine and Phil tied him up?'

'No, I wasn't there tha' day, Kathleen. Meself and Ma headed in to Meath Street early tha' mornin'. I only got bits and pieces about wha' happened off the kids. Go on – fill us in then, seein' as you were there for the whole thing.'

'Well, Da had just gone out and I was upstairs cleanin' around as usual when I heard Thomas whingein'. I didn't take too much notice – yeh know the way he was always cryin' about one thing or the other. Tha's when I heard Phil let out such a roar tha' the whole road must've heard him.

'"Yeh're startin' to do me head in, Thomas! Shut the fuck up, I'm tellin' yeh or yeh'll be one sorry little bastard."

'But did he listen, Carmel? No. He kept goin' on and on. "I want pancakes, Phil! Ma said tha' I could have pancakes. She said yeh'd make them for me." He kept goin' on and on, whingin'. Tha's when Phil lost the plot altogether. I was out on the stairs peepin' in, breakin' me heart laughin' at the goin's-on of the pair of them. Phil jumps up off the chair, runs into the kitchen to the press and grabs a few pairs of Ma's old tights. Thomas saw wha' was comin' and tried to run. He didn't stand a chance in hell of gettin' away from Phil. He had Thomas tied to the chair in seconds and wrapped in the tights, from his ankles right up to his shoulders. He couldn't move.

'"Yeh want pancakes, Thomas, is tha' wha' yeh're sayin'? Well, I'll give yeh all yeh want, and by the time I'm finished yeh won't look for a pancake for a very long time."

'"I'm sorry, Phil. Please let me out. I swear I'll be good," cried Thomas.

'"It's too late, yeh little fuck; yeh're goin' to pay the price."'

'Ah Jaysus, Kathleen, yeh should've gone in and helped Thomas,' said Carmel. 'I'd say he was shittin' himself at tha' stage.'

'Are yeh for real or wha', Carmel? Me try and stop Phil when he gets into one of his crazy moods? There's no way I was gettin' meself involved. Anyway, shut up and let me tell yeh wha' happened. Phil takes out one of the bowls from the press, puts the flour and milk into it, as yeh do when yeh're makin' pancakes. I thought to meself, tha' looks okay. Tha' was until I saw wha' came next. He mixed white puddin', beans, dog food, cod liver oil and a lump of drippin', and to top it off, yeh know tha' white chalky medicine Ma drinks when her stomach is at her with the acid? Well, tha' went in last.'

'Oh my God, Kathleen, I feel like gettin' sick just thinkin' about it.'

'Tha's nothin', Carmel. Wait 'til I tell yeh wha' he done next. He whisked it like mad, makin' it into a thick gooey paste. I have to say, me own stomach was turnin', just lookin' at the colour of it. He poured it onto the sizzlin' pan, which by the way was floatin' in drippin'. He made about six or seven pancakes, leavin' each one to cool down as he went on cookin', all the while breakin' his heart laughin' as he looked over at Thomas, who was goin' into a frenzy at this stage. He knew full well wha' Phil was goin' to do next and so did the rest of the kids, who weren't long about scarperin' out of the house.

'"Righ', Thomas," said Phil. "Yer pancakes awaits yeh. Now, open up."

'"I'm sorry, I'm sorry, Phil. Please don't make me eat tha'."'

'"But yeh wanted me to make them for yeh and tha's wha' I've done, Thomas. Now, open up and get it over with."

'Carmel, yeh want to see the dirty big grin on Phil's face as he forced those pancakes down Thomas's throat. He kept tryin' to spit them out but Phil wasn't havin' any of it so he held Thomas's mouth closed, makin' him swallow every bite. Thomas was startin' to turn a funny colour so I couldn't sit there any longer. I went into the kitchen when Phil tried to stuff the third pancake in Thomas's mouth.

'"Tha's enough, Phil," I said. "He's goin' to be sick. Yeh've made yer point, now leave him alone."

'"Ah, there yeh are, Kathleen. I was just tryin' to teach the little fucker a lesson. Maybe now he'll think twice about whingin' and cryin' in everybody's face when he doesn't get his own way."

'And tha' was it, Carmel. Ma and Da were none the wiser. Thomas didn't open his mouth or cry for ages after tha', which was great, and he definitely never ever cried in front of Phil again. He knew better not to. Jaysus, Carmel, surely yeh must have noticed how quiet Thomas was when Phil was around?'

'Ah, yeh know me, Kathleen, I was always busy playin' with me dolls. I never took much notice of anythin' tha' was goin' on around me. Except for the time tha' you and Phil had tha' big fight. Tha' always stuck out in me head. Yiz were always so close. I couldn't believe tha' yeh wouldn't talk to him for ages.'

'I know, Carmel, I was a stubborn bitch back then. It was stupid of me to keep it up for so long, but then again, I was only sixteen and thought I knew it all. I'll never forget tha' day meself, Carmel. Alan had bought me this little record player only the day before from Phil's friend Patsy, for nine pounds, which was a huge amount of money back then, as yeh well know. Anyway, there I was gettin' meself ready for goin' out tha' night with Alan. I was happy as anythin' with life while I blasted out Elvis's latest record. I was dancin' away, doin' a few twirls with one of the kids, when Phil walks into the kitchen.

'"Jaysus, Kathleen, there's a great sound comin' out of tha'. De yeh want to have a jive?"

'"Would yeh stop, Phil, there's no room in here."

'"I'll soon fix tha'," he said, pushing the table against the wall. "Come on, Kathleen, and I'll show yeh a few moves I'm after learnin'." There the two of us were, dancin' away while a couple of the kids clapped to the music. Then, all of a sudden, the song stopped.

'"Jaysus, Phil, wha's after happenin' there? Did any of yiz touch tha'?" I asked the kids.

'"We never went near it, Kathleen," they all chimed in together.

'"Hold on, I'll have a look," said Phil.

'"No, I don't want yeh to touch it. Alan will check it over when he comes down."

'"Would yeh give it over, Kathleen – it's probably a bit of dirt caught in the needle. I'll have it fixed in two seconds and then we can carry on dancin'."

'"I said yeh're not to go near it, Phil. Just in case yeh can't put it back together. And if it's not workin' righ' Alan can

43

bring it back to Patsy and get his money back. Now leave it." Before I could do anything, he slowly started to take the record player apart in front of me.

'I was startin' to grind my teeth at this stage. I don't know wha' came over me. I got meself worked up into a righ' frenzy. When I look back now, I suppose it was childish of me the way I carried on, but then again maybe not. I felt that it was my present, bought for me and nobody else, and I didn't want Phil messin' with it. That's when all hell broke out between us.

'It was our first time ever to have a serious fight. He kept laughin' at me, gettin' all worked up, ignorin' everythin' I was sayin'.

'"I'm tellin' yeh, Phil, if yeh don't leave the record player alone, I'll go upstairs and rip yer one and only shirt in half."

'"Would yeh get away, yeh mad thing, Kathleen. I know tha' yeh wouldn't do tha' on me."

'"Yes, I would," I said as I made a charge up the stairs. His black suit and snow-white shirt tha' Ma had got out of the pawn shop earlier on tha' day were hangin' on a nail in our bedroom, all ready for Phil's date tha' night. I know, I know – wha' I did next was terrible, but I couldn't help meself. This mad rage came over me. I not only ripped his shirt down the middle, I then got his suit and rubbed it under his bed in all the dust and God knows how many cups of tea tha' was spilt there.

'Phil was callin' up to me as he was makin' his way up the stairs. "Yeh were righ', Kathleen, I should've left it alone. I have all the bits in a bag downstairs. Maybe Alan can put it back together when he comes down." Then he stopped dead in his tracks. I was standin' there with half of his shirt in my hand.

'"I told yeh, Phil. Yeh should've listened to me. Yeh pushed me temper too far this time."

'He stood there with his mouth wide open in shock, not sayin' a word. Phil was built like a lion and as strong as an ox, so there was no problem for him to lift up my seven stone. Before I knew it, he had me up in the air, shakin' the livin' daylights out of me.

'"Yeh stupid fuckin' bitch," he kept roarin'. "There was no need for tha'. I've no clothes now." In the middle of all this mayhem I was still tryin' to get a dig in at him. I don't know what happened after tha'; all I know is I woke up on the bed with Phil at the end of it, laughin', ticklin' me feet.

'"Oh, me head. Wha' did yeh do to me, Phil Doyle?"

'"Yeh're a lunatic, Kathleen. I didn't do nothin' – you tried to head-butt me because I wouldn't put yeh down, and yeh knocked yerself out. Yeh gave me a terrible fright when yeh passed out. I thought yeh were after droppin' dead on me. By Jaysus, yeh're every bit of Ma with tha' mad temper of yers. I'll tell yeh one thing for nothin', I'll think twice the next time before I cross yeh."

'"I don't believe yeh – and there won't be a next time, Phil Doyle," I said as I stormed off to the toilet. "Because I'll never ever be speakin' to yeh again."

'I couldn't believe it when I looked in the mirror. My nose was double its size, with my eyes turnin' black already. Phil wasn't long gettin' his spoke in with Ma and Da as soon as they came home from town. I was lyin' on the bed in the dark when Ma made her way up to me, switchin' the light on as she came into the room. I could see by her face tha' she'd got a fright when she looked at me.

'"Before yeh open yer mouth, Kathleen, Phil just told me his side of the story and I'll hear yeh out, but I have just one thing to say – I won't be sidin' with either one of yeh and I told yer father to do the same. Yeh're big and hairy enough to sort this out between the pair of yeh. Now, havin' said tha', could yeh not have smashed a few jam jars or plates when yeh got yerself all riled up? I mean, the suit and shirt – for fuck sake, Kathleen, yeh could have left them alone. Now I have nothin' to pawn on Monday when I need an extra shillin' to get me through the week."

'I lay there crying my eyes out. Then I launched into my side of what happened. Ma sat there listenin', not sayin' a word.

'"Come on now, let's get yeh into the toilet and bathe yer eyes. See if we can get some of tha' swellin' down before Alan gets here. He's goin' to have a blue fit when he sees the state of yeh, and I wouldn't blame him one bit for gettin' annoyed. But as I said, it's best tha' it's kept between yerself and Phil and I'll be tellin' Alan tha' meself. Tha' way there'll be some chance of yeh makin' up."

'"Tha' won't be happenin', Ma," I said. "Me and Phil are finished. I mean, would yeh look at me face? It's gettin' worse by the minute. I won't be able to go to work. There'll be no wages for yeh and all because Phil Doyle, Mr Know-It-All, wouldn't listen to me. No, I'm sorry, Ma, but this is all his fault." Back then there was no way anybody could tell me that I did any wrong, which of course I had and was too stubborn to admit it.

'"Righ' then, Kathleen, we'll say no more at the minute. Come on downstairs and have a bite to eat."

'I was makin' me way into the kitchen when Phil came over to me. "Holy Jaysus, Kathleen, I'm sorry over the record player and the fight, but I didn't do tha' to yeh. Tha' happened when yeh tried to head-butt me. I'd never do anythin' like tha' to any of yiz and you should know tha' more than anybody."

'"I've nothin' to say to yeh, Phil Doyle, now or ever again."

'Da just looked over at the pair of us and shook his head from side to side, not openin' his mouth. It wasn't too long after the dinner when Alan arrived. Ma got her spoke in straight away, pulling Alan to one side, letting him know the ins and outs of what happened. "Best keep out of it, Alan," she said. "They'll sort things out in time themselves." I knew by the way he was looking over at Phil that Alan wanted to dig the head off him, but he held back and did what Ma asked.

'I was up with the doctor the next day and was relieved when he told me that my nose wasn't broken. It took the guts of two weeks for my face to come back to normal. Phil did everything in his power to try and get me to laugh and talk to him, telling his funniest jokes as soon as I would walk into the room, or hiding upstairs, waiting to pounce on me in the dark, but I wasn't having any of it.

'I kept it up for months on end, until one day when I came in from work and found Ma crying in the kitchen.

'"Jaysus Christ, Ma, are yeh all righ'? Wha's after happenin'?"

'"Oh, thank God yeh're home, Kathleen. It's Phil, he's after takin' bad in the hospital."

'"Ma, he's only gettin' his tonsils out – it's no big deal."

'"I know tha', Kathleen, but he's after bleedin' real bad. I was givin' him a sup of water to wet his lips, them being all dry after the operation, when next the blood spat out of his mouth nearly into me face. I nearly had a heart attack on the spot with the fright I got. The blood was everywhere. Yeh'd want to hear the roars of me, screamin' for help. The whole hospital must've heard me. Not tha' I gave two shites wha' anybody thought. I just wanted somebody to help me son."

'"Oh Ma, is he okay? Please tell me he's all right, tha' nothin' bad is after happenin' to him."

'"I have to say, them doctors and nurses are angels from heaven. They were in like a light. Now, mind you, it took a while before the bleedin' stopped. And yes, he's fine again. Thanks to the holy Mother herself, who has her own way of helpin' me sort things out when I need a bit of help. De yeh know somethin', Kathleen? The worry tha' I'm after goin' through today was worth every second of it, just to hear yeh say those words about yer brother. Me heart was broke lookin' at the pair of yiz driftin' apart."

'"I know, Ma, and I'm sorry. It was stupid, but the whole thing just seemed to get out of hand and then I didn't really know how to fix it without lookin' as if I was givin' in to Phil. Yeh know him, I'd never hear the end of it."

'"Well, this is yer chance now, Kathleen. Go up to the hospital to see him and make things righ' between yiz. I know Phil wants tha' more than anythin'. He's told me so many times how he misses yeh."

'That was all I needed to hear. I had myself ready in a flash and was down in the Meath Hospital just in time for visiting hour. I felt nervous because we hadn't talked for so long, and at the same time excited about all I had to tell him. Phil copped me as soon as I walked into the ward, and the big smile that he gave me said it all. That was enough for me. We sat there laughing and joking about the fight and how crazy I got.

'"I'm sorry about wha' I did, Phil," I told him.

'"Me too, Kathleen. I mean, the record player ended up goin' in the bin over me messin' and pullin' it apart, losin' half the screws along the way, but about wha' happened after tha' – I'm innocent, and I think yeh know tha' now."

'"I know, Phil, so let's make a pact tha', no matter wha' happens or wha's goin' on in our lives, we'll never fall out again." And we never did. We were the best of friends – always.'

* * *

'Jaysus Christ, Carmel, w...
got lost there for a while, g...
came down to give yeh a dig o...
I've ended up doin' nothin'.'

'Yeh're all righ', Kathleen. I'll get t...
on. Anyway, I enjoyed our little chat. It...
We should do it more often.'

'We will, Carmel, I promise. Now, where...
Jacinta and Patricia with me change? They see... ...ne
forever.'

With that, the pair of them burst in the door, with Da right
behind them.

'There yeh are, Kathleen,' said Da. 'Are yeh stayin' for a
bit of dinner?'

'I better not, Da, the time is gettin' on a bit now. I'd best
be on me way.'

'Well, at least stay and have a cup of tea with me.'

'All righ' then, go on, put the teapot on. I'll hang on for
another half an hour.'

'All the same, Kathleen,' said Da, 'the house isn't the same
without yer mother, with all her roarin' and shoutin' and
givin' out about one thing and another. I have to say I do miss
her around the place. She's the only one apart from yerself
tha' keeps the kids in hand from gettin' up to all sorts of
mischief. But havin' said tha', things have been very quiet
around here. They're all behavin' themselves. Isn't tha' righ',
Carmel?'

Carmel looked over at me with a big grin on her face. 'Yeh
never said a truer word, Da – they're all so good.'

6

Big Changes

I was expecting my third baby and was in and out of hospital for the first three months. I was unwell through the whole pregnancy, with the threat of miscarriage hanging over me all the time. I had to rest so much, which meant I wasn't able to go up to Ma every day and had to stay at home with Martina and young Alan. Ma would drop down to me, checking to make sure I was okay, always bringing a few of the kids with her, which I thought wouldn't be a problem.

I felt this was my home now, especially after Alan's granddad Pop sat the two of us down one day. He told us he had forty years' tenancy with the Corporation and that it would be a pity to let it go to waste. He suggested that we should put in to buy the house, saying he wasn't too far off eighty years old and wasn't going to last forever. He'd put his name on the form with us; that way, we would get it for little or nothing.

Alan didn't waste any time in bringing Pop down to the Corporation, and was told that we could get the house for as little as eight hundred pounds. We couldn't believe it; we were over the moon. We worked out all the bills and it was well within our means.

Of course, I got carried away as usual, making all sorts of plans about building on a new bathroom, maybe a new kitchen and definitely another bedroom. Alan would sit there listening to me rammaging on and laughing, knowing full well that wouldn't happen for a long time. He would never burst my bubble, though.

Pop, on the other hand, was listening and taking it all in. I don't know what was going on in his head, but it wasn't good for us. He always had his meals with us and there was never a bother with the kids playing around. But that all changed when I was sick and Ma started dropping in every day to me.

Pop didn't say anything, but you know when things are not right. He stopped coming down for breakfast and then I would hear him slipping out the front door. I would cook his dinner every day and it would be left there. I asked him one day, because it was getting the better of me.

'Pop, are yeh okay? De yeh not feel well? Yeh're not eatin' a thing.'

He didn't answer or look at me, just went about his business and headed out the door. I was left speechless, and believe me that doesn't happen very often. I told Ma when she dropped in to see me, but I was immediately sorry I opened my mouth.

'Wha' did I tell yeh, Kathleen? Didn't I tell yeh it never works out livin' on somebody else's floor? But would yeh listen to me? No.'

'He's probably a bit sick or somethin', tha's wha' it is, Ma. I'll get Alan to talk to him. He'll sort everythin' out.'

'I'm tellin' yeh, Kathleen, tha' oul' fella is up to no good. Mark my words, it'll all come out in the wash. Just wait and see.'

Ma kept going on and on about how we should have got our own house from day one. And she was so right, but I couldn't see that at the time.

Shortly after she left Alan came home. I didn't waste any time in telling him what had happened. He listened to me, taking it all in, not saying a word and not looking too surprised at what was coming out of my mouth.

'Alan, de yeh know somethin' I don't?'

Then he came out with the words which were the furthest from my mind.

'Kathleen, he wants us out. Pop wants us to leave.'

I heard what Alan said, but it didn't seem to connect with my brain. Not for a couple of minutes anyway. He went on to tell me what was going on.

'I didn't say anythin', Kathleen, with you being sick and all. Yeh've enough to be worryin' about there. But with yer Ma droppin' in, tryin' to keep an eye on yeh, and all the kids runnin' around playin' and makin' noise. It didn't go down very well with Pop. Me Da was tellin' me tha' he's been goin' up to him, givin' out like shite, and to top it off, when I told him that we had to go in and sign the final forms about buyin' the house, "No way!" he said. "I want yiz out." I couldn't believe it Kathleen.'

I nearly fell through the floor when he said that to me.

'But I don't understand, Alan – he's the one tha' wanted us to buy the house in the first place. And as soon as I have the baby, Ma won't be comin' down here anymore. It was only because I was sick – did yeh tell him tha', Alan?'

'I know all tha', and yes, I told him. There wasn't a bother on him until some of these oul' fellas he drinks with start sayin' that we'd probably fuck him into a home the first chance we get once the forms are signed.'

'Oh my God! We'd never do anythin' like tha'. How could he ever think such a thing, Alan?'

'Kathleen, me and me Da are after spendin' the last two weeks tryin' to convince Pop tha' would never happen, but there's no gettin' through to him. He has this in his head now and there's no changin' it. There's no two ways about it, we have to leave.'

'And go where, Alan? Where are we supposed to go with two children and another little one on the way? I can't believe this is happenin'! I mean, we're after buildin' our home here. We've spent every penny over the past six years on this house. Wha' are we goin' to do? We've no money behind us.'

'We'll have to go into the Corporation, Kathleen, and see if they can offer us somethin'. All I can say is, thank God yeh went in tha' time with yer Ma just after we got married and put our names on the list.'

I cried so many tears that night I could have filled a river. We went over and over it again, talking and talking, trying to make sense of what was happening. I was too upset at the time to realise how Alan must have felt about his own granddad doing that to him. That was hard.

* * *

I was up at the crack of dawn the next morning getting the kids ready. I didn't care how sick I was or how much I was supposed to rest; there was no way I wanted to see Pop. I was too upset and annoyed with him. So Alan dropped us off to Ma's and I wasn't long filling her in on everything. Well, all hell broke loose, just like I knew it would.

'The dirty, conniving bastard of a man! And him with nearly one foot in the grave as it is. He'll fuckin' rot in hell for doin' this to yiz, the pig. Didn't I tell yeh he was up to no good?'

'I know.' The tears rolled down my face once more. 'Please Ma, it's hard enough.'

She calmed down and pulled her horns back in.

'Righ', Kathleen,' she said, 'finish tha' cup of tea and, if yeh're up to it, we'll head into the Corporation righ' now.'

'Well, I have to be up to it, don't I, Ma? I've no choice in the matter.'

As soon as we got there I filled the lady in at the hatch about what had happened. Because our names had been on the list a few years, they offered us a flat straight away. She was nice enough to tell me that if I waited until my baby was born, which was only about three months away, we would be entitled to a house. I didn't get a chance to answer. Ma did that for me.

'Tha's great,' she said, 'put her down for the house.'

As we made our way home, Ma came up with a plan. 'Fuck tha' oul' fella, Kathleen. Alan can tell him yeh're not goin' anywhere until the baby comes into the world and if he has anythin' to say about it, I'll come down and sort him out. He can stick his house up his hole, so he can. Now wha' yeh do is, get Alan to drop yeh off in the mornin's before he heads off to work. Tha' way yeh won't have tha' long walk. Yeh'll be able to rest here. I'll take care of the kids; they can play out in the back garden with the rest of them. Yiz can all have yer bit of dinner here. Then yeh'll only have to sleep there. Things always have a way of workin' themselves out, Kathleen. So don't be worryin'. The only thing tha' should be on yer mind right now is keepin' yerself well so this little baby can be brought into the world safe.'

She knew I wasn't able for any more ranting and raving, but those last few words were so full of wisdom it made me put everything into perspective. I realised my baby was the most important thing. Everything else was just material things that could be replaced in time.

* * *

The next couple of months seemed to take forever. Then my little baby girl Amanda came into the world. She was so tiny, not even weighing five pounds.

I only had her with me two days and she was not feeding very well for me. I noticed her colour changing; she was turning orange. I called the nurse over. She took one look at Amanda and ran to get a doctor. He was up straight away and she was rushed down to the special baby unit. The doctor explained to me that her liver wasn't functioning and she also had a kidney and ear infection.

I watched through the glass as her lovely blonde hair was shaved off so they could put a needle into her head. I was frantic with worry. I could feel the blood draining from my face and my legs starting to go from under me. One of the nurses was over straight away.

'Sit down there, Kathleen, before you fall and hurt yourself. I'm sorry, but we have to get fluids into your baby fast to get her liver working and this is the quickest way. Believe me, it's not as bad as it looks, and I promise she didn't feel a thing. As soon as you're okay, I'll bring you in to her.'

'I'm fine, nurse, please bring me in now.' And she did.

'Look, Kathleen,' she said as we both stood by the cot, 'what did I tell you? There she is sleeping away, not a bother on her. And that's what you should be doing – getting yourself a good night's sleep while you can.'

Of course, I didn't get any sleep that night from the worry.

* * *

Amanda was kept in hospital for the next three weeks. Ma was great, looking after Martina and young Alan along with her own, while I spent all the hours I could in the hospital, getting as many feeds as I could into Amanda, helping to build her up. They finally let me take her home.

In the meantime, Alan didn't waste any time in getting her birth cert into the Corporation to prove we had our third child, making us eligible for a house. I knew as soon as Alan walked in the door that there was something wrong. The news wasn't good.

'Wha' is it, Alan? Tell me!' I asked.

'We can have a house now, straight away. The only thing is, it's over the northside of the city. A new scheme called Darndale. It's not too far from Portmarnock.'

'Jaysus, Alan, tha's miles away. I'll be out there on me own. I won't know anybody. Wha' will I do if one of the kids gets sick? Who will I turn to? I won't have me Da or Ma.'

'I know, Kathleen, and I did me best tryin' to see if they had any houses on the southside. They've nothin' and they won't be buildin' over here for another three years. We've no choice. We have to take it. I'm not stayin' in tha' house a night longer than I have to. It's hard enough as it is, but knowin' it's me granddad, me own flesh and blood tha's doin' this to us . . . No, I'm sorry, Kathleen, there's no turnin' back.'

* * *

And there wasn't. Within the next couple of weeks, we were in and signed for our house and were handed the keys on the same day. We drove out straight away to have a look. Alan was so excited, but I wasn't. We made our way up to Crumlin to tell the family our news.

When I told Ma and Da where I was moving to, Da got a bit upset.

'Yeh'll be missed around here, Kathleen, I can tell yeh tha' – and I don't only mean for all the cleanin' yeh do and keepin' them kids in hand for us. It's for yerself.'

It took me a big effort to keep myself from falling to pieces when Da said that to me. 'Don't worry, Da, I'll still be over, I promise.'

Ma was a different kettle of fish altogether. She went ballistic. I had a right job stopping her from going down and battering Pop. The fucking and blinding went on for I don't know how long. But eventually she calmed down, as she always did.

'I'm goin' to miss yeh around here, Kathleen. It won't be the same, you not droppin' in every day.'

'I'll still make me way over, Ma. Even if it's only two or three times a week. Sure I won't be able to stay away. Yeh know me; I'm glued to yiz all.'

I could see Ma looked and felt a bit better in herself then, for a little while anyway.

* * *

I was so upset over the next few days as I started to pack all the bits and bobs we had gathered over the few years since we had first moved in with Pop. I had come to love the little house that I had made my home, still hoping, even up to the very last, that he would ask us to stay. But that wasn't to be.

Pop had himself up and gone out of the house from early that morning. Alan had everything planned out to a T. He knew the way I felt about leaving, so he organised a lift with his Uncle Joe for me and the kids and sent us ahead of him. It all happened so quickly that I didn't have time to think, and maybe that was just as well.

I sat in silence the whole way out, listening to Joe giving out like shite about Pop, while Martina and young Alan giggled and played with one another. They were too young to understand what was going on; all that was on their minds was how soon we were bringing them to the seaside.

As soon as we got to the house, Joe didn't waste any time in hanging about and headed back over to give Alan a hand. I settled Amanda in her pram while the other two ran about.

It was a lovely house; it had three fine-sized bedrooms, a bathroom and toilet, which we hadn't had in Pops'. I should have been over the moon with this. There was a lovely big kitchen with plenty of built-in presses, and a huge sitting-room. I looked around me and none of it meant anything. All I wanted to do was to go home.

Alan settled in really well, as did the kids. But me? At first you might as well have put me on the other side of the world. I felt so isolated and lonely. Although I didn't realise it at the time, this move was to be a big turning point in my life, which, I might add, was for the better. At that particular time, I didn't mix very well outside my family circle. I was very shy but in time I learned to overcome that. Slowly but surely, I started to mingle, between the school and the local shops, which did me the world of good.

* * *

Amanda was nearly three months old on the day I got the letter from the Coombe. I got such a fright, as they wanted to see me straight away. I was only starting to get back on my feet again, after being so sick during the pregnancy. There seemed to be no end to my health problems, and I really didn't need to hear this news.

I got my sister Patricia to mind the kids while I made my way in to the hospital. I had myself in a right tizzy as I waited to be seen by the doctor, who looked very serious when I sat down in front of him. He read over my chart before he spoke.

'Hello, Mrs McGrath,' he said. 'I'm Dr Roche and I see here from your records that you have been in and out with us a lot over the past year.'

'Tha's right, Doctor.'

'Well, Mrs McGrath, I'm afraid you will be seeing us on a regular basis, because we are going to have to keep a check on you from now on. Your last smear test was very nasty, very nasty indeed. You have cells there that are not healthy. In normal circumstances, we would carry out a hysterectomy straight away, but since you're only twenty-six, we have decided that you are far too young to be going through the menopause. So we are going to go down a different route for the moment. You will have to come to the hospital every six weeks to get this particular procedure done, and then we will take it from there.'

I still found it very hard to talk to doctors in white coats, so I went along with what they said and did. When I think back now, I was such a gobshite. I never asked a thing. I should have been asking, 'How serious is this? What will you be doing? How long will it go on for? Could I die?' The most important question of all: could I die? But I asked nothing and was told nothing.

The word 'cancer' was never used – only, 'it's very nasty'. Maybe they just didn't want to frighten me. I really don't know. I remember on my first visit I asked one of the nurses what it was I was getting done. Her very words were, 'They're trying to burn off the unhealthy cells, Kathleen.'

Oh my God, I was so sore for days afterwards. It felt like I'd had a hot blowtorch down below. That went on for a good few months, and the doctor finally brought me back in for another chat.

'Now, Mrs McGrath, your last smear test results are much better than previous,' he told me. 'But – and I must stress this – they are still not as clear as we would like. So you must continue with the regular check-ups. I will see you again in six months and if that result is as positive as this, we can move to an annual visit.'

I wanted to jump up and kiss the face off him, but I wouldn't dare. All I said was, 'Thank you so much, Doctor.' Then I was gone like a flash.

Even though the news wasn't one hundred per cent, I was still happy enough with what he had to say, for that moment in time anyway. I was so happy that I didn't have to go back into hospital and have surgery that I slowly found myself starting to settle down a bit better.

* * *

I got to know a few girls around the estate, all like myself, each of us with a couple of kids, which meant we had something in common to give out and talk about. I could feel myself getting confident and more outgoing as the weeks and months went by, and it felt good.

I asked Alan if he would bring me into town one of the evenings when he finished work. I wanted to check out a hairdressing salon called 'The Witch's Hut'. 'One of the girls up at the school told me she had her hair done there by hairdressin' students. She said tha' they teach people in the evenin's to cut hair. So wha' de yeh think, Alan? If we could manage, I would love to do it.'

He sat there with a smile on his face, pleased with the big change in me. 'It's wha' yeh always wanted to do, Kathleen, so go for it!'

That was all I needed to hear. In I went the following evening, while Alan waited outside with the three kids in the back of the car. I was so nervous as I made my entrance – but determined. When I came back out I had a smile on my face that lit up the whole of Grafton Street. I had just booked my first three lessons, unsure how or where the extra money was going to come from; but knowing Alan, he would work things out and make it happen.

And that he did. By working two late nights and all day Saturday as overtime, he brought in enough to pay for my training.

* * *

I think when Ma brought me into this world I was given enough energy for a dozen people. I let nothing faze me. I would be up from the crack of dawn, always getting ahead of myself.

I was so excited that first evening I was to start my classes. Alan's dinner was in the oven. I had the three kids fed and ready in their pyjamas. Martina was five years old, Alan three and Amanda barely six months. I was ready to run with them as soon as Alan pulled up outside the house. I had to be there by seven o'clock, so there was no time to waste.

I sat in the back of the car; Amanda was on my lap, with Martina and Alan either side.

'Now, Martina,' I said, 'yeh're to be a good girl for me. Mammy has to work, so I want yeh to hold Amanda in yer arms real tight for Daddy when he's driving yiz home. And wha'ever yeh do, don't let go of her.'

'Okay, Ma,' she smiled, delighted with the bit of responsibility.

As we pulled up outside the salon, I sat there for a minute, getting myself together. I was nervous as hell, but, as always, Alan said the right words just when I needed them most.

'Yeh can do this, Kathleen; all yeh have to do is believe in yerself, because I know I do. Now run along; yeh don't want to be late for yer first class. And don't worry about the kids, I'll take care of all tha'.'

So in I went with those words in my head, ready to take on the world.

* * *

I took to hairdressing like a duck takes to water. I had a great teacher called James, who I got on very well with. He only had to show me something once and I could do it. He would tell me all the while that I was a born hairdresser, which helped build my confidence more and more.

The days that I didn't have classes I would make my way over to Ma, just as I promised, practising what I had learned the night before on all the kids, which helped me move forward faster. The more models I got, the better I became. There was no stopping me. Every chance I got, I had my scissors in my hand, cutting everyone and anyone's hair that I could get my hands on.

In less than two years, with the help of a few courses in between, I had perfected the art of hairdressing. I followed my dream and it came true for me at last.

I now felt I was ready to start making some money and reap the rewards for all my hard work. That's when I put my first plan into action, telling Alan what was going on in my head.

'Alan, yeh know the way the sittin' room is really big? Well, de yeh think tha' yeh could put a wall along there, takin' part of it away? I'd just need enough room for one mirror and a chair. I could put a hooded hairdryer over there in the corner behind the door. Tha's all I need for doin' me perms and sets. So wha' de yeh think?'

I showed my pearly white smile from ear to ear, bursting with excitement at the thought of starting my own little business.

'I knew yeh were up to somethin', Kathleen. I've been watchin' yeh, sittin' there starin' into space, schemin' away to yerself, wonderin' wha' yeh were goin' to come out with, and I have to say it sounds good. I'll be able to do the work meself; tha' way, it won't cost too much. Yeh'll be up and runnin' in no time.'

* * *

Alan did a great job on dividing the sitting-room, giving me enough space to work in, but still leaving plenty of room for us to sit in as a family. Because the houses had their own back entrances, it made it very handy for me to keep the hairdressing separate from the house.

I didn't waste any time in telling all the girls at the school and the neighbours nearby, asking them to pass the word around, which they all did. I built myself a nice little business over the few years we lived in Darndale, working every hour that I could, doing as many haircuts as I could while the kids were in school. As soon as they were in bed, I'd start all over again. With Alan's overtime and the money I was making, we were starting to get a nice few pound behind us, enough for our first holiday abroad.

7

Spain

We decided on the sunny island of Majorca for our first holiday
– just Alan and myself. My sister Carmel came out to Darndale
with a few of my younger brothers and sisters to mind our three
kids for us. I wanted to make sure they had plenty of company
while we were away and wouldn't miss us too much. I did feel
a bit guilty about not bringing them with us, but I also felt Alan
and I needed some time for ourselves. We had been chasing our
tails over the past couple of years, between one thing and
another. There never seemed to be any time for us, and maybe
now we could have the honeymoon we'd never had.

There were loads of waves and kisses from all the kids as
we drove away from the house. I was so excited as we pulled
up to the airport. It was my first time there because I had
never been outside Ireland before. I couldn't believe the
numbers of people all heading off to different parts of the
world. There was such a buzz around the place and it felt
great because we were part of it. I have to say, I was a bit
nervous when the plane took off, but that soon passed. I
talked away like mad through the whole flight.

'Isn't this great, Alan? Did yeh ever think tha' we would be headin' off on our own for our first holiday?'

'To tell yeh the truth, Kathleen, I couldn't believe it when yeh came out and said no kids. Yeh know yeh're always worryin' about them – not tha' I ever mind, but it is nice just the two of us for a change. It'll be like old times. We'll hire a bike and go all over the island together. I promise yeh, we'll have a great week.'

'I know, I know, Alan. I can't wait. I just can't wait to get there.'

I was like a child heading off on a big adventure. Before I knew it, the pilot was announcing, 'Fasten your seat-belts, ladies and gentlemen. We'll be landing shortly.'

I couldn't believe the heat as I walked down the steps of the plane. It nearly took my breath away. It didn't take us too long to get through the airport and in no time at all we were on our way. My mind was blown as the coach drove us to the hotel. I'd never seen the likes of it before, except maybe on the telly, but this was real and I was here in the middle of it all. I soon let everybody on the bus know that too.

'Oh my God, Alan, would yeh have a look at the height of them buildin's? And did yeh ever see so many flowers in yer life? Look how tall all them palm trees are. They're massive. I'd love one of them in our garden. Christ, Alan I just saw a swimmin' pool. Did yeh see, Alan, did yeh see it? Oh, there's another one . . . and another one.'

Alan was laughing his head off at my excitement. 'I have to say, Kathleen, it's the business all right. Now, will yeh try and calm yerself down – the whole bus is listenin' to yeh.'

I hadn't realised I was jumping up and down, shouting and roaring all over the place. With that I slowly slipped back down into my seat, embarrassed as hell, blushing all over.

Then I felt someone tap me on the shoulder. It was the woman sitting across from me. She was wearing this big flowery hat, with the fuzziest blonde curls you ever saw underneath, bright pink sunglasses with lipstick to match, and a big friendly smile to top it all off.

'Yeh're all right there, love. I have to say I enjoyed every minute listenin' to yeh,' she said as she put her hand out to shake mine. 'By the way, I'm Maggie. Yer first holiday?'

'Tha's righ'. I'm Kathleen.'

'It brought back memories to me, so it did, of when I came on me first holiday. Yeh think you were bad, I was like a ravin' lunatic, runnin' up and down the aisle of the bus, askin' people did they see this and tha'. Marty said I made a holy show of meself, but fuck it, I didn't care. Marty is me husband, who's sittin' here next to me – he was mortified. Marty, tell the girl – weren't yeh mortified?'

Maggie's husband, who was reading his paper, looked over at me, not saying a word, shook his head from side to side, rolled his eyes in the air and turned away.

'He gets a bit shy at times. But don't mind him.' She went on talking about all the different places she'd been to. I listened, taking it all in, but still trying to have a peep out along the way. I didn't want to miss a single thing.

The bus finally pulled into our hotel, with Maggie shouting as we got off. 'Enjoy yerself, love, and remember wha' I said – once yeh get a taste of this kind of livin', there's no turnin' back. And believe me, I know wha' I am talkin' about. Isn't tha' righ' Marty?' I could hear her saying as the bus pulled away.

She was so right. It opened up a whole new world to us, which both of us agreed we wanted.

I had to keep myself from screaming when we walked in the hotel entrance. It was really big and plush. There were cream leather sofas throughout with matching stools on either side. The coffee tables were made of glass with thick chrome legs and the most beautiful spray of flowers on each one. The gleaming tiles on the floor were a champagne colour. I was half afraid to walk on them as we made our way over to the reception to book ourselves in.

Everybody was so nice and friendly. We were shown to our room straight away. I couldn't believe it when I looked around – a big king-size bed, more sofas, shower room, bathroom. Everything was perfect and seemed too good to be true.

'Alan, would yeh have a look at this? I don't remember the rooms lookin' anythin' like this in the brochure. I think they're after makin' a mistake and bringin' us to the wrong hotel.' Alan started laughing. 'No, I'm serious, Alan. Look around at this place, it's really posh. We'll end up gettin' a big bill at the end of the week and we won't be able to pay for it. We'll have to say somethin'.'

'Kathleen, stop rammagin' on, will yeh, or yeh'll end up blowin' a fuse. I changed the hotel, just before we came away. I wanted it to be a surprise. I got a bonus in me wages tha' I wasn't expectin' and I knew if I gave it to you it would end up gettin' lost in with the bills along the way. So I decided, with this being our first holiday, tha' we were goin' to do it in style, and I have to admit it is class. Now, will yeh go and get yerself ready and we'll have a swim in one of these famous swimmin' pools tha' yeh were screamin' about all the way here.'

'I'm speechless, Alan.'

'Well, tha' doesn't happen very often, so yeh must be pleased.'

We had ourselves changed and down to the pool in no time at all. The place was packed, with not a sun-lounger to be got anywhere. Not that we minded; we spent the best part of the morning in the swimming pool, taking out only enough time for a bite to eat before we headed over to the beach, which happened to be across the road from the hotel.

'This just keeps gettin' better and better, Alan. Would yeh have a look at tha' water – it's as blue as the sky, and the beach is so clean. Yeh know wha', the kids would love this. We'll have to bring them on a holiday.'

'I was wonderin' how long it'd take before yeh mentioned the kids.'

'I know, sorry, Alan, I can't help it.'

'If the truth be known, I was thinkin' the same meself. Now, come on and let's see wha's happenin' around here tonight.'

There was plenty to do, between the bars, clubs and every type of restaurant you could think of. I thought I was in another world. You would have needed a month to get around them all. Having said that, we managed a fair few, enjoying every one of them along the way.

Alan hired a bike and, with me on the back, off we went day after day, making sure we saw every inch of the island, always getting back in time to have a swim, which for me was a great finish to the day.

* * *

One of the highlights of the week was the 'Spanish Night', which I'll never forget. You could drink and eat as much as you liked. It was Alan's first time to drink wine and he was knocking it back like it was water. He was pissed out of his brains before I knew it and had the whole place singing 'Is This the Way to Amarillo?' along with him. The atmosphere was brilliant.

It wasn't too long before the show started and the flamenco dancers were on. We were all standing up on the tables, clapping like mad, when Alan decided to get up on the stage. He grabbed one of the flowers off the table, stuck it between his teeth and danced away with them, and they didn't mind a bit. The place was hopping, with everybody cheering him on.

'Are yeh righ', Kathleen?' he roared over to me. 'Come on, help me out here.'

There was no way I was getting up there in front of all those people, me with not a drink on me – no way! But before I knew it, this gang of young fellas who were sitting at the table with us, who just happened to be Irish, all started banging the table and shouting, 'Kathleen! Kathleen! Kathleen!' They too were pissed and with that the whole place started calling my name. I kept laughing, but then I thought, *Wha' the heck – fuck it!* I stuck a flower between my teeth and danced all the way over to Alan, not realising that all the young fellas were dancing behind me, doing the same. With that, everybody was up on the floor.

'Yeh know somethin', Alan, yeh're a mad thing when yeh get goin'. Them flamenco dancers didn't get a look in once yeh started. Now, havin' said tha', the craic was ninety lookin' at yeh.'

'Tha's wha' it's all about, Kathleen – lettin' yer hair down and havin' a bit of fun. Now, come on, dance with me!'

We had one of the best nights of the week and such a laugh we had on the bus back to the hotel, a right sing-song got going. Between 'Molly Malone' and every rebel song you could think of, everybody had to be Irish.

While all this was going on, Alan downed another bottle of wine, which wasn't good and soon changed the course of the night.

Our hotel was the first stop.

'Are yeh righ', Alan?' I said. 'Here we are.'

He didn't see or hear me and was lost in noddy-land at this stage. With the help of two fellas, I managed to get him off the bus. There were loads of waves and goodbyes as I stood there trying to hold him up.

'Come on, Alan, let's get yeh up to bed before yeh fall down. It's after three o'clock in the mornin'.'

'Jaysus, Kathleen, is tha' yerself? I was wonderin' where yeh'd got to. Give us an oul' kiss.' He was slipping and wobbling all over the place.

'I will in a minute, Alan. Now, stand up straight against the wall while I look for the key before we go in.'

I only took my eyes off him for a few seconds, but when I looked up he was gone. I tried not to shout out too loud as I went around calling for him.

'Alan, stop yer messin', will yeh? I'm tired.'

I kept expecting him to jump out from one of the bushes. I was starting to get scared, walking around on my own. There wasn't a sinner to be seen anywhere. Then it dawned on me, 'Oh my God, the swimmin' pool! Wha' if he's after fallin' in there?' I was shaking as I walked around to look, and was relieved to see that the pool was empty.

I was in floods of tears as I made my way into the hotel, only to find out that the night porter couldn't speak a word of English. I was like a traffic warden, standing there doing hand signals. But no matter how hard I tried, there was no getting through to him.

I was too afraid to go up to the room in case Alan would wander in and go back out again, so I sat there, frantic with worry, thinking only the worst. It was starting to get bright outside and it was a big effort for me to stay awake. There was hustle and bustle as the hotel started to come alive as the workers arrived. With that the porter came over to me with a young girl who could speak some English.

'Hello, my name is Anna. My friend tells me you are upset. Can I help you?'

I was so happy to hear those words and told her what had happened, crying and sobbing as I tried to speak. She explained to the porter what I'd been trying to tell him. They spoke together for a couple of minutes before coming back to me.

'Señorita, we have decided, before going to the police, if you can come please with us and we will check the grounds of our hotel first. Then the surrounding area.'

'Thank you. Thank you. Thank you so much.' I nearly took the hand off her I shook it so much. She went around and gathered some of the staff to help us with the search.

It was now coming up to midday and there was still not a sign of Alan anywhere. I didn't know if I was coming or going and was starting to feel really ill at that stage. We were on our way back to phone the police when I heard my name being called.

'Kathleen, is tha' you?'

I looked down the road and there was Alan in the distance, walking towards me. I thought my heart was going to jump out of my body, I was so happy to see him.

'This is your husband?' said Anna.

'Yes, yes, tha's him.'

'Good!' She gave me a smile before heading back to the hotel with the rest of the workers.

I could feel a mad rage coming on me the closer I got to Alan. Instead of hugs and kisses, he got such a dig off me and a right kick in the ankles.

'Where the hell were yeh?' I screamed. 'I'm after bein' up the walls, sick with worry over yeh. I was just goin' back to the hotel to ring the police.'

'I don't know where the fuck I was, Kathleen. I'm after wakin' up in a ditch. Look at me! I'm eaten alive by them bloody mosquitoes. The last thing I remember was gettin' on the bus – after tha', everythin' else is a blank.'

No matter what, I could never stay annoyed at Alan for very long, so I calmed down and took a good look at him. He was in a right mess. There were lumps all over his face and arms. I couldn't help but laugh.

'Come on, Alan, some of them bites look very nasty. We'd better go find a chemist and get yeh sorted out or yeh'll end up in hospital.'

'I'm sorry, love, yeh know I'd never leave yeh on yer own like tha'. It was tha' bloody wine. Never again, Kathleen, I mean it. I'll just stick to me shandies. Tha' way I know wha's goin' on around me.'

'And believe me, Alan, I'll make sure yeh do.'

We bought a big bunch of flowers for Anna and some chocolates for the staff, to thank them for all their help.

* * *

Other than that little hiccup, we had a great holiday, the best time ever. We had meals out every night, dancing the night away until the early hours of the morning. Blue skies and sunshine every day. What more could you ask for?

The week went by so fast that we were back on the plane heading for Dublin before we knew it. I sat there, lost in my thoughts as Alan slept, and I made a promise to myself: no matter what, I would work my arse off for us and our family, to give us a piece of this life.

8

The Snip

Alan came in from work one evening, looking very serious in himself, which is not like him; he's usually so happy-go-lucky, but not that night. I waited until the kids were asleep in bed before I said a word.

'Yeh're very quiet, Alan. Wha's the matter? Did somethin' happen in work? Is yer Da okay?'

'No, it's nothin' like tha', Kathleen. I want us to have a chat about havin' more kids.'

'Jaysus, Alan, yeh want me to have another baby? Amanda's only a couple of months old. Are yeh mad!'

'No, no, tha' came out wrong. Wha' I mean is – and I've been thinkin' about it for a while, but I'm not too sure how yeh feel about this . . . all I know is, I don't want any more kids, and if we keep goin' the way we're goin', we'll end up havin' as many kids as yer Ma.'

'Well, Alan, if tha's wha' has yeh all serious in yerself, yeh've nothin' to worry about there. I'm happy with the family tha' we have and certainly don't want any more. But wha' are we to do? I seem to get caught very easy.'

'Tha's wha' I want to talk about, Kathleen. There's this fella in work, he was tellin' me he got this job done on himself. Yeh know, down there. It's called a vasectomy. Well, in other words, the snip.'

'Jaysus, Alan, wha' exactly gets snipped?' I was cringing just saying the word and imagining all sorts of bits being 'snipped' off.

Alan went into the ins and outs of what it all meant, finishing off by saying, 'It's permanent. There'll be no going back once I get it done.'

'Tha' won't be a problem, Alan, once it's safe for yeh.'

'Yer man said it was just a little nick. He was back in work the next day.'

'How and where does all this happen?'

'There's this doctor, he flies in from Holland every few weeks. He has a clinic in one of the houses down there in Wicklow. He does a couple of fellas over the weekend and then he's gone as quick as he came. I have a phone number here to ring, to get me name put down on the list. So wha' de yeh think, Kathleen?'

'It sounds great, Alan, and it means I won't have to worry any more, watchin' meself all the time, wonderin' every month am I pregnant or not.' Then I thought of something else. 'But how much is this all goin' to cost us?'

'Around a hundred pound.'

'Oh my God, Alan, where are we supposed to get tha' kind of money?'

'It's all right, Kathleen. I've it all worked out. I'll get a loan off me Da, tellin' him the car is givin' me trouble, and yeh know wha' he's like. There'll be no rush havin' to pay him back all in one go. I'll give him a few bob every now and then when we have it. He'll be none the wiser.'

'Jaysus, Alan. Yeh gave me a fright there for a minute. I thought yeh were goin' to say yer Da knew wha' yeh were up to. I'd never be able to look him straight in the face again. Yeh know wha' they're all like about religion.' I thought about my own side of the family then. 'Christ, Alan, I just got a flash of me Da there. Wha'ever yeh do, never tell him about this. I'd never hear the end of it, with him tellin' me I'm flyin' in the face of God. And then there's Ma. I don't think she'd bat an eyelid, and knowin' her she'll be happy enough tha' I'm not bringin' any more babies into the world. There'll be some lame excuse made by her, glossin' things over as usual when it suits, of course.'

'Right then, it's settled. Yeh're happy enough with everythin' I've told yeh, Kathleen?'

'Would yeh have a look at me face, Alan, I can't get the smile off it. Believe me, I'm more than happy yeh're gettin' this done.'

* * *

A few weeks went by before the appointment came through. Alan thought he'd never get there, to get it over and done with. Not really knowing what to expect and just in case he felt a bit ropey on the way home, he brought my younger brother Thomas with him for a bit of company, swearing him to secrecy.

The night seemed endless and they seemed to be gone forever. I paced the floor as I watched the clock every few minutes. Finally the car pulled up. I was so relieved when Alan walked in the door, looking very pale, I might add, but also very pleased with himself.

'Sit down there, Alan, and I'll make us a cup of tea. Then yeh can tell me all about it.'

75

He filled me in on what had gone on at the doctor's. 'Now yeh know all the gory details of what was said and done, Kathleen. I'll tell yeh the good part,' he started laughing his head off, not able to get the words out.

'Are yeh goin' to tell me or wha'?'

'Righ', are yeh ready? We've to have sex, sex, sex, and sex again, as often as we can, as much as possible.'

I started laughing. 'Will yeh stop yer messin', Alan.'

'I'm tellin' yeh, Kathleen. The doctor told me there's millions of them little swimmers down there tha' I have to get rid of, or it won't be safe for yeh. Yeh'll end up gettin' pregnant again, and we don't want tha', do we? So it's up to us how long it takes before we get the all-clear.'

Once I heard that, there was no stopping me. Alan would only be in the door and as soon as I got the kids out of the way and the coast was clear, I would be giving him the nod, the eye and the wink. There was no way I was having any more babies, so whatever it took, I was on for it. Having said that, we had the best fun along the way, and Alan had a permanent smile on his face.

After about two months we finally decided to have a test done, which meant Alan had to fill a little bottle. I won't go into the details!

'Righ', Kathleen, today's the day.' He handed me the bottle.

'Why are yeh givin' it to me, Alan? Yeh're bringin' it to the hospital, not me.'

'Jaysus, Kathleen, I don't want to go in there with all them nurses and all. Anyway, I can't be late for work. Yeh know I have me name down on the transfer list for Tallaght and I don't want them thinkin' I'm acting the mick. Yeh know tha' this will have to be done a couple of times, just to be on the safe side. So it's best tha' you go from day one. Go on, Kathleen . . . please.'

'Righ' then, Alan. Wha' do I have to do?'

'Well, it has to be kept at body temperature. So yeh'll have to put it on yeh somewhere until yeh get to the hospital. Yeh can't delay, Kathleen; yeh'll have to get in there as quick as yeh can. We don't want any of them little swimmers dying before yeh can get them tested.'

'Well, I'll tell yeh one thing for nothin', Alan, it won't be goin' down me knickers, and tha's for sure. I'll stick it in between me diddies. It'll be safe enough there.'

I got a quick kiss on the cheek and Alan was out the door like a light, in case I changed my mind. I dropped Martina off to school, and got myself into town in no time. So there I was, charging up O'Connell Street, heading for the Rotunda Hospital, pushing Amanda in the buggy and dragging young Alan along the way, all the while checking that the little bottle was still there. Only to be told, when I phoned up a few days later, that the results were still positive.

'I'm afraid, Mrs McGrath, that everything is still very much positive. Come back again in a month's time.'

* * *

And that's what I did, for the next couple of months, with the results the same each time – positive.

'Alan, I don't think tha' this is after workin'. One of the nurses was sayin' to me tha' yeh should be gettin' negative results by now. She said for us to go along to the family plannin' clinic and have a chat with them there.'

'Kathleen, the reason I didn't go there in the first place was because of our age. Yeh're only twenty-six, I'm twenty-seven. They won't do it, I'm tellin' yeh. One of the fellas was sayin' he knew somebody tha' was turned down because they were too young.'

'Come on, Alan. It's worth a try. Wha's the worst thing tha' can happen? Only that they say no.'

* * *

So in I went and made the appointment, which we weren't too long waiting on. I remember the morning we were heading in to see the doctor. Alan seemed to be nervous and never stopped talking, which is unusual for him.

'We have to get this righ', Kathleen. So I want to talk to yeh about a few things before we get there.'

'Wha' about, Alan? '

'Now don't get annoyed with me when I say this, but yeh know the way sometimes yeh can come out with things without thinkin'? Yeh just say wha's on the tip of yer tongue. Well, when the doctor asks yeh a few questions, will yeh try and not be so blunt? Just go along with wha'ever he's sayin'. I don't want anythin' to go against us here.'

'Yeh mean yeh want me to suck up to him. Is tha' wha' yeh're tryin' to say, Alan?'

'Yeah, if tha's wha' it takes, Kathleen. So, will yeh just be careful how yeh phrase things?'

'Yeh're worryin' yerself too much, Alan, but if it makes yeh happy, I'll try and not be too outspoken. Now, come on, let's go in and get this over with.'

It wasn't long before we were sitting in front of the doctor, who was very nice and didn't waste any time in launching into what he had to say.

'Well now, Alan, I see here from your form that you had a vasectomy carried out less than a year ago.'

'Tha's righ', doctor. But it doesn't seem to have worked. Tha's why we're here.'

'In you go there behind the curtain, Alan, so I can examine you.'

They were in there for a while, and I could hear Alan talking away, telling the doctor all about who did it and where he had it done. The doctor didn't say very much on the subject, only to confirm what we already knew – it hadn't worked.

'Now,' said the doctor as he sat back down in his chair, 'I have just one or two questions I would like to ask both of you. Why do you want to get such a permanent job done? I mean, you're very young to be thinking along those lines.'

'Well,' said Alan, 'we had a good talk about this, doctor, and both of us decided tha' we definitely don't want any more kids and tha's for sure.'

'I understand that, but there are contraception methods out there you could use. For instance, Alan, there's Durex; or Kathleen, you could take the pill.'

'Excuse me, doctor,' I said, 'if it's okay, can I say somethin' here?'

You could see Alan breaking into a sweat, not knowing what I was going to say.

'By all means, Kathleen, I would like very much to hear what you have to say.'

'Well, first of all, I can't take the pill – it makes me go crazy mad. I wanted to kill everybody around me when I was on it and tha's not good. And about them Johnny Overcoat things, it's all righ' usin' them now and again, but not forever. Anyway, they're not tha' easy to get.'

'I have to say, Kathleen, that's the first time I've ever heard them called that. Anyway, carry on.'

'No, tha's it, doctor. This is the route we want to take.'

'Hmm, I see. Now, I have just one more thing I would like to ask.' He was looking straight at me as he spoke. 'What if, in a few years' time, you get the longing for another baby? You might be sorry.'

I looked over at Alan while I thought for a second or two. I could see the panic on his face, not knowing what I was going to come out with. I didn't know myself; the words just seemed to flow out of me.

'I don't think tha' will happen, doctor. But if for some reason it does, well then, we'll adopt. Isn't tha' righ', Alan? We did talk about this, doctor, and most definitely tha's wha' we would do.'

'Both of you seem to have your minds made up about this, but because you are so young, I will have to consult with my colleagues and we will let you know in a day or two.'

We must have given the doctor all the answers he wanted to hear, because a few days later Alan had his appointment to get the job done once more, with the results being negative on the first go. Alan was so relieved when I told him, but not half as much as I was.

9

The Priest and the Pay Packet

I had made a good few friends and got to know so many people around Darndale through the hairdressing, and I had tried really hard to settle, especially since the holiday, knowing that I was able to make good money where we were living. But I still longed to live back over near Ma and Da in Crumlin. I missed my brothers and sisters so much; no money could put a price on that. I also knew that if I was able to set myself up once, well, why not again?

With that thought in my mind, I was more determined than ever to move. Alan was happy enough to go along with the plan, which was to save every penny we could and try to get a deposit to buy our own house. But in the meantime, he came in one evening, excited as hell.

'Kathleen, I've great news. Not only for meself, but for you as well. I got me transfer. I'm movin' up to the factory in Tallaght. This not only means tha' I'll be on better money, but we'll be eligible for a house – back over on the southside of the city. It'll be like killin' two birds with one stone.'

'How come, Alan? I don't understand. Why would the Corporation let us change houses just because yeh're movin' in yer job?'

'I found out tha' once yeh live so many miles away from where yeh work, yeh can put in to move. So wha' de yeh think of tha', Kathleen?'

'Oh my God, tha's great news, Alan. Tha' means with the money we have saved we'll be able to do the new house up really nice, and maybe have enough over to buy a shed for me to do the hairdressing in. It doesn't have to be big, just enough room for meself and one or two clients.'

'Jaysus, Kathleen, there's no flies on you. Yeh're always two steps ahead of yerself. Always plannin' away in tha' head of yers, which is no harm at the end of the day.'

'Will yeh mind movin'? I mean, after all the work yeh done in the house, Alan.'

'I knew yeh'd never settle, Kathleen, no matter how hard yeh tried. It's just too far for yeh. So I think it's best tha' we make the move while the chance is there and as yeh said, we have the few bob to do it up straight away. I'll go in first thing in the mornin' and get the forms.'

* * *

There was no way we could get a house in Crumlin or anywhere in or around there. They were like gold dust. The only place that was on offer to us was Tallaght – a place called Killinarden, which we took in the end.

Ma was a bit upset when I told her where we were going to move to.

'I've been prayin' to the Holy Mother herself, mornin', noon and night. I've been askin' her to try and get yiz a little house beside me.'

'I know, Ma, and I would have loved nothin' better, but at least this house is only one bus run for me. Sure I'll be down to yeh all the time. Just wait and see.'

'Every time I think of tha' oul' Pop fella and wha' he did on yiz – havin' to walk away from the lovely home yeh built around yerselves, and not even six months gone by when the fucker went and died, with the house goin' back to the Corporation. May he still be burnin' in hell for wha' he done.'

'Jaysus, Ma. Will yeh keep yer voice down! If Alan hears yeh, no matter wha', he was his grandda.'

'Ah, I can't help meself, Kathleen. When I think back to the way things were. The two of us always together, goin' up and down to the shops, pickin' up our few bargains. Alan droppin' in every other evenin' to pick yeh up. Me and him would sit there havin' a smoke and an oul' yap. De yeh not think I miss all tha'?'

'I tell yeh wha', Ma. We've to pick the keys up in the next couple of days. Why don't yeh come with us?'

That cheered her up a little. 'I suppose I could do tha'. It'll let me see how far it is for when I want to drop out to yeh.'

Just then, Clare came charging in. 'Ma, Ma, Ma – look wha' I have for yeh.' She handed over a little brown envelope. 'I found it up the road. It was lying there on the ground – it's full of money!'

Sure enough, when Ma opened it, it was full of pound notes.

'Phil!' she roared in to Da, who was sitting in the kitchen with Alan, the pair of them talking away, lost in conversation as usual. 'Phil, did yeh hear me?'

'I heard yeh the first time, Lil. Now, wha's all the racket about?'

'Have a look at tha'. There's a name on the front. De yeh know who it is?'

'I can't say I do, but whoever he is I'd say he's frantic by now, after losin' his wage packet.'

Ma sat there thinking for a minute or two as she held on to the money.

'Righ', Kathleen,' she said, 'de yeh want to come for a walk with me?'

'Okay, Ma, but where are we goin'?'

'We'll go up to the priest, see wha' he has to say. Maybe he'll say somethin' about it after mass in the mornin'. Clare, get me coat – yeh're comin' with us, yeh can tell him exactly where yeh found it.'

'Ma, why don't yeh just keep it for yerself? If yeh give it to the priest, tha's probably wha' he'll do,' said Clare.

'I wouldn't have an hour's luck if I did the likes of it, and if yer father hears wha's after comin' out of yer mouth, we'll never hear the end of it.'

'But I was only sayin', Ma.'

'I know, I know, and yeh were a good girl to bring the money in to me, but there's just some things tha' yeh don't do and this is one of them. Now, hand the coat over here to me. Are yeh righ', Kathleen? It'll be dark before we know it, best we make a move.'

So off the three of us headed to the priest's house, while Alan and Da kept an eye on the kids. I looked around as we went through the big iron gates. The grass was neatly cut and there were lots of fresh flowers planted throughout the garden. Not a pebble out of place. Snow-white lace curtains hung perfectly through the gleaming glass windows.

Ma stood there as proud as Punch as she knocked on the door, telling us, 'Wait 'til yeh see Father's face, how pleased he'll be when I hand him the pay packet. He won't be able to thank me enough for being so honest.'

She knocked and knocked again, giving the door a good hard bang on the third go. With that the lights went on and the door was opened. It was the priest, who stood there in all his black, looking as cranky as hell and not a glimmer of a smile on his face. He lashed out at us before Ma could get a chance to open her mouth.

'What is it? What are you looking for at this hour of the night? Can it not wait until tomorrow?' I looked over at Ma and I could see that she was really taken aback. It was far from what she expected and it took her a few seconds before she opened her mouth.

'Is it beggin' tha' yeh think I'm up here for, Father? Is tha' wha' yeh're thinkin'? Well, shame on yeh, tha's all I have to say. God help any poor craythur tha' would be needin' a bit of help, if this is wha' they have to listen to. Shame on yeh again, Father!' With that Ma took out the pay packet and placed it in his hand. 'If it's not puttin' yeh out too much, me child found this a little while ago and I'm sure the poor man is at his wits' end with worry as to how he and his family will get through the week, with not a penny in his pocket. I'd like for yeh to mention it after mass in the mornin' – of course, without sayin' whose name is on it. I don't want any Tom, Dick or Harry tryin' to put a claim on it. And I'll be there meself, of course, if tha's okay with yeh, Father.'

Well, he started to suck up to Ma then, but she wasn't having any of it.

'How kind of you for being so honest. You will get your rewards in heaven for this. What was it you said your name was?'

'I didn't – and yeh can forget yer fancy words and yer airs and graces, it's too late.'

She turned her back and beckoned for us to follow. He was left standing there with his mouth open, and rightly so. We were only out the gate when Clare got her spoke in.

'I told yeh. Yeh should've kept it.'

Ma took no heed of Clare. She walked along in silence, too upset to say anything. As soon as we got home, I told Da what had happened. But of course, he made all sorts of excuses for the priest. They could do no wrong in his eyes. Religion played a big part in Ma and Da's life; the church and priest were always up there on a pedestal, never to be questioned.

The priest wasn't long finding out where Ma lived and made it his business to drop in to see her, letting her know how thankful the man was for the return of his money. He knew how wrong he had been and glossed things over well.

'Well, seein' yeh put it like tha' . . .' said Ma. 'Would yeh like a cup of tea, Father?' All was forgiven.

* * *

A few days later, we picked up the keys from the Corporation and collected Ma on the way. We were up in Tallaght in no time. It was like driving onto a building site. There were no roads, no shops, no schools – nothing. Just a couple of rows of houses plonked in the middle of the mountains.

'This can't be it. Yeh must've taken a wrong turn, Alan.'

'No, I didn't, Kathleen. Killinarden was on the sign as we drove in. Come on, let's see where number seventy is.'

Ma was puffing away on her Woodbines as we struggled through the muck. 'De yeh know somethin', Kathleen?'

'Wha's tha', Ma?'

'This brings back memories to me, so it does, of when I saw me house in Crumlin for the first time. It wasn't too far off like this and I have to say it was the best feelin' ever.'

Just then Alan called out to us. 'Are yeh righ'? It's this one over here.'

There must have been a couple of pounds of muck on the soles of my shoes by the time I got to the house, but I didn't care. I was so happy with what I saw. It was a big corner house, with a fine-sized front garden and a driveway for the car. The inside was just as impressive, but what really got me going was the back garden. It was huge. My brain started ticking over like a race car. I was planning everything out by the second.

'Alan, would yeh have a look at this? We could put a shed along tha' wall for me hairdressin'. I could plant loads of flowers over there. Good Jaysus, there's a back entrance as well. The clients could come in tha' way. Tha' means they won't have to come near the front of the house. I can't believe it, Alan. This is great. It couldn't have turned out any better if we'd planned it!'

'Yeh're gas, Kathleen, most women would be goin' on about doin' the inside of the house up, but not you. Yer business brain always gets in there first. Anyway, I'll have tha' up and runnin' in no time for yeh. Now, we'd better get back inside to yer mother, before she lets out one of her famous screams. She'll frighten the shite out of the builders if she starts.'

Ma wasn't long getting her spoke in. 'I have to say, it's a fine house – there's no way yeh'd get the likes of it anywhere around Crumlin. Yeh have three fine bedrooms there, and would yeh have a look at this kitchen? It's twice the size of mine and then there's tha' big long window in the sittin' room – right down to the ground, with the sun beamin' through it. Yiz landed on yer feet all right. I'm more than happy for yeh.'

'Tha's great, Ma. Tha's after takin' such a load off me mind, just to hear yeh say tha'. Yeh were so upset the other night when I told yeh about the new house. I had meself up the walls with worry, thinkin' about yeh going up and down to the shops on yer own and missin' us and all.'

'I feel a lot better in meself, Kathleen, now tha' I see where yeh're goin' to be livin'. And it's not as far as I expected, so we can take turns droppin' up and down to one another. Tha's if it's okay with yerself, Alan, and knowin' me, half of the gang will tag along.'

'Tha'll never be a problem, Lil. Yeh'll always be more than welcome and I think yeh know tha'.'

'Good. Now we better get back before yer father tears the little bit of hair out tha' he has left on his head, mindin' all them kids.'

As Alan and Ma made their way back to the car, I stood in the garden for a minute or two, giving the house a final look-over. I knew straight away that it was going to be our home for many years to come.

'I know I will definitely settle here.'

10

The Shed

I felt a bit sad when we were moving from Darndale. Even after four and a half years, I still hadn't really settled in, but I knew in the long run that it was best all round for us.

It didn't take us too long to get everything organised. We had moved and were living in Tallaght within the week. Because we had a good few bob saved, we were able to do up the inside of the house straight away. Alan did most of the work himself, so we saved a fair bit of money there.

After about nine months, when most things in the house were done, I had just enough left over to set myself up with my hairdressing business – which, by the way, was to be in a six-by-ten-foot Barna shed. I know, I know; how could you work in something so small? Well, I did, and that's what got me started in my career.

I was so excited the day we went out to buy the shed. We were out for hours, looking everywhere we could think of, trying to get the best deal. I kept getting drawn over to the big fancy sheds. My mouth was watering, thinking of all I could do with the big windows and porch to the front. In my mind

I could see it all done up with snow-white blinds on the windows, a couple of hanging baskets here and there, and maybe a few terracotta pots stuck over in the corner on the porch, all bursting with flowers of every colour you could think of.

But Alan wasn't long bringing me back to reality. He tipped me on the shoulder.

'Come on, Kathleen, yeh're only annoying yerself lookin' at these. There's no way we could afford anythin' like this. Tha's more wha' I had in mind.' He pointed over to the six-by-ten-foot Barna shed.

I sighed. 'Yeh're righ', Alan, tha'll have to do me to get started. As they say, yeh have to creep before yeh walk. And I could always put one hangin' basket beside tha' little window, couldn't I?'

'Tha's my girl. We'll ask yer man how soon he can have it delivered.'

* * *

That happened to be bright and early the very next day.

'Righ', Kathleen,' said Alan, 'they have the shed put together and I've arranged for two fellas to come later on to put the water and electricity in. Now, show me where yeh want everythin'.'

'I have it all worked out in me head, Alan. Put the hooded hair dryer and chair there to the left as I open the door. In the middle I want me dressin' mirror and chair; tha's where I'll work on the clients. Put the sink over there to yer righ' in the corner and I want two shelves above it. They'll hold the shampoo bottles and me bit of stock. Oh, I nearly forgot, Alan – some lino for the floor. Will yeh try and get some of tha' heavy-duty stuff? It'll help keep the heat in and with tha' small heater we have it'll be nice and cosy. So wha' de yeh think?'

'Jaysus, Kathleen, it's goin' to be very tight. Yeh'll barely be able to move, but knowin' you tha' won't stop yeh. Anyway, it won't take me long, I'll have all this done in a couple of days.'

* * *

When it was finished it was tiny but looked really well. That was me ready and rearing to go. All I needed now were a few clients. That was going to be a bit harder this time around, since there was absolutely nothing in the area whatsoever. Only a shop van selling groceries, which just happened to be parked on the road we lived on, which turned out to be lucky for me in the end.

'Alan, you were up buyin' cigarettes off yer man in the van. Wha's he like?'

'He seems friendly enough. Why?'

'De yeh think he'd let me put up a sign about me hairdressin'?'

'Sure all yeh can do is ask him, Kathleen, but I don't imagine there'll be a problem.'

And there wasn't – he was so helpful. The following morning I dropped the kids off extra early to school and was over at the van as he opened the doors.

'Howyeh, mister. I'm Kathleen and I was wonderin' if yeh could put this sign up on the door of yer van for me? I'll throw a free hair cut in for yerself if yeh do.'

'Certainly, love, hand it in here to me. By the way, I'm Paddy. Is it on this road yeh live or the houses at the back of the estate? So's I can tell people when they ask.'

'Jaysus, tha' would be great if yeh could do tha' for me. It's the last corner house on the righ'-hand side at the end of the road – see, there.' I pointed down. 'And I'll tell yeh wha', Paddy, I'll trim yer beard for yeh as well. So don't forget to drop down.'

He did just that and seemed very pleased with the results, telling all who came to his van about me.

Martina and young Alan went to school over on the far side of the main road, through a settled estate called Springfield, which had been there for the past couple of years. It was a good distance from our house, so I made sure I got my spoke in as I walked along chatting to all the other mothers.

It took a while but the word started to spread around and in no time at all I had my first client.

* * *

I'll never forget the first morning I opened up. I was feeling a bit nervous as it was, but when I heard the back gate open, my insides did a somersault. A very tall woman walked in – and I mean tall. I thought to myself, *Good fuck, she'll never fit in me shed*. I didn't get a chance to open my mouth; she launched straight in.

'Righ',' she said, 'are you the wan tha's doin' the hairs? Yer man at the van said I was to come in the back gate – is tha' okay?'

'Yeah, yeah, tha's fine. I asked him to tell people for me.'

I was sweating as she sat in the chair, hoping and praying that she would be looking in the mirror and not at the roof of the shed. I could just about see her face in the mirror and got away with it.

I went to introduce myself but got stopped in my tracks again. 'Now,' she said, 'I just want to say a few things before I let yeh near me. I've had me hair done many times over the years and was never happy. So I started doin' it meself and, as yeh can see, I've made a righ' fuckin' mess of it. I couldn't give two shites about the rest of me, but when it comes to me hair, it's me pride and joy. So I hope yeh get it righ' on the first go.

Cause yeh see this mouth of mine? Well, it'll either do wonders for yeh or it won't. So am I clear in wha' I'm sayin'?'

I was starting to shit myself at that stage and I hadn't even touched a hair on her head, which was a canary yellow colour with about six inches of black roots – and she said she was fussy!

I cleared my throat, hoping that what I wanted to say would come out right. 'First of all, before we go any further, I'm Kathleen. Yeh're very welcome; and yer name is?'

'Me name is Rosalina, but everybody calls me Ro.'

'Well now, Ro, wha' we're goin' to do first is have a little chat. You tell me wha' yeh like and don't like and I'll throw a few suggestions in along the way and I'm sure we'll come up with a nice style between us.'

She had settled down by the time I was finished talking. I worked for the best part of the morning transforming her hair. I was very happy with the results; all I needed now was for Ro to feel the same.

I stood there anxiously waiting as she checked the colour out, played around with her fringe and fluffed the back of her hair out a few times, still not saying a word.

'Well, wha' de yeh think, Ro? De yeh like it?'

'It's massive, Kay. I fuckin' love it. Wait 'til all me sisters and friends see this. I'm tellin' yeh, yeh'll be out the door with work by the time I'm finished.'

Thank God, I thought. The relief – I was able to breathe again!

'Oh, by the way, Ro, as I said, me name's Kathleen.'

'Well, I hate long names, righ', so I'll be callin' yeh Kay.'

It didn't matter how many times I said it, she always called me Kay and that's what I became known as in the hairdressing business.

* * *

Ro went on to be one of my best clients and a good friend over the years, spreading the word about me to all she knew. After that first day I couldn't believe the number of people who were knocking on the front door or coming in the back gate.

I was so busy and, with the shed being so small, I had to start taking appointments, which was better for me in the long run. I would try to do as many haircuts as I could while the kids were at school. If I couldn't fit a client in at that time, I would work the odd evening when they were in bed.

There was one evening in particular that always sticks out in my mind. Josie, who became a regular client, asked me if I could do her perm after hours, which wasn't a problem – or so I thought. She arrived on the dot of eight as planned.

'There yeh are, Kay, thanks for fittin' me in at this late hour. I would have come durin' the day, but I just couldn't get anybody to mind the four kids for me and there's no way I'd go into hospital lookin' like this. So make sure tha' yeh give me a nice tight perm tha' will last me a while, because as soon as this baby comes into the world, God only knows how long it will be before I'll be around to see yeh again.'

'Josie, yeh seem to be goin' around forever with tha' bump. When exactly are yeh due?'

'I should have been gone two weeks ago, Kay. I don't know wha's wrong this time. I'm always bang on me dates. If this keeps up they'll have to put a bomb up me arse to shift me.'

'Two weeks, yeh say, Josie? Tha' means yeh could go any minute . . . No, I don't think I should give yeh a perm. Just get a cut and blowdry until afterwards.'

'Ah, for Jaysus' sake, Kay, don't say tha'. I've been lookin' forward to gettin' me hair done all day. Sure come on, don't be worryin', yeh'll have it done in no time at all. Yeh know you – yeh're like Flash Gordon when yeh start.'

So I went against my better judgement and started the perm. 'Righ' then, Josie, lie back there at the sink and I'll get yeh washed.' She had tons of hair, which meant I had a good few hours' work ahead of me.

I was halfway through the perm when I saw Josie bite her lip and make a few faces. I didn't want to keep going on about it, so I didn't say anything but kept working and chatting away, trying to get the perm done as quickly as I could. That was, until she let out such a roar and then went into the heavy breathing sound.

'Holy Jaysus, Josie, yeh're after frightenin' the life out of me. You didn't just start gettin' pains now – when did yeh go into labour?'

'Kay, I'm sorry for lyin', but I hate me hair straight and I really wanted me curls back in. I knew if I told yeh there was no way yeh'd do it for me.'

'Josie, tell me, when did yeh start?' I was actually grinding my teeth at this stage as I spoke.

'Me waters broke early this afternoon. Ah! Ah! Ah!' she roared, over and over again.

'Oh my God, oh my God! That means yeh're not far off havin' this baby. Wha' am I goin' to do? I'll have to get the ambulance.'

'I want me hair finished. Yeh can't let me go into the hospital with me hair straight on one side and curly on the other.'

'Fuck yer hair, Josie! Who de yeh think yeh are, the Holy Mother herself? De yeh want to deliver yer baby here in me little shed? Now please, come on, I'll have to get yeh to the hospital."

I screamed in for Alan to come out to me while I tried to calm myself and Josie down. He didn't waste any time in phoning for the ambulance.

Josie was rocking and roaring in the chair but I managed to take the rollers out and was spraying water like mad to rinse the lotion out.

'I promise yeh, Josie, when yeh come home I'll come round to yer house and do yer hair.' I was doing and saying anything I could think of to pacify her. At this stage she was bent over in pain and didn't give two shites what I was saying. 'Now, come on, yeh know wha' to do – big deep breaths. In and out, in and out, tha's it.'

I was never so happy to hear an ambulance siren. The two men were so friendly and took charge straight away.

'There you go, madam, your chariot awaits.' One of them helped her into the wheelchair and took her out through the back gate to the ambulance.

'Don't worry, Josie,' I shouted after her. 'I'll slip around and tell Eddie tha' yeh're gone to the hospital.'

I made my way around to the house straight away. Eddie wasn't too happy when I told him what had happened.

'For fuck sake, Kay – I told her not to go around, but would she listen? No! Sorry about all this, I'd better make me way down to the Coombe. I'll let yeh know what happens. Thanks again.'

I couldn't believe it the next day when he told me the news – that their little baby was born in the back of the ambulance as they drove down the Greenhills Road, less than ten minutes' drive from my house. I got the shakes just thinking about what could have been.

I gave Josie a couple of days after she came home from the hospital before I made my way around to do her hair. She was well pleased when she saw me standing there. It was far from funny at the time, but we had a good laugh about how easily her baby boy could have been born in my little shed.

* * *

Over the next two years I saved every penny I could, cutting corners every which way I could, always with the help of Alan. I had a goal set in my mind, which was to expand my business. So I decided it was time for me to get a proper building out in my back garden. It looked like a real hairdressing salon by the time Alan was finished, with plenty of room this time, which helped me to go from strength to strength, building up a very good established business. But it was my little shed that got me off the ground, and that I will never forget.

11

The Runaway

I was very lucky to be able to work from home. That way I was there all the time for the kids, who were starting to get a bit older and needed a good eye kept on them, especially Martina. She was around eleven and a half at that stage, as cocky as they come, trying to be more grown up than her years, but I wouldn't be long putting her in her place.

Except for one occasion. It was Saturday afternoon. I was busy working on a client's hair when in she walked.

'Hi, Ma, can I go down to the roller rink in Crumlin? There's a whole load of girls goin'.'

'Yeh know yeh're not allowed, so the answer is no. Now, go back out to the front of the house and play around. And keep an eye to Amanda when yeh're there.'

'Ah, Ma! Please? Go on. Yeh never let me do anythin'.'

That's when I gave her the look, which should have been enough; but no, she kept it up, going on and on at me, hoping I would say yes in front of the client. There was no way that was going to happen.

'I'm sorry about this, Mary. I'll be back in two minutes.'

I took Martina by the hand, half-dragging her out the door, with the client shouting after me, 'Don't worry about me, Kay. I know wha' they're like. I have a few little fuckers at home meself. Do yer head in, they would.'

'Martina, wha' did I tell yeh about goin' on and on at me when I'm workin'?'

'But Ma, they're all goin'.'

'I don't give two shites who's goin' where – *you're* not. Now get yerself back out there and don't move off the road. De yeh hear me?'

As I made my way back to the client, little did I know the worry and upset that was ahead for me that night.

* * *

It was around half past five when I finished work and locked up for the night. My younger sister Patricia arrived just as I was about to call the kids in.

'Howyeh, Kathleen. Any chance of a haircut? I would've been up earlier than this only I missed the bloody bus.'

'Go on in, Patricia. I'll be with yeh in a minute.'

I turned to young Alan. 'De yeh know where Martina is?'

'She said tha' she was goin' up to the shops, Ma.'

'Did she now – well, I'll sort her out as soon as she comes in. It'll be straight up to bed for her for goin' against me. Now, come in, the pair of yeh. It's startin' to get dark out.'

'Wha's wrong with yeh, Kathleen?' said Patricia. 'Yeh're all fired up. Is it me comin' late?'

'Jaysus, no, Patricia. It's Martina; she's gone off the road and I told her not to move. She keeps wantin' to do things tha' she's too young for. I swear, when I get me hands on her . . .'

'Yeh know somethin', Kathleen, yeh sound exactly like Ma. Now, will yeh sit yerself down and I'll make yeh a nice cup of tea. Wait'll yeh see, she'll be knockin' on the door in the next half-hour, suckin' up to yeh. I used to do it with Ma all the time.'

'Ah, I suppose yeh're righ', Patricia. De yeh really think I'm like Ma?'

'Yeah!'

I had the dinner on in no time, while the other two watched the telly with Patricia. I was still uneasy, so I slipped up to the shop, checking to see if Martina had been in. The women said no. She wasn't to be found anywhere. I had myself in a right tizzy as I walked back to the house, thinking all the while, *If tha' little bitch is after makin' her way down to tha' roller rink, I swear to Jaysus I'll fuckin' kill her. No, she wouldn't do tha'. Sure where would she get the money from?*

Then it dawned on me; that's when my blood really started to boil. As soon as I got to the house, I went straight upstairs to where I kept my bill money and, sure enough, thirty pounds was missing. Talk about being worked up! I was doing somersaults in my head.

It was just as well Alan walked in then because I was getting ready to let out such a scream that I would have frightened the life out of the other two kids. I was ranting and raving so much, Alan couldn't make sense of what was coming out of my mouth.

'Good Jaysus, Kathleen, will yeh calm yerself down and tell me wha's after happenin'?'

So I went into the goings-on of the day. I was convinced in my mind that Martina was down in the roller rink. Alan checked straight away – not a sign of her there, or at any of her friends' houses. Up to this, I had been so angry at her for not doing what she was told and then, to top it off, robbing money!

There was no way Patricia was going to get her hair done that evening. Instead, she ended up looking after the younger kids for me.

My anger soon changed to fear as we walked the streets looking in every nook and cranny of the estate, with not a sighting of her anywhere to be found. I was frantic and sick to the pit of my stomach, as was Alan.

It was now ten o'clock and we were starting to think the worst. It was rare back then to hear of a child going missing and never to be found, but it did happen. With that thought in both of our minds, we decided to go to the police, only to be told that she had to be missing for twenty-four hours before they could do anything about it. But they asked us for a description of Martina and what clothing she was wearing, letting us know that the local cars would keep an eye out for her.

I don't know how Alan drove the car home that night. He was green in the face with worry, but still trying to keep a front up for me. I was falling to pieces, thinking only the worst.

'Come on, Kathleen, she's probably in somebody's house tha' we haven't checked. I'll go around again when we get home. Now, try and pull yerself together. Yeh'll only be upsettin' the other two kids.'

'Yeh're righ', Alan. Tha's wha' it is. She's hidin' out in somebody's house, too afraid to come home after wha' she's done.'

When Alan dropped me off to go and check once more, I tried really hard to keep that thought in my mind, at the same time hoping and praying that she would be there when I walked into the house. But there was only Patricia sitting there, with young Alan and Amanda asleep beside her.

Martina was nowhere to be found. Alan paced the floor, smoking his brains out while I drank cup of tea after cup of tea.

* * *

It was coming up to midnight when the phone rang. I had it in my hand before Alan could get to it.

'Hello? . . . Hello!' I said. There was silence at the other end. 'Martina, is tha' you? Please tell me where yeh are and we'll come and get yeh.'

A young girl's voice answered me – not Martina. 'Yeh're all righ', Mrs McGrath, we're okay.' And that was it – she hung up.

I stood there with the phone in my hand, my mouth open, unable to speak. Alan was frantic.

'Kathleen, will yeh say somethin', for Jaysus' sake! Was tha' Martina?'

'No, no, Alan, it wasn't her. It was some young wan, sayin' they're okay, and then she hung up. Wha' will we do? Should we phone the police and tell them?'

'Yeh heard wha' they said, Kathleen, we'll have to wait it out and hope tha' she's safe in somebody's house.'

'We can't just sit here, we have to do somethin'. I'm going back out again to look for her.'

Alan came over and put his arm around me. 'Come on, love, there's no point. I've been everywhere. Anyway, it's best tha' we're here, just in case she comes home.'

* * *

That was one of the longest nights of my life. I never closed my eyes for one second. I cried and cried so much, thinking the worst all the time. Eventually the light shone through the sitting-room windows. It was morning at last. I looked over at Alan, who looked tired and worn out with worry, but still trying to keep a front up for all of us.

Patricia looked after the kids while we both walked the streets once more, looking everywhere and anywhere we thought she might be. Still she was nowhere to be found. My legs were starting to go from under me as we made our way back to the house. I couldn't help myself. I was falling to pieces. Alan got me to lie down on the couch, trying to calm me down.

'Please, Kathleen, try and keep it together. Yeh're upsettin' the other two kids.'

'I know, I know, I'm sorry, Alan. Amanda, come over here, pet. Young Alan, sit down here beside me.'

I sat there with my arms around both of them for I don't know how long, as I watched the minutes on the clock tick by.

Then the phone rang. I nearly jumped out of myself, I got such a fright. Alan answered it this time. I was sitting there with my hands up to my mouth, not knowing what to expect as I listened to him speak.

'Yes, yes, tha's righ'. I'm Mr McGrath. Okay, could yeh hold onto them for me? It'll take me about fifteen minutes to get there.' He hung up. 'Come on, Kathleen, she's okay. Tha' was the receptionist up in the Downshire Hotel in Blessington. They booked in there last night.'

'Did I hear yeh righ', Alan? Martina's been in a hotel all night? Is tha' wha' yeh're sayin'?'

'Kathleen, let's just go and get her. We'll talk about this later.'

'Wait 'til I get me hands on her, Alan. I'm goin' to fuckin' kill her for wha' she's after puttin' us through.'

* * *

Alan drove so fast there was smoke coming out of the wheels. We were there in no time at all.

Just as we were walking in the front door of the hotel, Martina and another girl whom I recognised – she lived in a house on our estate – were walking down the stairs, with not a care in the world and looking none the worse for wear. They stopped dead in their tracks, not knowing where to look when they saw us and at the same time getting ready to run. Of course, they didn't get a chance to do that; Alan made sure of it.

Out of the corner of my eye, I happened to get a glance over at the reception area, where two wans were standing there, giggling to one another. I was fit to be tied and wasn't long letting them know how I felt.

'I'm glad yeh're amused. De yeh realise the night we're after havin'? Why didn't one of yeh get the police to check them out? Surely to God yeh knew they were too young? And by the way, where did yeh get our phone number from?'

'One of the young girls phoned down to reception for an outside line. The number was in the log,' one of them replied.

'Well then, why the hell didn't yeh ring us last night?'

Neither of them knew what to say or where to look.

'Leave it, Kathleen,' said Alan. 'Take the pair of them out to the car while I talk to the women.'

My first reaction was to hug Martina, as any mother would do. I was so happy that she was okay and safe. Then my blood started to boil as I sat there in the car thinking about the night we had just been put through. All I kept hearing was 'Sorry Ma', 'Sorry Mrs McGrath'. I would neither look at nor answer either one. I was afraid that if I opened my mouth, I wouldn't be able to hold back. I thought it best to wait until I got into my own house; then I'd explode.

There wasn't a word spoken all the way home. We dropped the young girl off outside her house, making sure she went in. As soon as we got inside our door, Alan sent Martina to her room, before I got a chance to lose the plot altogether. And he was so right; screaming and shouting wasn't the answer. So I calmed myself down and we both made our way upstairs to

Paul and Mano, the tough guys

On the boats at Butlin's: Mano,
Paul, Patricia and Martina

A fun day out: Martina, Jacinta,
Paul, Mano and Patricia

Ma and Da in Canada

Philip Doyle

Phil the Champ

Phil's boys, Philip, JJ and Andrew

Ma in Crumlin

Amanda on her first communion, with myself, Ma,
young Alan, Martina and baby Treasa

My three kids, Martina, Amanda
and young Alan

Growing up: myself with Amanda,
Martina and King the dog

Martina with little Danielle

Martina with Alan and the ice-cream van

Kathleen and Danielle when
I first because a granny

Myself and my other
granddaughter, Jessica

Granddaughter, Robyn

The wild one: Clare's son Dominic on the "funny farm"

Clare's youngest, Romano

Hot wheels: Alan and I on holiday

Ma

Ma with her great-granddaughter, Danielle

The whole gang: Clare, Marion, Noel, Carmel, Mano, Jacinta,
Paul, Patricia, me and Thomas. Only poor Phil is missing

Baby Conor with his great-grandmother and
great-great-grandmother

Myself and Alan, still in love

Martina to talk and try to find out what brought all this about.

She sat on the end of her bed and told us, point-blank to our faces, 'Yiz never let me go anywhere! Every time I ask yeh, it's always, "no, no". I made up me mind that I wanted to be like the hippies and see wha' it's like without all yer rules.'

Just at that very second I wanted to give her such a clatter, but I stopped myself because I had promised Alan I wouldn't. So I bit my lip and listened until she was finished.

'Now,' said Alan, 'and how did yeh like it out there without us and our rules?'

'I didn't, Da. Because nearly all the money was gone. We bought fish and chips and loads of bars of chocolate and had a party in the room and then Tara bought a brush for her hair, 'cause it goes all fuzzy and I'd forgot mine, and then the women wanted money off us. And there was hardly any left, so she made us pick up all the leaves around the hotel, and I didn't know wha' to do next. I'm sorry, Ma. I'm sorry, Da. I'll never do anythin' like tha' again, I promise.'

'Well,' I said, 'I certainly hope not.'

I could feel the anger leave me as I moved over to put my arms around her. I was only glad to have her home safe and sound but, at the same time, if only to teach her a lesson, I made her pay us back every penny out of her weekly pocket money – which took her a very long time.

As I was walking out the bedroom door, I couldn't believe what she said next.

'Ma, it was lovely in tha' hotel. Any chance we could all go back up sometime?'

'No problem, pet – when *you're* payin'!'

12

The Party

Da was sixty-six now and coming up for retirement soon. He had worked all his life, taking very little time off work for himself, so we all decided that we were going to have a big night out. Nothing but the best for our Da, so we booked Clontarf Castle.

You could see he was well pleased when we told him, but he put up a front. 'Now wha' did yiz go and do tha' for?' he said. 'Spendin' all tha' money when there's no need for it.'

'Ah, would yeh listen to yerself, Phil Doyle,' said Ma. 'Puttin' on the act when I know, and so does everybody else, tha' yeh're only delighted with yerself.'

'Yeh always have somethin' to say to me, Lil, don't yeh? Will I ever see the day tha' somethin' nice will come out of tha' mouth of yers?'

'Go and ask me arse and don't be annoyin' me,' said Ma as she made her way into the kitchen.

'I swear, Kathleen, one of these days tha' mother of yers is goin' to push me too far. I mean it, too far.'

'Yeh're worse, Da, to be takin' any notice of her. Yeh should let it roll off yeh like wha' we all do. And if the truth be known, I think she does be windin' yeh up most of the time just to get yer back up'.

'Well then, if tha' be the case, Kathleen, there's no need for it, no need at all.'

'Come on now, Da, forget about all tha'. We have another little surprise for yeh before yer big night out. Noel is goin' to bring yeh into town on Saturday to kit yeh out with all the trimmin's – new suit, shoes, shirt and tie, and to top it off, a new trilby hat. So wha' de yeh think of tha'? And before yeh say anythin' about money, Da, we all chipped in, costin' each of us only a few pound.'

'Well, I suppose when yeh put it like tha', Kathleen, I'll be lookin' forward to me big night out. But wha' about yer mother – will she be gettin' a new frock?'

'Don't worry about Ma, tha's all sorted. Carmel and Jacinta are bringin' her in to Meath Street to pick up a few nice bits. Anyway, yeh're gas, Da, less than five minutes ago yeh wanted to kill her.'

'Hmm,' he said, 'well, tha' was different.'

'The pair of yiz will be like film stars when yiz make yer entrance.'

And so they were, with both of them looking really well on the night – and what a night it turned out to be.

* * *

I had to laugh at Alan that night as we were getting ready to go to Da's party. Every time I looked at him, he was stuck in front of the mirror admiring himself.

'Are yeh lookin' at yer pearly whites again, Alan?'

'I know, I can't help it, Kathleen. The difference these new teeth make, it's unbelievable, after all the problems I've had over the years.'

'And so they bloody well should with the price of them!' I laughed and gave him a nudge. 'Now, will yeh come on or we'll be late.'

The night started off well, with a nice big fancy meal. Ever so posh it was. There was a big show after, which Da was very impressed with, followed by a bit of dancing, with every one of us up on the floor, having the best craic ever. Even Ma and Da got up to dance together, which was great to see.

I was breathless from jumping around dancing with them all and had to sit down for a minute or two, when out of the corner of my eye I copped Alan, heavy into conversation with Paul, one of my younger brothers, who had just turned eighteen. I could see that Paul was getting himself into a right tizzy. As I watched, he turned on his heels and went outside. I made my way over to Alan who at this stage was swaying from side to side, just about keeping himself off the floor.

'Jaysus Christ, Alan, this is not like you. Yeh're langered. Come over here and sit down. Now, wha' did yeh say to Paul?'

'I was just tellin' him a bit of home truth. He was sayin' he's goin' to start bringin' yer Da for a pint now tha' he's old enough and I told him tha' will never happen – as soon as tonight's over he'll go about his business and won't bother his arse, just like the rest of them. So he got annoyed and stormed off.'

'Can yeh blame him gettin' annoyed? It's a wonder he didn't give yeh a dig. I can't believe yeh said all tha', Alan! You of all people tha' never has a bad word to say about anybody – and of all the nights yeh pick to speak yer mind!'

But I might as well have been talking to myself. He wasn't minding a thing I was saying. He was away with the fairies, which I wasn't used to looking at and didn't like one bit. I made my way out to Paul, who had a right sup on him as well and was giving out like mad.

'Paul, don't be mindin' Alan, tha's just a load of shite-talk comin' out of him. It's the drink, tha's all it is. He'll be sick tomorrow when I tell him wha' he said to yeh, and he'll be even sicker when I'm finished with him.'

I thought it was all going to be left at that, so I made my way back in to Ma and Da, who were just finishing off the last dance of the night. They both said that they'd had the best night ever. The place slowly started to empty. People were gathering their belongings and making their way home and in no time at all the crowds were gone, leaving only our family standing around outside the castle.

I looked over and there were Thomas, Paul, Mano and Patricia's husband Josh, with Carmel's boyfriend Shay. I could see that there was something brewing; their voices were getting louder and each of them was trying to talk over everybody else.

I called Noel over. 'Get Ma and Da into a taxi, quick. I think there's goin' to be trouble.'

'Where, Kathleen, where? With who?' said Noel.

'I'll fill yeh in in a minute; just get them off side.' Noel got it sorted and they were gone before I knew it, giving me enough time to tell him what Alan had said.

'He's a stupid little fuck, Kathleen. Of all nights, he decides to say his piece! I mean I don't know wha' he's scutterin' about. Paul and Mano were too young to go to the pub and meself and the Thomas fella have been out many a time with Da for a drink.'

'I know, Noel, yeh don't have to tell me. I want to fuckin' kill him meself.'

Just then I saw Alan making his way over to all the fellas. Josh and Shay walked away, with Carmel taking them and the other girls home in her van – leaving me with all these lunatics.

That's when the pushing and shoving started. Alan got knocked to the ground. I ran over as Noel tried to stop them. I got a fist in the face myself and landed on the ground beside him.

At that, Alan said, 'Now, wha's going on here, fellas, for yeh to be all fired up, hittin' me and threatenin' me like tha'?'

Can you believe it? And him after starting the whole thing! I wanted to punch the head off him myself. Well, one word borrowed another and soon they were all punching and killing each other. Alan got a dig in the face that knocked his false teeth out and sent them flying in the air, teeth we had just paid two hundred pounds for the previous week.

I let out such a scream: 'Stop, stop!' And they all did, for a split second. 'Don't move! It's Alan's teeth,' I said, 'don't walk on them, wha'ever yeh do.' When I looked, they were lying right beside Thomas's foot. I bent down, picked them up and stuck them in my pocket.

I thought that might have stopped them, but, no, the fight carried on. This time Noel was the one who got the full force of a punch in the nose, even though he was the one doing everything in his power to stop them. The blood poured down his face and you could see at this stage that he was really pissed off. Noel is quiet enough when left alone, but when pushed he has the temper of a lion.

I knew if he got involved, they should all look out, so I ran over to one of the bouncers and asked if they would please help me break the fight up. One of them turned around and said, 'Are you mad? Look what they're doing to one another, and they're family! No way!' Instead, they went in and locked the doors behind them.

When I turned around and looked over, Noel had Alan up in the air. He was like King Kong, twirling him around.

Before I could stop him, he threw Alan over the wall of the grounds and then made a run at the rest of them, with each one running to get away from him. I don't know how Alan didn't break his back because he fell across the stump of a tree and screamed in pain. Between the roars of him and the noise of the police sirens arriving, I don't know who was loudest, but it wasn't long bringing the fight to a stop.

We all stood there, me with my swollen eye; Noel with the blood still pumping from his nose; Thomas, Mano and Paul with their lips and eyes cut to bits, and all of their shirts hanging off them covered in blood; and last but not least, the upstart of the whole thing, Alan, bent over in pain, with not a tooth in his head, still mumbling away to himself, talking a load of shite.

'Right,' said one of the gardaí, 'my colleague here tells me that he has spoken to the manager and there is no damage done to the premises. So, do any of you want to press charges against the others?'

'Now, why would we do tha', guard?' said Thomas. 'We're all brothers.' Each of the others said the same.

'Okay then,' said the gardaí, 'none of you are in any fit state to drive, so all cars will be left here – and I mean this, if any of you attempt to drive, and we will be keeping an eye out, I'll throw the book at each and every one of you, so bear that in mind. Now, my advice is, get yourselves home and sleep it off.'

'I don't drink, guard,' I said. 'I'll make sure to get them all home.'

And off they went, leaving us standing there. We all scarpered over to my van as quickly as we could in case they came back and changed their minds. As I drove home, with Alan asleep in the front, all I could hear from the back was who got the better digs in at one another, and then the singing started.

Alan was in a right mess the next morning and couldn't remember a thing, but I filled him in about the goings-on of the night. I showed him the black eye that I got, all because of him.

'Yeh better go around them all and make yer peace, Alan McGrath. Because I'll never hear the end of it if yeh don't. And believe me, neither will you.'

'Kathleen, are yeh sure yeh're not addin' a bit more on here than wha' really happened? I mean, yeh know you and yer family – arms and legs are added on before things get around.'

'Yeh needn't start all tha', Alan. There's no way yeh're gettin' outta this. So yeh may head off now and start doin' yer rounds, makin' Paul's yer first stop. And he won't be long tellin' yeh wha' happened.'

And off he went, with egg all over his face and his tail between his legs, having to suck up to each and every one of them.

They all made sure he never forgot it. With the slagging that they gave him, for such a long time afterwards, Alan made sure that he was on his best behaviour for future parties to come.

13

The Crasher

It was two weeks before Christmas. Martina and young Alan had gone to school. I was getting myself ready to go into town with Amanda, to get her Christmas clothes, when Alan's brother Paul knocked on the door.

'Howyeh, Paul. Come in. Wha' has yeh up here so early?'

'There yeh are, Kathleen. Is Alan around?'

'Yeah, yeah, he's out in the garage.'

'I was goin' to ask him would he give me a hand doin' a bit of paintin'. Yeh know the way he's good at the decoratin'. I'm hopeless when it comes to all tha'.'

'I'm sure he won't mind givin' yeh a dig-out, Paul. Here he is now, ask him yerself.'

The two of them sat in the kitchen yapping away while I tidied around the house before I headed off myself. They decided to take my small van, leaving Paul's brand new car parked in our driveway, and the keys in full view on the kitchen table, which shouldn't have been a problem.

That was until young Alan, who was thirteen at the time, came home on his lunch break from school and decided to take the car out for a drive – which, of course, he couldn't do.

* * *

I was in town the best part of the day and it was coming up for around five o'clock when I got off the bus. Amanda was skipping along in front of me, while I was lost in my thoughts, planning the dinner.

Just as I came around the corner onto our road, I was stopped dead in my tracks. I couldn't believe my eyes. There was Paul's brand new car, crashed through the front garden of a neighbour's house, only inches away from their front door, with walls knocked down all over the place. Never in my wildest dreams would I have suspected that young Alan would have anything to do with this, but as soon as I knocked on the door I found out the truth. Our neighbour lashed into me straight away, screaming and shouting at me, and I couldn't blame him one bit.

'Where the hell have you been? Look wha' yer son's done – look!' he said. 'De yeh realise he could have killed me or me wife if one of us had been standin' in the garden – or, for tha' matter, a child playin' around out there.'

I stood there with my mouth open, not knowing what to say. The only words that eventually came out of my mouth were, 'I'm sorry, I'm so sorry.'

'I've been waiting hours for one of yous to show your face. You will be sorry by the time I'm finished – because it's the guards I'm ringin' now!' He closed the door in my face.

I made my way over to the house in a complete daze. I ran around looking for young Alan but he was nowhere to be found. I was only in the door a couple of minutes when my sister Patricia, who lived nearby, knocked on the door. I broke down crying when I saw her standing there.

'Before yeh say anythin', Kathleen, young Alan is in my house. But don't worry, he's not hurt, and neither is anybody else.'

'Thank God for tha', Patricia. I didn't know wha' to be thinkin'. I can't believe he's after doin' this. Oh my God, wait 'til Paul sees his car. Alan is goin' to go mad when he hears about this. Christ, wha' am I goin' to do?'

'First of all, Kathleen, come up to my house and talk to young Alan. He has himself in an awful state; he's green in the face with worry.'

'And so he should be, Patricia, for bringin' all this trouble on us. And for wha' – a jaunt in a car? I'll fuckin' kill him when I get me hands on him'.

As soon as I got to Patricia's house I made a run to give Alan a dig, but he was like lightning and I couldn't catch him. All he kept saying was, 'Sorry, sorry Ma', as I chased him around. I was breathless and had to sit down.

'In the name of Jaysus, Alan de yeh realise how serious this is? Yer man is gettin' the police for yeh. Wha'ever possessed yeh to do such a thing?'

'I'm sorry, Ma, I just wanted to see wha' it was like to drive. I didn't mean to do any harm. Me foot slipped and I hit the accelerator instead of the brake. Sorry, sorry.'

'Listen to this, Kathleen, it might put a smile back on yer face,' said Patricia. 'De yeh know wha' he did after he crashed the car? Put the keys back in the house and went back to school – can yeh believe tha'? He was hopin' yiz might think somebody robbed it. And he would've got away with it, only yer man was up on the roof of his garage lookin' at him drive the car through his garden.'

'How de yeh know all this, Patricia?'

'Well, Alan told me everythin' when he came up and one of the neighbours stopped me when I was goin' in to yeh earlier on – sure yer man was tellin' everyone.'

I shook my head and looked over at young Alan, giving him 'the look'. 'I'd better go back down to the house, Patricia. Can he stay here with yeh for a while? There's goin' to be blue murder when Paul sees his car, never mind when Alan finds out how it happened.'

'You go ahead, Kathleen; I'll drop him down in a couple of hours. Things might have cooled down a bit by then.'

'I don't think so, Patricia, but we'll see. And listen here, Alan McGrath,' I roared, shaking my fist into his face, 'don't move outside this house, de yeh hear me?'

He just looked at me, not saying a word.

* * *

Just as I got to our house, Paul and Alan were driving around the corner. The look on both their faces said it all – they were in shock. Paul jumped out of the van first.

'Holy fuck! Look at me car – wha's after happenin' here, Kathleen?'

I didn't get a chance to open my mouth, because the neighbour was out straight away, screaming and shouting again. We tried to talk to him, saying that we would pay for the damage.

'Bloody sure yeh'll pay,' he said, 'and so will yer son because I'll be pressin' charges against him.'

I nearly fainted when I heard that. I made my way over to the house with Amanda, who was starting to get upset with all the carry-on, leaving Alan and Paul to see if they could change his mind about bringing the police into it. There was no way they could reason with him, so they followed me over.

Alan was in the height of it. I had never seen him so angry before. 'Kathleen, where is he?' he asked.

'Up in Patricia's house, Alan. He went there after school.' I told them the full story. I could see a grin coming on Paul's face, which I was so happy to see.

'Come on, Alan,' he said, 'at least nobody got hurt. The wall and the car can be fixed and maybe when yer man calms down he won't go ahead with the charges.' That helped, but only a bit. Alan sat there brooding in silence.

Then there was a knock on the door. I jumped up with the fright. I could see through the glass as I went to open the door that it was the police and I could feel myself shaking inside as I called to Alan.

'We would like to speak to you about the incident down the road, concerning the car in the garden.'

'Come on in, guards,' said Alan. 'This is me brother Paul here, who owns the car, and it was our son who tried to drive it.'

'I see,' said the guard, 'and where is your son now?'

'He's up the road in me sister's house. Will I go up and get him for yeh?' I asked.

'No, leave him there for the moment.' He asked us all about young Alan. Had he ever been in trouble before? What kind of a boy was he? Even though Alan was still very annoyed, I could see how proud he was telling the guards about our son being on the hurling team in the school, playing matches every weekend and also being into the soccer. I was taking everything on board, but at the same time praying like mad, asking all my guardian angels to please make all this go away, which of course they didn't.

The guards seemed to be happy enough with what we told them, but they made it clear how serious it was. 'Even if the gentleman decides not to press charges,' said one of the guards, 'more than likely we might have to. Your son did steal a vehicle and drove with no tax or insurance.' I could feel the blood drain from my face.

'Can I say somethin' here, guard?' said Paul, 'I won't be reportin' tha' me car was taken.'

'Is that so, sir? Now what you're telling me is you gave your car to a minor, to take out on the road to drive, and if that is the case, then we will be charging you.'

Holy Jaysus, I thought to myself, *this is gettin' worse by the minute*.

That's when Alan stepped in. 'Guard, me brother is just tryin' to help out here, tha's all. It happened like I said. Our son will have to pay the price for wha' he did and, believe me, he won't be gettin' off lightly with us. So if yeh can try and keep him out of the courts, I'd very much appreciate it.'

'Right then, Mr McGrath,' said the guard as he got up to leave, 'bring Alan down to the station tomorrow evening around seven o'clock and I'll have a talk with him and we'll take it from there. But in the meantime, go over and get the car out of the gentleman's garden and see if you can come to some sort of an arrangement about getting the walls fixed straight away, and any other damage that was done.'

'I'll do tha' now,' said Alan, 'and all I can say is I'm sorry about all this bother me son is after causin'.' Alan was sucking up like mad to the guards.

It wasn't too long after they left that Patricia walked in with young Alan, who was shitting himself. He got lashed out of it by both Alan and Paul, with the pair of them ranting and raving to beat the band. And that was the easy part. Then he had to run the gauntlet with me. I would usually scream, shout and maybe throw a few fucks in along the way, but this was too serious and had to be handled with great caution. So I was very calm, which surprised even me, never mind everyone else.

'Alan, go to yer room,' I said. 'I'll speak to you later. Martina, take Amanda upstairs with yeh. I'll call yiz down as soon as dinner is ready.' The pair of them thought they'd never get up the stairs fast enough to find out what their brother had been up to.

After Paul and Patricia left, I sat there with Alan trying to work out the best way to handle the situation.

'Kathleen, he's definitely grounded,' said Alan. 'At least for a week. No, I changed me mind – two weeks.'

'I agree with yeh, Alan, and tha' will happen, but tha's not enough for me. Wha' I'd really like to do now, at this very minute, is to run up them stairs and give him such a dig, but tha' would be over too quick. Anyway, I'd only end up hurtin' me hands with the size of him now. We'll have to make him realise how serious this all is and tha' he's goin' to pay for the damage – not us.'

'And how are we goin' to tha', Kathleen?'

'Well, first of all, yeh know the money tha' I have put by to dress him for Christmas? And, believe me, he needs new clothes badly, with the height he's after gettin'; nothin' fits him – well, tha' won't be happenin' now. So tha' money and the money tha' he would be gettin' for his Christmas present will get tha' wall fixed. I'm tellin' yeh, Alan, tha' won't go down well with him. Havin' to go out on Christmas Day in front of his friends with all his old clothes on and not a penny in his pocket. Tha' will hurt him more than anythin'.'

'Righ' then, Kathleen, yeh seem to have it all worked out in tha' head of yers as usual. But I do have to agree with yeh – he won't like this one bit.'

And he didn't. As soon as the dinner was over, we sat him down. You'd want to see the look on his face as we dished out his punishment. He sat there quietly, with the biggest mush on him you ever saw.

'Young Alan, are you listening to me?' I said. 'If this is all tha' happens, yeh can thank yer lucky stars, because if the guards go ahead and charge yeh, there'll be a black mark on yer record forever. And tha's not good for yer future.'

He finally spoke up. 'All I can say is tha' I'm sorry, righ', and I'll never do anythin' like tha' again. I don't know wha' else to say to yiz.'

I thought to myself, *Typical fuckin' teenager!* I was starting to get a bit worked up at this stage and wanted to clatter him. But I held back once more. What can you do? You can't keep going on and on, so I just hoped that he would take heed of what we were saying and prayed that there wouldn't be a next time.

I have to say, the guard was great when we went down to the police station the following evening. He was firm in everything he had to say, giving Alan a good caution, but also very fair. There was great relief on all our faces when he said the police would not be bringing any charges against him.

'I will talk to the gentleman,' he said, 'and I'm sure when he calms down he won't take things any further. Just remember everything I've said, Alan. Keep your nose clean and stay out of trouble or you won't get off so lightly the next time.'

'I will, guard. Thanks,' said young Alan, and then he was gone out of that police station like a light, as we were after thanking him ourselves, in case he changed his mind.

Our neighbour finally calmed down. We had the wall fixed in record time, which he seemed to be happy enough about in the end. All was forgiven and the charges were dropped.

* * *

By this stage young Alan had been grounded for the best part of a week and I could see that it was starting to get to him, even though he tried to pretend it wasn't. School had just finished for Christmas, so he was in the house all day, every day.

I was upstairs tidying around and he was in his room, lying stretched out on the bed with his hand behind his head.

'I have to say, Ma,' he said, 'this is the life. Wha' more could yeh ask for? I think I'll do this more often. I'm really enjoyin' the rest.'

'Is tha' righ', Alan?' I said. 'Well now, seein' as yeh're havin' such a good time with yerself there, I'm addin' another week onto yer punishment.' Well, you'd want to see his face! 'Now, wha' de yeh think of tha'?'

I strolled out of his room with a big smile on my face. After a while I called out for him to come for his dinner. There was no answer, so I called out again.

'Alan,' I said, 'get yer arse down here now, while the food is still hot.'

Still not a sound, so I raced up the stairs, taking them in twos, only to find him gone and the window wide open.

'Holy Jaysus, I don't believe this. He's after jumpin' out the top window. Tha's it, I'm going to fuckin' kill him when I get me hands on him!'

Then I copped a note on his locker. 'I'm sorry, Ma,' it read. 'Your rules are too strict. I won't be back. Goodbye.'

I didn't know whether to scream my brains out or laugh my head off. I charged down the stairs, only to fall over the Hoover in the hall. I fell flat on my face, and banged my head against the door. Well, if I hadn't been in a temper before, I certainly was now. We had this big Alsatian dog called King, who followed me everywhere I went. He jumped on top of me and had me pinned to the floor, licking the face off me. I pushed King off me, grabbed one of the tubes off the Hoover and stuck it up the sleeve of my coat as I went out the door to look for young Alan, with King hot on my heels.

It didn't take me long to find him and as soon as he saw me he ran straight over.

'Ma, don't say anythin' in front of me friends.'

'Is tha' righ', Alan?' I pulled the tube out and made a run at him, giving him a right bang on the shoulders. While I was doing this, King was jumping on top of him, trying to bite the arse off him. You'd want to see the shock on his face as he tried to get away from me.

'Yeh'd better make yer way home, Alan.' I was screaming my head off at this stage as I chased him down the road and on into the house.

'Yeh didn't have to do tha', Ma,' he was roaring. 'I'll be the laughin' stock of the place tomorrow.'

'Yeh should have been happy enough to take the punishment tha' was dished out to yeh,' I said, 'and you were gettin' off light for wha' yeh did. But I'm tellin' yeh here and now, there'll be no more pussy-footin' around here, Alan McGrath. From now on, if yeh bring any more trouble to this door, tha's nothin' compared to wha' I'll do to yeh. So bear tha' in mind. Now, get back up to yer room.'

* * *

I won't say that young Alan didn't get up to more mischief along the way – far from it, but there was nothing too serious that Alan and myself couldn't handle.

14

Little Girl

Martina was driving me nuts. She wanted to leave school altogether. There was no way I was having any of it, as she was only fifteen. Because I had very little education myself, I wanted our children to get as much schooling as possible.

Martina worked with me on the weekends, washing hair and tidying around for her pocket money. Even though she was a great help to me, I felt it would do her good to get out there and work with girls her own age, not having her stuck out in the back garden working with me all the time. So I decided to see if I could get her a Saturday job in the hairdressers where I got my own hair done, which happened to be in the city. I got on very well with the girls there. I asked if there were any openings; luckily enough there were.

'Righ', Martina,' I said, 'sit down there. I have a bit of news for yeh and I think yeh'll be pleased. I'm after gettin' yeh some weekend work. It's the same as wha' yeh're doin' here for me, washin' hair and cleanin' around, so it shouldn't be any bother to yeh. Tha' way yeh can see if tha's wha' yeh'd like to do when yeh leave school – after yeh do yer exams, of

123

course. It'll give yeh a little sample of wha' life is like out there in the real world.'

'Oh, Ma,' she screamed, 'tha's great, I can't believe it! When do I start? When do I start?' She was jumping up and down with the excitement, hugging and kissing me at the same time.

'This comin' Saturday. Now, I have just one or two things to say on the matter, Martina. The rest will be up to you. Keep yer head down and do the jobs yeh're given. Listen and take in everythin' tha's been said. And most of all, zip yer mouth up and have nothin' to say about anybody. And I mean anybody – there's people out there tha' get pleasure in carryin' stories, addin' their own little bits along the way, so take heed in wha' I'm saying – de yeh hear now?'

'I will, Ma, I promise, I promise. I swear!'

'Other than tha', love, enjoy yer adventure.'

There were more hugs and kisses. I watched her skip along out to her friends. She thought she'd never get out to tell them her news. With that I could feel myself starting to get a bit upset, looking at my little girl, who was now starting to grow up. I hoped that life would be good to her along the way.

* * *

She settled in really well and took to the hairdressing just as I did. She worked all her school holidays and loved every minute of it. So much so that, as soon as her Inter Cert exams were over the following year, she asked us if she could leave school. There was a full-time job going and it was offered to her.

I was dead set against it in the beginning. But then Alan said to me, 'If tha's wha' she really wants, Kathleen, remember you at her age – tha's all yeh wanted to do and yeh were stopped for different reasons. I know tha' couldn't be helped, so before yeh say a flat-out no, have a good think about it first.'

'Please, Ma, please!' Martina kept saying, over and over again. 'It's wha' I really want to do.'

'Are yeh sure? Yeh're not doin' this just to get out of goin' to school? Because if yeh are, Martina, I'm tellin' yeh' . . .'

That's when she stopped me dead in my tracks and looked me straight in the eye.

'Believe me, Ma, I know this is wha' I want.'

When she said those words to me, for a split second I got a flashback to nearly twenty years earlier when I said those very words to my own Ma and how upset and disappointed I felt when I was told no. So I made up my mind there and then, with the support of Alan, and said yes.

That was it; Martina was on her way to follow her dreams.

* * *

Martina loved her job and was as happy as anything, making lots of new friends along the way. She came home one evening with a grin on her from ear to ear.

'Yeh're lookin' very pleased with yerself, Martina. Wha's happenin'?' I asked.

'A fella asked me out on a date, Ma. Can I go?'

'And who is this young fella? Do I know him?'

'His name is Rob. He's not from around here, Ma. He lives in town. I met him at the roller rink the other night. We had a great laugh. He was chasin' me all over the rink. We had the best time ever. Please, Ma, can I go out with him?'

How could I say no? It was like looking at myself when I asked Ma the very same thing, and I was even younger. So that was it; we said yes and Martina had her first date.

I didn't force her to bring him home to meet us. Alan and myself decided that we would let her do that in her own time, when she was good and ready. And she did, after a few weeks. He seemed nice enough, so we didn't overdo it by asking too many questions. We left the pair of them sitting there chatting away to young Alan and Amanda.

Over the next couple of months, Rob was up at the house more and more, so much so that he was there nearly every night. I pulled Martina to one side one night after he had gone.

'Sit down there, love. I want to have a talk with yeh.'

'Wha's wrong, Ma? Yeh look all serious.'

'Everythin's fine, Martina. It's just . . . I don't really know how to say this to yeh.' I hummed and hawed for a few seconds. 'Ah, to hell with it, I'll just come righ' out and say wha's on me mind. Are yeh doin' anythin'? Yeh know, like sex and stuff. Because if yeh are, we'll go down to the doctor and I'll get yeh the pill.'

She was trying to be serious and not laugh in my face but at the same time couldn't keep her face straight.

'Jaysus, Ma, will yeh not be askin' me things like tha'. Of course I'm not doin' anythin'! How could yeh even think such a thing?'

'Well, yeh're goin' out with this young fella a good few months now and I'm worried about yeh, tha's all. Everythin's so different now, Martina, as to when I was yer age, and I'm not too sure wha' yiz get up to these days.'

'Yeh worry too much, Ma,' she said, as she gave me a kiss, and off she went to bed.

Was that a good sign or not? I wasn't sure. But that's the way things were left over the coming weeks. I went around with not a care in the world, thinking everything was okay.

* * *

Martina arrived home early from work one day.

'Wha' has yeh home at this hour, Martina? Have yeh not got classes tonight?'

She just sat there and looked at me, not saying a word, which was unusual for her, as she is nearly as bad as myself for talking.

'Are yeh in trouble at work? Don't tell me yeh're after gettin' sacked. Jaysus Christ, Martina, I hope yeh haven't lost tha' job.'

There still wasn't a word coming from her, only plenty of tears. Then the penny finally dropped with me.

'Well, then,' I said, 'there's only one other thing tha' would have yeh this upset. Yeh're pregnant, aren't yeh?'

She looked up at me with such a lost look in her eyes as she sobbed out the words, 'Yes, Ma.'

I thought I was going to faint, I got such a shock. I stood there for a few seconds, looking at my very young daughter, who had just turned sixteen not too long before, only a child herself, telling me she was going to have a baby. I wanted to scream the house down – but I didn't. I took a deep breath and sat down beside her, putting my two arms around her. We both sat there and cried together.

'I'm sorry, Ma,' she kept saying. 'I'm sorry.'

'We won't talk about it now. Just let me sit here and hold yeh for the minute while I try and get me head around all this.'

That wasn't easy to do. I sat there thinking, for I don't know how long. Part of me wanted to box the head off her for being so stupid and not looking after herself. The other part wanted to keep holding on to her and not let go, knowing the pain her tiny body was going to have to go through, the responsibility that lay ahead, taking all of her youth with it along the way. Was I angry? Yes, very.

I came back from my thoughts with Martina shaking me.

'Ma, I think I can hear Da comin'. I can't face him. Please, will yeh tell him for me? Please!'

'Go on then, up to yer bed. Yeh look as if yeh could do with a good night's sleep. I'll talk to yer Da.' I got a quick kiss on the cheek and she was gone like a light before I could say another word.

I waited until they were all asleep and we were alone before I said a word. Alan knew me so well. I'm a cleaning freak at any time but when I'm in a temper or feel nervous I go on the rampage altogether, taking the place apart. I had myself in such a state I was only short of scrubbing the ceilings.

'Righ' Kathleen,' he said, 'spit it out, wha's wrong?'

I kept humming and hawing for a few seconds. 'Hmm, hmm . . . I don't really know how to put this, Alan. I mean, I know how to say it, tha's not wha' is hard; it's how to put it in a way tha' it doesn't sound too bad. If I just say it . . .'

'Kathleen, wha' have I told yeh over and over again? When yeh want to say somethin' will yeh just come righ' out and say it, instead of pussy-footin' around for God knows how long.'

'Okay, Alan – Martina's pregnant.'

He was drinking a cup of tea and he nearly choked right there and then in front to me with the shock. I had to bang his back like mad until he got his breath back.

'Jaysus, are yeh all righ', Alan? Yer tea must have gone down the wrong way. This is why I was tryin' to build it up to yeh.'

'Fuck the tea, Kathleen,' he roared, 'fuck, fuck, fuck and fuck again.' It wasn't very often you would hear Alan swear. I usually did enough of that for both of us, but I suppose that night it was his way of letting his anger out.

We sat there the best part of the night, talking and crying, trying to work out in our minds what the future held, both for us and for Martina, and how it was going to change all our lives so much.

Alan could never stay angry at any of our children for very long, so as soon as Martina walked into the kitchen the next morning – and God love her, she was waxy in the face – he put his arms around her and said, 'Don't worry, love, we'll work things out.' There was such relief on her little face when she heard her Da say that.

* * *

And we did work things out. Not to say that it was easy, far from it. I remember the day she brought Rob up to see us, about two weeks after we found out. He stood there acting all shy, with the 'I'm sorry' bit. I wanted to give him such a fucking dig. I know it takes two to tango, but for a split second to me it was all his fault, which of course it wasn't. But that's how I felt.

Then there was the first visit to the Coombe. Oh my God, I didn't know where to be putting my face when the nurse told me to stand on the scales. I had a quick look around to see if anybody was listening as I whispered, 'It's not me, nurse; it's me daughter Martina.'

Martina looked about twelve. She was wearing these little black pump runners, three-quarter-length leggings and the brightest orange shirt you ever saw, which looked as if it was three times too big for her, and her crazy pink Mohawk hairstyle to finish it off. Talk about standing out in the crowd.

Anyway, when all was said and done, she was well on her way – three and a half months pregnant.

I made sure that I was on my own the day I told Ma and Da they were going to be great-grandparents. I thought Da was going to have a fit. Because he was so religious and worrying about what the neighbours thought, he had to blame somebody, which of course was me.

'This is all yer fault, Kathleen,' he said, 'lettin' Martina dress in all them mad-lookin' clothes. I don't know wha' she's like goin' around. As for tha' stupid-lookin' haircut . . . is it any wonder she got herself into trouble?'

I sat there and let him rammage on and on. I wasn't in any humour to get into an argument with him. At the end of the day he was just letting off a bit of steam and would calm down in time.

I had myself all ready to run the gauntlet with Ma, expecting her to lash me out of it too, but to my surprise she didn't.

'Yeh got her checked out then, Kathleen?' she said.

'I did, Ma, and everythin's fine.'

'Good, tha's all tha' matters. Once her and the baby are well, everythin' else will fall into place. Don't be mindin' wha' yer father or anybody else thinks, because it's nobody's business only yerself and Martina's. Now, tha's all I'll say on the matter.'

* * *

Martina worked right up to the last couple of weeks, not losing a day of work. I went in and spoke to her boss, who I have to say was so nice. He let me know her job would be there for her when she was ready to come back, which I was well pleased about. I wanted her to finish her apprenticeship, no matter what. I felt there would always be a future both for her and the baby.

The night finally arrived when Martina went into labour. I kept her with me for as long as I could, checking on her pains, just like Ma did with me all those years ago. But unlike Ma, I was a nervous wreck and was trying really hard not to let Martina see it.

As soon as she said, 'Ma, I think me waters are broke', I nearly fell out of the bed.

'Hold on, Martina, I'm comin' to yeh. Don't get out of bed.' I grabbed a big bath towel out of the press on my way into her room. 'Quick, stick tha' between yer legs and try not to let it get on the new carpet.' God love her, she wobbled into the toilet with me holding onto the towel before the big gush came.

'Quick, Alan,' I roared, 'Martina's in labour.'

He had himself dressed in a jiffy. Martina was bent over in pain as we helped her into the van. Alan had us at the doors of the Coombe in the blink of an eye. 'Alan, will yeh go down for Rob? He said he wants to be at the birth.'

Because he was living nearby they were back in no time at all. Alan went on home to the kids while I sat there. I'll never forget what I did and said next and I still don't know if I was right or wrong, but at the time I felt very strongly about it. One of the nurses came over to me and asked me to sign a form for Martina to get the epidural needle. I didn't even think twice about it; 'No' came out of my mouth. You could see that she was taken aback with my answer.

'First of all, nurse,' I said, 'I don't know enough about this needle tha' yeh want to give to me child. I hear tha' sometimes it can have side-effects. The other reason is, I don't think a bit of pain will do her any harm. She'll know now tha' makin' the baby is the easiest part, but it's a different kettle of fish when yeh're bringin' them into the world. So we'll leave it at tha'.'

I went in a couple of times to sit with Martina and fell to pieces as I looked at her in so much pain. Finally the nurse told me I was only upsetting her and it would be better if I waited outside. I had myself in a right state, worrying all through the night if I had done the right thing. Should I have made the birth easier for her?

It seemed to take forever for the morning to arrive and it wasn't too long after that the hustle and bustle of the hospital started. I jumped every time I saw a nurse come out of the labour ward. Each time I was told, 'She's nearly there.'

Finally, after the guts of another hour, Rob came bursting through the doors and told me that Martina had a baby girl. I couldn't hold back the tears any longer.

'Thank God, thank God, thank God,' that's all I could hear myself saying over and over again. 'Are Martina and the baby okay?'

'She's great. There's not a bother on her and the baby is gorgeous. Go on into her, Kathleen, I'll wait out here,' Rob said.

'Will yeh ring Alan and tell him? I'm sure he must be frantic by now.'

I got myself together and made my way in. I stood there and looked at my little girl as she held hers. I could see straight away, young as she was, that she was going to be a great mother. All the worry and anger that I had felt for months on end left me as soon as I held my two little girls.

I suppose some mothers would have gone mad at the thought of becoming a granny at the age of thirty-eight, but I have to say, I totally enjoyed every minute of it. I loved my little Danielle.

15

The Van

Alan always seemed to be happy enough in himself, working away in Gallagher's, but as the years went on I could see that he was getting tired of the long hours.

'Yeh know somethin', Kathleen?' he said one day. 'I'm sick and tired of bein' on the clock and havin' to answer to people all the time. I wish, I just wish tha' I could get meself somethin' to work at and be me own boss.'

'Yeh have a very good job there, Alan. De yeh really hate it tha' much, tha' yeh want to give it up?'

'Yeh don't understand, Kathleen. It's the system I want to get out of, not the work. I mean, there's you, for example; I know yeh work most days, but if yeh really want to take a day off from doin' hair, yeh can just go ahead and do it. There's nobody breathin' down yer neck if yeh're a few minutes late. Then there's the shite tha' I have to go through when the holidays are given out. It's when they say I have to take them, not when I want to.'

'Jaysus, Alan, I never knew yeh felt like tha'. Yeh should have said somethin' instead of lettin' it get on top of yeh like this. Well then, wha' about openin' up yer own shoe repair shop, like wha' yer Da use to have?'

'It's a dyin' trade, Kathleen. I'd never make a decent wage out of it. No, forget about tha'. Ah, don't be mindin' me, Kathleen, it'll pass. I'm just lettin' off a bit of steam, tha's all.'

* * *

I kept my eyes and ears open, hoping that something would come my way that would help Alan get out of this rut that he felt he was caught up in. Then, out of the blue, to my surprise it did.

My sister Clare was over with me one day and I was filling her in on what Alan was saying and how he was feeling.

'Yeh know wha', Kathleen,' she said, 'I might have the very thing for him. There's this girl I know, and her sister is headin' off to Australia with the husband and two kids to start a new life there, sellin' every screed they have so's tha' they'll have as much money as possible for when they get there . . .'

'Clare,' I interrupted her, 'wha' are yeh tellin' me all this for, and about somebody I don't even know?'

'Will yeh wait and listen to me, Kathleen. I'm buildin' up to it. I know yeh're goin' to be over the moon when I tell yeh about this . . .'

'In the name of Jaysus, Clare, will yeh stop pussy-footin' about and just say it.'

'His ice-cream van – they're sellin' it. Alan could buy it! So wha' de yeh think?'

I stood there for a moment, my brain clicking in and out all over the place. This could be the very thing that Alan was looking for.

'Clare, are yeh sure about this? They're definitely goin' away?'

'I'm tellin' yeh, Kathleen, I was up in their house only the other night buyin' a few bits of furniture. Sure I got the stuff for half nothin', tha's how I know about the van.'

'Alan will be in soon, Clare. Will yeh hang on for a while and tell him about this?'

'Sure don't yeh know I will, Kathleen.'

While the two of us sat there yapping, I kept glancing over at the clock every few minutes, thinking about how Alan would feel when he heard the news. I was getting butterflies in my stomach just thinking about it.

Alan was only in the door and didn't even have time to take his coat off before I launched into everything. 'I have the best news ever, Alan! Wait 'til yeh hear wha' Clare just told me. Yeh'll be able to be yer own boss – tha's if yeh want it, of course! I mean, maybe yeh might not want to drive an ice-cream van? I never thought about tha'. But if yeh do, we know a fella tha's sellin' one and Clare said tha' yeh'll probably get it real cheap because yer man needs the money fast because they're all goin' to Australia and Clare was sayin' . . .'

'Kathleen!' said Alan. 'Stop talkin' for a minute and take a breath before yeh faint. Now, first of all, I haven't a clue wha' any of tha' meant, so yeh're goin' to have to slow down and fill me in on wha' yeh're talkin' about.'

'I'm just excited for yeh, Alan, tha's all.'

'I know tha', love, so will yeh come on and tell me, nice and slow, and I might get a bit worked up with yeh.'

I could see Alan's face light up when I went into the details of what Clare had told me. He listened, taking everything on board that I was saying. As soon as I finished talking, to my surprise, Alan didn't waste any time in asking Clare if she would bring him over to meet the fella.

'Come on, Alan,' said Clare, 'we'll go over now. There's no time like the present.'

'I'm comin' with yiz,' I said. 'Yeh're not leavin' me here. Hold on 'til I get me coat.' I went running out after them.

It didn't take us too long to get there. While I sat in the car, Clare went into the house with Alan. I was on tenterhooks. It seemed to take forever before they came back out. Alan stood talking to the fella for a few more minutes as Clare made her way out to me. She was giving me the nod and the wink and a huge smile to go with it.

'Jaysus, Clare, will yeh hurry up and tell me wha's happenin'. I'm burstin' here to know.'

'I'm saying nothin', Kathleen. It's not me place. I'll let Alan tell yeh himself.'

And he did, as soon as he got into the car. 'Well, tha' went very well, I have to say, Kathleen. Joe – tha's yer man's name – said he'll take me out in the van with him at the weekend and one or two nights next week to see wha' I think of it, and then we'll take it from there. Now, if it's a thing tha' I do like it, then you and me will have to sit down and have a good talk about me givin' up the good job tha' I have.'

'Well, the way I see it, Alan, I know yeh make good money and yer job is permanent, but it's no good to you or me for tha' matter if yeh're not happy. Wha'ever yeh decide, I'm behind yeh all the way. So there's no need for us to have any big talk.'

I could see by the big smile he gave me that he was well pleased with this.

Alan went out on his few test runs and was as happy as anything each time he came home. So he ended up buying the van and becoming the local ice-cream man of our area.

* * *

It took Alan a good few months to get the hang of things. He had to learn so much about the ice-cream machine and the running of the van – and that was before he faced the gangs of kids in the streets. But none of that was a problem to him. Once he made his mind up to do it, he'd make sure that he would master anything that would come his way; and he did. Nothing fazed him.

So life was good. Alan was happy and contented in himself. He was his own boss at last. He must have been nearly a year in the ice-cream business and was working away, day in and day out, with not a care in the world.

That was until one evening when he came in early from work. He looked very pale and was very quiet.

'I have yer bit of dinner ready, Alan. Will yeh have it now?'

'Ah, just leave it there for a minute, Kathleen. I think I'll go up and lie down for a while. I'm feelin' a bit off.'

'Jaysus, tha's not like you, Alan. Yeh're never sick.'

'It's probably a flu or somethin' comin' on me. I'll be grand once I get a couple of hours sleep.'

Of course, he wasn't all right, as I found out very early the next morning. I was up at the crack of dawn. Amanda was going to England for a few days' holiday with Clare. When I went back upstairs, Alan was sitting up in the bed holding his chest.

'Jaysus, wha's wrong with yeh, Alan? Oh my God, look at the colour of yeh!' He looked as if every drain of blood was gone out of his body. 'I'm phonin' for an ambulance. Oh my God, Alan . . .' I was frantic.

'Will yeh stay quiet, Kathleen. I don't want yeh upsettin' the kids. Look, there's Clare over to pick Amanda up. Say nothin' until she's gone.'

I flew back downstairs and had Amanda on her way in no time at all. As I stood there smiling and waving her off, I was telling young Alan to get his arse up to his Da. As soon as Clare's car was out of sight, I was back up to Alan in a flash. He had himself up and dressed.

'I don't care wha' yeh say, Alan, I'm gettin' an ambulance righ' now.'

'I can't wait, Kathleen; just get me to a hospital, quick.' By this stage he was bent over and nearly on his knees with the pain.

'Ma, I'll run down and start the van up. You help Da down the stairs,' said young Alan.

At the time I had a small Suzuki van I used as a run around. I got in the back of it with Alan while young Alan drove. The nearest hospital was St James's and in my mind it seemed to be a million miles away.

Young Alan drove so fast down the Greenhills Road. He had lights flashing and his hand on the horn all the way down. He was screaming out at all the cars to let him pass. Most of them moved over – they could see there was something wrong. For the few that wouldn't move, he drove up on the paths and around them. We had no seats in the back of the van so, as you can imagine, we were getting thrown all over the place. I was trying to get Alan to lie down but he kept pushing me away. He was boxing himself in the face.

'Holy Jaysus,' I screamed to young Alan, 'yer Da's goin' mad back here. He's punchin' the head off himself.'

'Leave him, Ma,' roared young Alan, 'he know's wha' he's doin'. He's tryin' to stop himself from goin' unconscious. Look, we're nearly there. I'm goin' to drive right up to the front door. You jump out and get the first doctor yeh see.'

I fell around the casualty department, roaring for a doctor, and grabbed the first person I saw in a white coat, who happened to be a woman. I couldn't speak, I was crying so much. I just pointed to the door and kept pulling her along with me. She knew straight away it was something serious, as she called over to one of the nurses to come with her.

Alan was unconscious when we got there. I thought he was dead. I was hysterical. The doctors and nurses were great. In seconds, he was taken into the emergency room and given oxygen straight away. I was told to stand outside the door.

I could hear the doctor saying, 'Stand back; one, two, three.' I knew when I heard this that they were trying to get Alan's heart going. I was never so frightened in my whole life. I couldn't move. Young Alan put his arm around me as we waited patiently on someone to come out to us.

'Don't worry, Ma,' he said, 'Da will be okay. Yeh know him – he's as tough as nails.'

'I hope so, love, I just hope so.'

We seemed to be standing there forever. When the doctor finally came out to talk to me, I was so afraid of what he was going to say.

'Your husband had a very severe heart attack, but don't worry, we have him stable now. Getting him here as fast as you did saved his life.'

'Oh my God,' I said, 'Alan's never sick. How did this happen, doctor?'

'We will be doing some tests over the next few days and I will let both of you know then. You can go in now but only for a few minutes. He is very tired and needs to rest.'

'You go on in, Ma,' said young Alan. 'I'll wait out here for yeh.'

As I made my way in and looked at Alan lying there, I got such a fright. He was like death warmed up. It took me all my time to keep myself from falling to pieces. Alan took my hand and held it so tight.

'Come on, love,' he said, 'keep it together.' He tried to give me a little smile. 'Anyway, yeh won't be gettin' rid of me tha' easy.'

'Don't you die on me, Alan McGrath. De yeh hear me? I swear, I'll kill yeh if yeh die on me.' I couldn't hold back the tears any longer.

The nurse came over to me just then. 'I'm afraid you will have to go. Your husband has to go up to intensive care now and I need to get some general information about him from you.'

I gave Alan the biggest hug ever before I had to walk away. I wasn't too long with the nurse, then we headed on home. I sat in the van while young Alan drove.

'De yeh know somethin', love?' I said. 'I'm so proud of yeh. The way yeh held yerself together, gettin' us to the hospital so fast. Now, mind you, I thought we were gonners a few times when yeh started goin' up on the paths and all, but no matter. Yeh got us there, tha's the main thing. I don't think yer Dad would have made it only for yeh.'

'As I said, Ma, he's tough as nails, so don't be worryin'.'

He was so like his Da in many ways. There he was, barely seventeen and he handled something so serious in such a grown-up way. What would I have done without him?

Poor Martina was up the walls with worry by the time we got home. With all the upset, I had forgotten to ring her. It was only when I walked into the house that it entered my head.

'Please, Ma,' she said, 'tell me tha' Da is okay!'

I told her the news and she was a lot happier by the time I had finished. I got on the phone to Amanda straight away, filling her in on everything and reassuring her.

* * *

I thought that the next day would never come so I could go to see Alan. By the time I got there, some of his tests had been done and he was sitting up in bed, looking a lot better.

'Well, Kathleen,' he said, 'as yeh can see I didn't die, so come over here and give us a kiss.'

'Yeh nearly killed me with the fright yeh gave me, Alan McGrath, never mind yerself.' We gave each other a big hug. 'Well, tell me wha's happenin', Alan. Have they found out wha's wrong with yeh?'

'The doctor was in with me just before yeh got here. The bottom line is, I have a couple of blocked arteries around me heart and maybe – now only maybe, so don't start gettin' yerself all upset – I might need to have an operation.'

I took a deep breath and held myself together and started rammaging on about God only knows what, just to keep my mind off this. Then Alan started going into the details of a test they had done called an angiogram.

'Yeh want to see it, Kathleen. I was sittin' there lookin' at the doctor puttin' this tiny little wire through me veins, startin' at the top of me leg righ' up to me heart. It was connected to a tiny camera and I could see everythin'. I'm tellin' yeh, it was really somethin' else.'

Just at that very moment, without any warning whatsoever, I could see Alan turning a dreadful colour and going unconscious – right in front of my eyes. I was off screaming all over the place again, and two nurses came in straight away, putting me outside once more.

'Oh my God, oh my God . . .' was all that kept coming out of my mouth as I walked up and down outside the ward. I don't know how long it was before one of the nurses came out to me.

'Don't tell me anythin' bad, nurse, please, please don't!'

'It's okay, Mrs McGrath, try and calm down, everything's under control. This can happen sometimes after the angiogram. There was a clot, but we've managed to disperse it now and everything's fine. You can go back in now, and make sure Alan stays lying down flat. We have some sand bags on his legs to make sure it won't happen again.'

I made my way back inside and true enough, there he was flat on his back, looking the colour of a Granny Smith apple.

'Jaysus Christ, Alan, yeh'll have to stop doin' this or I'll be havin' a heart attack along with yeh.'

'Ah, don't be givin' out to me, Kathleen. Sit yerself down there and talk to me. Did yeh think of gettin' young Alan to wash the machine and clean the van out for me before he locked it for the night?'

'Are yeh for real or wha', Alan? Here yeh are, nearly at death's door, and yeh're askin' me was I thinkin' of yer van last night? No – I don't think so and neither was he. Anyway, tell me wha' else the doctor was sayin'.'

He told me all he was getting done over the next few days, which turned out to be very much in his favour, as he didn't need to have surgery. He was nearly a week in hospital by the time he got the good news.

'Well, Alan,' the doctor said, 'we have decided not to operate because you are so healthy in every other way, and very fit I must say for a forty-year-old man. You have all that going for you, but for one thing – and I think you know what you have to do there: stop smoking.'

I listened to Alan lie through his teeth, promising the doctor the sun, moon and stars about how he would never let a cigarette pass his lips again. Which, of course, he did, only the very next day. He had me watching out to make sure none of the nurses were around so he could have a quick puff out the window.

No matter how much I would give out, it didn't matter. Alan's outlook on life was, and still to this very day is, 'Wha's goin' to happen, will happen, no matter wha' yeh say or I do, Kathleen, so why worry about it?'

When Alan came home from hospital first, I was a nervous wreck, keeping an eye on him all the time, phoning for every little thing. He couldn't breathe without me watching him. I was so scared that he would take bad again and this time be taken from me for good. But in time I learned to take a step back, not worry so much and let him enjoy life. Which he did. Alan didn't look or ask for much for himself ever. Everything was always for me and the kids.

So I was very happy to watch him doddle out every day in his van, knowing that, for once, he had got what he wanted, which was to work for himself and be his own boss.

16

The Markets

When Alan decided to give up his job and buy his ice-cream van, it was great for him, he was so happy. But we didn't really think it through or realise, with the long winters we get, how bad things could get and that there would be times when his income would drop considerably.

I was down in Ma's one day and I was telling my sisters, Jacinta and Carmel, that things were very tight with us and that I was finding it hard to keep up with my bills. They were dressmakers and worked for themselves, making all their own clothes through the week and selling them in the markets over the weekends.

'Yeh know wha', Kathleen,' Jacinta said, 'why don't yeh do the markets with us on Sundays? Yeh could make yerself a grand few bob there.'

'But how? Wha' would I sell, Jacinta?'

'Clothes, of course! Yeh bloody gobshite, Kathleen. We'll bring yeh down to the wholesalers; I know one or two of them real well. I'll get yeh some stuff on tick to get yeh started. We'll pick out some nice trendy dresses and jeans, they sell quick, and then yeh can pay the bill off as yeh're goin' along.'

'I have a spare rig there and a cover,' said Carmel. 'Yeh can have tha'. And yeh know somethin' else, Kathleen? When yeh're doin' yer bit of hairdressin', yeh could have a rail of clothes out there with yeh, tha' yer customers could be rootin' through while they're waitin' to get their hair done.'

'Jaysus, tha's a great idea, Carmel. I can't believe I didn't think of tha' meself.'

* * *

True enough, between the pair of them they got me started in the markets. I would check out what was in fashion in the bigger shops and then, after taking my own few bob out for myself, I would go in every Monday and buy as much as I could, selling it on to my clients throughout the week. They were all well pleased, since I was a lot cheaper than the shops.

I would be up at the crack of dawn on Sundays, with Alan helping me load the van, before heading out to the Finglas market for eight o'clock, and then on out to the Stardust for the afternoon. Carmel and Jacinta were always ahead of me and would help me get set up as soon as I arrived. I never would have managed without them. They were great.

It didn't take me long to get the hang of things. I think it was something that was in all of us – the gift of the gab, which we got from Granny Kitty. Between the hairdressing and then the markets, by the time I was finished I could have sold sand to the Arabs. I actually used to look forward to Sunday and meeting up with my sisters. We would have great craic throughout the day.

I remember one day in particular, we were in the Stardust market and I had just finished hanging the last of the clothes on the rails, when the crowds all started to gather. It was a lovely sunny day, so there were plenty of people out and about and I thought to myself, *This is great, I'll make a grand few bob today.* And sure enough, everybody seemed to be buying that day.

'How are yeh doin' over there, Kathleen?' asked Jacinta.

'I'm doin' really well. See all them trench coats, they're gone bar one. And wha' about yous – have yeh made a few sales?'

'Would yeh have a look at the rails, Kathleen? We're nearly cleaned out and we have about twenty orders between the two markets for next week.'

On the chit-chat went between us and before I knew it the day was nearly over. I was starting to pack up the few bits I had left when these two wans came over to me.

'Can I help yiz?' I asked.

'Could you kindly tell us, how much is that blue trench coat, please?'

'It's twenty-five pounds, miss. But seein' as it's the last one, and the day is comin' to an end, yeh can have it for twenty. Now, is tha' a bargain or wha'?'

The younger one of the two tried the coat on.

'Mummy,' she said, in an ever-so-posh accent, 'I think it might be slightly too long for me. What do you think?'

I jumped in straight away, before the other wan could get a word in.

'Tha's the latest fashion,' I said. 'They're just in from France, love, and I mean, they know their stuff. If they say tha's the length, well then tha's gospel.'

'I'm not really sure, Mummy,' she said. 'There's no mirror for me to look in to judge.'

Now, this is when 'Mummy' put her plan into action. I couldn't believe afterwards that I fell for it, with me always being bang wide, but nevertheless . . .

'Would you mind awfully letting us go around to our house,' she said, 'which is right at the back of the market, so that my daughter could have a quick look before she pays you? It will take us all but five minutes.'

Now, talk about being a gobshite. Instead of saying, 'I'll hold onto the twenty pound until you come back,' which is what I should have done, I went and handed the coat over, and that was the last I saw of them. I think it was the posh accent that put me off guard, making me think they'd have money and that there was no way they were pulling a scam. But as they say, you live and learn. It wasn't even the money at the end of the day that got up my back. It was that they made a fool of me, and I didn't like or forget that.

Well, you'd want to hear Carmel and Jacinta rammaging on at me as soon as I told them.

'Are yeh a thick or wha', Kathleen? I can't believe yeh broke the golden rule,' said Jacinta. 'Always, money in the hand first, before anythin' is given over. Isn't tha' wha' Ma taught us all? Never, ever, trust no one when it comes to money, because tha's when people can change their tune.'

'I know, I know now! Don't keep goin' on at me about it, Jacinta.'

* * *

But, of course, she did, and into the bargain told everyone else in the family that I had been taken for a sucker. None of them let me forget it.

'Go to Kathleen's stall,' they kept saying. 'She gives clothes out for nothin'.'

They all made a right laugh of me.

Every single week after, I was on the look-out. I watched and watched. I knew there would come a time when they'd breeze back into the market. And they did, six months later, in the depths of winter. Everyone was wrapped up really well, with their hats, gloves and heavy coats on. I was standing there with a hot cup of soup in my hand when I copped the same two wans walking towards me. They had themselves well muffled up, but that didn't matter to me. Their two faces were stuck inside my head, which I never forgot. They must have seen me because they side-tracked really quickly in between a couple of the stalls, thinking that I hadn't seen them.

'Quick, Jacinta,' I roared, 'them wans tha' done me outta the money are in the market. Go over to the entrance and don't let them out. Carmel, watch me stall, will yeh?'

I ran after them and tipped 'Mummy' on the shoulder.

'Remember me?' I asked as I stood there face to face with them.

'I beg your pardon, do I know you?' I could see she was starting to get herself into a bit of a tizzy.

'I'm fuckin' sure yeh know me. Yeh robbed me a while back – remember, the trench coat? "It's too long, Mummy",' I mimicked, as I glared into the daughter's face. 'All tha' shite tha' yeh gave me.'

'Oh, tha's right. I think I vaguely remember now,' said Mummy. 'We came back down with the money and you were all gone. Isn't that right, pet?' She turned to her daughter, who at this stage was shitting herself. 'And we came in a few times over the months, checking to see if you were here, but you weren't to be found.'

'Yeh know wha', yeh're not only a robber, but yeh're a bare-faced fuckin' liar as well, because I hung around here for the guts of half an hour tha' day, waitin' on yiz to come back, and I haven't missed a week since then. Now, hand over me money.'

The two of them went to walk away; that's when I grabbed Mummy's arm.

'De yeh see her over there?' I pointed over to Jacinta who was standing at the entrance to the market with two men. 'Yeh'll have to go through them to get out, and believe me, tha' won't be happenin'. Now, as I said, me money. Thirty pounds, if yeh don't mind.' I stretched my hand up to her face.

'If I recall properly, it was only twenty pounds.'

'Is tha' righ?' I said. 'Well, the other ten pounds is for six month's interest.'

As I stood in front of the pair of them, she looked over at Jacinta and then at me.

'Don't even think about makin' a run for it,' I said.

That's when the daughter stepped in. 'Mummy, will you just pay the money, please, and let's get out of here now. I'm absolutely mortified.'

Mummy bashed the thirty pounds into my hand and stormed off, and I have to say it felt great. I was jumping up and down, waving over to Jacinta, letting her see I'd got paid and to let them pass.

I made my way back over to Carmel with a smile on me the length and breadth of the market.

'Well done,' she said, as I got a big pat on the back. Word wasn't long getting around, and I got a big round of applause from the rest of the traders. I was well pleased with myself.

It's a hard enough job to have to do, especially during the long hard winters, standing out in the cold for hours on end. I often thought my fingers were going to fall off when I would be breaking my stall down at the end of the day. Sometimes the canopy and bars would be covered with thick frost, sleet or snow. Then, for the likes of those wans to come along and take your bit of profit! Worst of all, I felt like a bloody thick because I'd trusted them. Money wasn't the issue; it was more of a pride thing with me. I had broken the golden rule, which didn't happen very often, and never happened again.

I thought I'd never get up to Ma to let her know what had happened. I could see by her face that she liked what I told her.

'Hmm,' she said, 'and yeh tell me yeh made yerself an extra ten pounds, Kathleen?'

I started laughing, knowing full well what she meant.

'Tha's righ' Ma,' I said. 'Tha's for you.' I handed her a few pound. She nearly took the hand off me as she spat on it for luck.

'Tha'll get me a grand few messages tomorrow.'

We were all happy bunnies that day, thanks to those two wans. I stuck with the markets for a couple of years, making a good few bob along the way, which made life a lot easier for Alan and myself. It was only when I opened my first salon that I decided to give up the markets, but I never ever forgot how good they were to me through those years.

17

Da

I dropped down with Danielle one day to see Ma and Da. I told them about how well Martina was doing in her apprenticeship.

'De yeh know wha', Kathleen?' said Ma. 'Tha's the best bit of news yeh've told me in I don't know how long. It'll do her the world of good to get out there and not just be sittin' at home, playin' with the baby. Keep her busy, tha's wha' I say, and maybe she won' get up to any more mischief. Isn't tha' righ', Phil?'

Da just looked over at me, rolling his eyes when Ma wasn't looking.

'Kathleen, I'm after makin' a nice pot of stew,' he said. 'Will yeh have a bowl?'

'I could smell it as soon as I walked in the door and thought yeh'd never ask me, Da. No matter how hard I try, I don't seem to get it as good as yers. I'm just listenin' to yeh talkin' there, Da, yer voice sounds very dry and hoarse. Yeh want to go and get tha' checked out by the doctor.'

'I keep sayin' tha' to him,' said Ma. 'But does he listen? No!'

'It's only a bit of a cold, tha's all. Anyway, never mind all tha', Kathleen. How's young Alan? Is he behavin' himself?'

'Well, he seems to be keepin' his nose clean but yeh know yerself, Da, yeh can't watch them twenty-four hours a day. But I tell yeh one thing, I'm not too far off. I have all me clients keepin' an eye out for me and if he's carryin' on or actin' the mick, I get a phone call and I'm out like a light and don't be long sortin' him out. Yeh'd want to see him run when he sees me comin'.'

'Just give him a good fuckin' dig, if he gets out of hand,' said Ma, 'because if I bring meself up to Tallaght, I swear to Jaysus I'll run amok and kill him if he brings the police to yer house again.'

'Please, Lil, don't be interferin'. And another thing – there's no need for tha' language,' said Da. 'Will I ever see the day tha' yeh'll hold a conversation without cursin'?'

'Ah, me arse, Phil Doyle, would yeh ever give it over, with yer frog voice on yeh.'

* * *

I laughed that day, but it was far from funny, as we were to find out over the coming months. I kept at Da each time I came down to the house to get himself checked. His answer was always the same: no.

'Please, Da,' I said. 'I was tellin' Dr Johnson about yeh the other day and he said tha' there's probably a few little nodules at the back of yer throat. They'd be like small warts tha' can be treated no problem, but if they're left it can get very serious.'

He just sat there listening to me, taking it all in, not saying a word; not that he was able to say much at that stage, with his voice nearly gone.

'Come on, Da, wha' de yeh say? Everybody's worried about yeh. Even Ma said to try and get yeh to go to hospital. I mean, is tha' not sayin' a lot?'

With that I got a nod of the head and a big smile. He agreed at last to go to the doctor and get a few tests.

As soon as the results came back, there was no time wasted. Da was taken into hospital and operated on straight away. The hospital didn't know what hit them when the whole gang of us came in to see Da. I slipped out with my brother Noel to speak to the doctor, not expecting what I was about to hear.

'We have taken all the nodules off,' said the doctor. 'Now, having said that, there were traces of cancer present. Hopefully we got it all but I can't promise what the future holds. We will just have to wait and see.'

I was so upset I couldn't speak, so Noel stepped in.

'Doctor,' he said, 'would yeh mind not tellin' me Da wha' yeh told us? He's a terrible worrier. Tha's why it took us so long to get him here, he was afraid of being told the likes of this.'

'I won't say anything for the moment,' said the doctor, 'but you must bring him for regular check-ups so we can keep a close watch on him.'

'Tha' won't be a problem,' said Noel, 'You tell us the time and the place, doctor, and we'll have him there.'

After the doctor had gone, I sat there with Noel for a few minutes, talking.

'Well, wha' de yeh think?' I asked.

'The first thing we should do is keep this to ourselves, Kathleen. No point in worryin' Ma and the rest of them unless we have to, and with a bit of luck all will go well for Da and nobody will be the wiser. Now, let's get back to the ward before he starts smellin' a rat. And will yeh ever put a smile on yer face, for Jaysus' sake, or yeh'll have Ma askin' twenty questions, and before yeh know it one of us will trip up.'

You'd want to see the big smile on Da's face when Noel told him everything was clear, but letting him know that he had to be checked out every now and then. I thought he was going to jump out of the bed and do a jig, he was so happy. And that's the way we left things, with only Noel and myself unsure of what the future held for Da.

* * *

I kept myself busy all the time, trying not to think about what might happen to Da, but it was always there in the back of my mind. Little did I know all the things that were about to happen over the following couple of years.

I went back to the hospital for months on end with Da for his check-ups. Even though the results seemed to be good each time, I could see that he was pale and had got very thin. He was such a worrier that none of us passed remarks about how he looked, and neither did he.

I spoke to Noel and we decided that we would go and talk to the doctor ourselves. He suggested lots of tests, which Da wasn't happy about and refused to have. I sat up in the bedroom for hours one day, trying to convince him it was for his own good. That's when I said the words that I know he didn't want to hear, but I couldn't help myself as I broke down crying.

'Please, Da, I don't want yeh to die. The doctors can help yeh. Please come to the hospital with me.'

He sat there for a while before he spoke. 'Okay, Kathleen, I will, because, yeh know somethin'? I'm not ready to leave yiz all yet or for tha' matter this earth.'

I threw my arms around him and held on so tight, not wanting to let go.

* * *

They did so many tests, showing up clear each time.

'How can this be?' I asked the doctors. 'Me Da looks so sick, there has to be somethin' wrong.'

'We didn't want to say anything until we were absolutely certain, but your father has what we call a hiding/moving cancer. It showed up in his lungs once and then when we looked again there was nothing there.'

'Tha's good, doctor. No, I mean, tha's great,' I said. 'Tha' means it's probably gone now for good and it won't come back and me Da will get better and everythin' will be like always.' I was trembling as I spoke.

The doctor listened to me going on and on. I so wanted to believe the words that were coming out of my mouth and not his. 'I am very sorry,' he said, 'we have one more test to do and then we will know for certain what is wrong with your father.'

* * *

It seemed to take forever for the day to come to go back to the hospital for the results. I was very nervous but didn't let Da see it. He held onto my arm as we walked down the long corridor.

'De yeh know somethin', Kathleen?' he said in a very low voice. 'Wha'ever the doctor has to say to me today, it doesn't matter wha' it is, once I'm not told tha' I have cancer. Other than tha', I'll handle anythin'.'

'Of course yeh will, Da. Haven't we all got over so much through the years between the whole lot of us? This is just a little blip along the way. Now, come on, straighten them shoulders up and let's see wha' this fella has to say to us.'

I made it my business to speak to the doctor before I brought Da in.

'Doctor, I'm Mr Doyle's daughter, Kathleen. I need to speak to yeh first.' He listened as I spoke. 'If me Da has cancer, please don't tell him.'

'I am sorry, Kathleen, but I have to give the proper results if he asks me.'

'He won't ask yeh, doctor; he doesn't want to know. Please, he won't be able to take it.'

The doctor said no more except, 'Bring your father in.'

I was sick to the pit of my stomach as we sat facing him, not knowing what was about to be said.

'Mr Doyle, we now know what is wrong with you.' He looked over at me as he spoke, 'You have tuberculosis – more commonly know as TB.'

Da jumped off the chair before he heard another word and nearly took the hands off the Doctor, he shook them so much. 'Thank you, thank you, doctor. I had meself in an awful state, worryin' tha' yeh might tell me I had cancer.'

'You are still a very sick man, Mr Doyle, and will have to be on a lot of strong medication.'

'No matter wha' yeh say, doctor, with tha' bit of news yeh just gave me I could take on the world.'

'Right, Mr Doyle, I'll get you to sit outside while I talk to your daughter about your prescription.'

As soon as Da left the room, the doctor didn't waste any time in telling me the truth. 'I am afraid your father has lung cancer and he has only a matter of weeks left.'

I couldn't believe what I was hearing. Deep down, I suppose I knew, but I didn't want to know. I had been in complete denial, as had the rest of the family. I couldn't keep myself together; I fell to pieces right there and then.

'Will you just give me a minute, doctor? I can't let him see me cry.'

'Take all the time you need. I have this form filled in and ready for you to sign for him to go into the hospice.'

'Thanks, doctor, but no thanks. If we were to do tha', then he would surely know he had cancer. I think I can speak for all the family when I say this: we'll take care of our own Da. But, if need be, when it comes to the time tha' we need a bit of help, I'll let yeh know. And thanks for doin' tha' for me Da.'

I stood up, took a deep breath and went out with a smile to Da. He was like a different man walking out of the hospital compared to the weak frail man who had held onto me only a short time earlier. He had straightened up, his shoulders pulled back, walking a few steps ahead of me.

'Will yeh hurry yerself there, Kathleen,' he said as I got a big smile. 'I can't wait to get home to tell them all me bit of good news.'

* * *

To this very day, I don't remember driving my car home that day. I could hear Da talking away to me in the distance, but my mind was still trying to take in what I had just been told. *My Da is dying – he won't be around anymore. How can this be? There is no way I'm ready for this. No way at all.*

I barely had the car stopped outside the house when Da was out and heading for the front door. All I could hear was cheering as I walked in. I stood there and looked at everyone. So happy, hugging and kissing Da.

'Kathleen, isn't this the best news ever?' they all kept saying. 'Da is goin' to be okay!'

I got a glimpse of Noel standing in the background. I shook my head and gave him the nod. He knew what had to be done, before I could say anything to the rest of the family.

'Yeh look a bit tired, Da,' he said. 'Why don't yeh lie down for an hour before yer dinner?'

'Now tha' yeh say it, Noel, I think I could do with a bit of shut-eye. I'm after drainin' meself with all the excitement of the day.'

I waited for a few more minutes, making sure that he was settled and asleep before I came out with the words I didn't want to say.

'Stay quiet, everyone, I have somethin' to say.' I could feel myself shaking as the tears rolled down my face.

'Jaysus, Kathleen,' one of the girls said, 'wha' the hell is wrong with yeh? Yeh're cryin' when yeh should be happy and laughin'.'

'I'm sorry, there's just no other way to say this . . . Da has lung cancer. He's dyin'; he has only a few weeks left to live.'

'But Da said . . .' they all kept saying. 'Da said . . .'

There were tears and hysterics when I told them what had happened in the hospital. Ma sat there, not saying a word. She seemed to be lost in her own world. I wasn't sure if she had taken in what I had said and wanted to be left alone. I thought that she might have cried, even a little. But there was nothing; there didn't seem to be any response from her at all. Everybody was too upset, so I said nothing about Ma and let it go for the time being.

When everyone had calmed down we had a talk amongst ourselves.

'This is how I feel,' I said, 'and I think Noel agrees with me. Da doesn't want to know wha's wrong with him. He made that very clear to me today. So, if you all agree, and I know it's goin' to be very hard, we'll try and carry on as normal.'

And that's what we all did, as best we could. When Da came back down that evening for his dinner he was so happy and had such a big smile on his face that we all knew immediately we'd made the right decision.

* * *

Over the next couple of days, whenever I went down to Crumlin, Ma seemed to be asleep a lot of the time and when she was awake she wasn't her usual self. She was too quiet. So I made it my business to speak to my sister Carmel, who spent more time than any of us with Ma and Da, as she had never left the family home.

'Carmel, de yeh think Ma is goin' a bit strange? I'm not sure the news about Da has her like this or if there's somethin' else wrong.'

'Yeh know wha', Kathleen, I kept meanin' to have a talk with yeh about Ma, but with yeh runnin' to the hospital so much with Da, and then with one thing and another, I forgot. Yeh know wha' I caught her doin' one of the days? Now this is before yeh told us about Da. He was givin' out to her about somethin', I don't know wha' it was. Anyway, she was makin' him a sandwich and then I saw her crush a couple of her sleepin' tablets and put them on the bit of corn beef, smotherin' it with brown sauce. Only I caught her, God knows wha' could have happened.

'"Ma," I said, "wha' the hell are yeh doin'?"

'"Tha' fuckin' oul' fella is annoyin' me," she said. "He's givin' out all mornin' like I don't know wha', so this will shut him up for a while." It took me all me time to stop her givin' it to Da. And then the other mornin' I came down and she was sittin' there with about three sets of clothes on.'

'Ah, for Jaysus' sake, Carmel, how could yeh not tell me tha'?'

'Everybody thought it was real funny, Kathleen. I mean, she never done anythin' like tha' before. And then, as I said, it went out of me head.'

I didn't waste any time in getting Ma to the doctor and then on to the hospital to be checked out, only to be told they could find nothing wrong. She sat there chatting away to the doctor, with not a bother on her. The way he was looking at me, I think he thought I was the one who needed help. I was told to come back in six months and they would assess Ma again.

* * *

In the meantime, Da was getting weaker by the day, so we put one of the single beds down in the sitting room. That way there were always a couple of us with him at all times. It was now time to let the doctor know we needed some help, which we got straight away. The nurses from the hospice were so kind to Da. They made sure that he was in as little pain as possible.

My sister Marion, who had married and settled in Canada, came home with my brother Phil to spend the last few days with Da. Although it was such a sad and heartbreaking time for us, we were all together as a family and that's what got us through.

Phil and I were sitting at Da's bedside on the evening he passed away. Phil, as usual, was joking and telling a few yarns. Then, just out of the blue, he held Da's hand and said, 'Don't be afraid, Da. Yeh won't be on yer own for long. I'll be with yeh soon.'

'Jaysus Christ, Phil,' I whispered, 'will yeh not be sayin' such things.'

He gave me one of his big smiles and said no more.

We all stayed together that night, sitting on the floor in front of the fire, just like when we were kids, crying and laughing at the same time as we all went down memory lane, before we all eventually fell asleep.

* * *

I woke up to the sound of someone sobbing. It was still night. Phil was sitting beside Da's bed and crying so hard as he held Da's hand. I made my way over to him and put my arm around his shoulder.

'De yeh know somethin', Kathleen? All those years away – wha' was it all for? A bloody house and a fancy car tha' I would have got here anyway in time? Me Da is dead and Ma hardly knows who I am half the time. I should've been here to look after them. Half of me brothers and sisters I don't even know. They're like strangers to me, they were so young when I took off.'

'Come on, Phil, don't be beatin' yerself up like tha'. Yeh were just followin' yer dream, like all of us.'

'I know tha', Kathleen, but did mine have to be on the other side of the fuckin' world? I've missed out on so much because of it.'

'For Jaysus' sake, Phil, will yeh not be cursin' like tha', or yeh'll have Da jumpin' up there givin' out like shite to the pair of us.'

I got a tiny little grin when I said that.

'All the same, Kathleen, wouldn't tha' be somethin'? I'd give the world to have him back, even just for a little while.'

'Wouldn't we all, Phil? Now let's go into the kitchen and I'll make us a nice cup of tea.'

My own heart was bursting, but I was trying so hard to keep up a front, Phil was falling to pieces that much. We sat there through the night talking and laughing as we went over the past once more and then crying as we were brought back to the present.

Before we knew it the morning light was breaking through the curtains and the rest of the family were starting to wake up. It was going to be a long, hard day ahead for each and every one of us.

* * *

There was hustle and bustle over the next couple of days with Da being laid out in the house. There was no end to the people coming to pay their respects.

Ma sat in her chair staring out, not saying a word. I knew deep down in my heart there was something seriously wrong with her, especially when she turned around without the blink of an eye and said, 'I want me telly on. I want to look at the funnies.' 'The funnies' were the cartoons.

Everyone in the room went quiet for a few seconds, with a few of the neighbours giving the eye to one another. There was our Da, laid out in his coffin, ready to go and meet his maker, and all Ma wanted was to watch Mickey Mouse on the telly. I looked over at Phil and Noel, not knowing what to say or do. I could see that Noel was in shock like the rest of us. But Phil, being Phil, was laughing his head off. He got up and put the telly on, saying, 'Wha' harm is she doin'? If it makes her happy, wha' the heck.' And that was it; the funnies played as the wake went on.

The priest came down that evening to say mass. We had to move all the furniture around to make as much room as possible. We had a parrot called Rocky, who was supposed to be put upstairs out of the way, as he had a terrible mouth on him and never stopped cursing. But, of course, somebody just happened to put his cage behind the very chair that the priest was standing in front of. There we were, all upset, crying and sniffling, when suddenly we heard the words, 'Yeh're only a bollocks, yeh're only a bollocks!'

We all looked at each other, not knowing what to do, biting our lips, trying not to laugh. The priest didn't bat an eyelid; he just gave a little cough and carried on with the mass, while Clare took Rocky upstairs, apologising on the way out.

The funeral went off as well as any funeral does. We were all grieving in our own way, but all feeling the same loss inside, now that our Da was gone. After a few days, we said our goodbyes to Phil and Marion as they headed back to their lives so far away, and then we all settled back into our own lives. Little did any of us realise the trauma and pain that lay ahead for Ma.

18

Ma

After Da died, I used to dread going down to Crumlin, walking into the house, with him not being there. I loved and missed him so much.

I used to get into some debates with him over the years, mostly about religion, which I started to find many faults with as I got older. He would go mad when I pointed out different things that he had no answer for, about the priest or where all the money was going and so on. His response was always the same: 'Mark my words, Kathleen Doyle' – when he used my full name I knew that he was really pissed off with me – 'one of these days yeh'll be struck down dead for flyin' in the face of God.'

We would either hammer it out, hot and heavy, or if he saw that he wasn't getting the better of me, he would storm off up to his bedroom and sulk for an hour. If he didn't come back down, I always made it my business to go to him, making the peace with a smoke and a cup of tea.

'Yeh're an awful girl, Kathleen,' he would say, 'gettin' me all roiled up like tha'. Yeh really know how to get me goin'.'

Oh, how I miss those times.

I suppose if Ma had been her old self, going around ranting and raving, throwing the odd 'fuck' in here and there, the house wouldn't have been so quiet and maybe I wouldn't have felt the loss so much. But that wasn't to be. She just sat in her chair saying very little, like someone lost in another world. She never cried once for Da and when we would ask her where he was, she'd shake her head and turn away, not saying a word.

It had been a couple of months since I had last been at the hospital with Ma and in that time she had got a lot worse. I thought to myself as I waited to see the doctor, *Surely to God this time they will be able to see that there is something wrong?* I had asked over and over again if they would do a brain scan for me. The answer was always the same: 'I'm afraid your mother will have to go on the waiting list like everyone else.'

'But, doctor,' I would say, 'if it's the money, tha's not a problem. There's plenty of us in the family to pay for it.' But they didn't listen.

It was only on her last visit, after I insisted that they do a test for diabetes, that somebody finally listened to me. I knew by the doctor's face that Ma's results must have been serious. His words to me were, 'I'm afraid your mother's sugar levels are quite high. As soon as the first bed becomes available, she will have to come into hospital for further tests.'

'Yeh mean they're sky high, is tha' wha' yeh're tryin' to tell me, doctor? I've tried to tell yeh for I don't know how long tha' there was somethin' very seriously wrong with our Ma. And it's not only diabetes; there's somethin' else there, I know there is.'

'And you would know this how, Mrs McGrath?' he asked smartly.

'Well, I don't pretend to know the medical terms, doctor, but in my line of work I deal with people every day and I *listen* to my clients telling me about their mothers and families, and the different symptoms they would have. Tha's how I knew my Ma had diabetes and tha's why I'm fightin' to get a brain scan, because I think there's something wrong there. I know by the way she's goin' on.'

I could see that he was getting annoyed at me for speaking out to him like that, but at that stage I didn't care. I was sick and tired of them passing me around from Billy to Jack and not one of them coming up with any answers. Anyway, I got the usual little cough off the doctor, and I could tell he didn't know what to say. He kept his head down as he wrote on Ma's chart while he mumbled out a few words to me.

'The nurse will tell you about your mother's medication and she will also make arrangements about her coming in for the test as soon as a bed is ready.'

I didn't have anything else to say to him, so I took Ma by the hand and left.

Incredibly, I was only in the house ten or fifteen minutes when the phone rang. It was the hospital, asking if we could bring Ma straight back in, as they had a bed for her.

Good Jaysus, I thought to myself, *I should have got annoyed with them months ago.*

'Carmel,' I said, 'run upstairs and pack a bag with Ma's few bits in it and I'll get her back down to the hospital as quick as I can. We don't want them changin' their mind now, do we?'

'Thank God they're takin' her in, Kathleen. I don't know wha' she's goin' to do from day to day. I came down the other mornin' and the front door was wide open; Ma wasn't to be found anywhere. I was frantic. De yeh know where she was when I did eventually find her? Up the top of the road, not dressed, still in her nightdress. And tha's not all; she's gettin' up in the middle of the night to make herself a cup of tea, which is no harm I know, but she's puttin' the gas cooker on and not lightin' it. Only I woke to go into the toilet and smelled the gas, we'd all be dead today.'

'I know it's hard on yeh, Carmel. Yeh're with Ma more than the rest of us. But I promise we'll get to the bottom of it this time. Now, I'd better go. Will yeh ring around the rest of the family and tell them wha's happenin'? I'll stay with Ma until one or two of yeh come up and then I'll go on home and have a break.'

* * *

I was only in the door of the hospital when Ma was seen to straight away. They had her settled in a ward in no time at all. I was sitting there talking to her, trying to get her to understand that she was only going to be there for a couple of days.

'The doctors want to do a few tests,' I said, 'just to make sure you're okay, Ma. And then yeh'll be straight back home, I promise.'

Not a sound came from her. She was yellow in the face and had this glazed look in her eyes. You know, like when someone is looking at you but they're not seeing you. She looked as if she was lost in another place and couldn't find her way back.

My brother Noel arrived. The two of us were sitting there talking away when suddenly Ma started twitching and shaking. Then she went into a major fit. Noel jumped up with the fright.

'Good Jaysus,' he roared, 'quick, Kathleen, get a nurse, get a doctor!'

He was trying to put Ma on her side while I ran out screaming for help. Two nurses came straight away with the doctor following minutes after, putting Noel and myself out in the corridor while they looked after Ma. Then the rest of the family starting to dribble in one by one and there was no way any one of us would be allowed back in to Ma.

She continued having more fits through the night and into the early hours of the morning. Then and only then was the decision made to send her for a brain scan, over to Elm Park Hospital. The brain scan showed that she had a brain tumour the size of a large egg, pressing on her memory bank, which was causing her to be so confused. When we spoke to the brain surgeon we were told, 'Your mother has a fifty-fifty chance of pulling through the operation, and even then I can't promise anything. But if she does make it through, don't expect too much. She will never be the same woman again.'

'So wha' yeh're sayin', doctor, is Ma will be the same as she is now,' I said, 'and still not know any of us?'

'I'm afraid so. But without the operation she will surely die, and it will be sooner rather than later.'

We were all in shock, trying to take it all on board. Our Da was only two months dead, and now Ma . . . I was screaming inside my head, *Why is all this happenin' to us? It's not fair. It's just not fair!* Such a hard life Ma had had rearing us kids. Now, at the age of only sixty-three, when she should be starting to enjoy life, all this was happening to her. We didn't want our Ma to leave us, so each and every one of us gave the go-ahead to operate.

They operated straight away. Such a long day it was, taking nearly eight hours before they were finished. We all handled it in our own way. Some wanted to be on their own; some paired off together. Myself and Clare sat in the little church in the hospital. Both of us knew full well that if one of us was sick, that's where Ma would be. I couldn't help but let my mind wander back in time, thinking about all the mad things us kids used to do on her. How she put up with us I'll never know. I was laughing and crying at the same time as I spoke to Clare.

'Remember the day we made the swimmin' pool in the house, Clare? God, she nearly killed us all tha' day. I don't know how one of us didn't end up in the hospital, she was throwin' tha' many rocks at us.'

'She never caught me, Kathleen, ever, not even on the day tha' priest came down to the house – yeh know, the one tha' made Ma cry over the purse. I swore I'd get me own back on him for doin' tha'. He was a righ' pig, so he was. Well, he was down knockin' on the door one day, givin' out shite about me being cheeky. I wasn't long about sortin' him out. I fucked a load of potato skins, tea leaves and any rubbish I could get me hands on out the top window all over him and then scarpered over the back wall before Ma could catch me.'

'Jaysus, yeh were a mad bitch, Clare. I'll never forget tha' evenin'. I was only in the door from work when Ma launched into tellin' me wha' yeh did. Now, havin' said tha', yeh could see tha' she was tryin' to keep a straight face herself. If the truth be known, Clare, she was probably pleased with wha' yeh did after the way he treated her. But, of course, she couldn't let us know tha' at the time.'

Both of us sat there laughing about the past, but at the same time crying as we waited to see what the future held for Ma.

The doctor told us that the operation went well but the next twenty-four hours were crucial. We were to leave it until the following evening before coming in. We phoned all the family, letting them know that Ma had pulled through.

I was so tired and drained from all the running around that I had done with Da the previous few weeks, up until he died, back and forward to Crumlin, up and down to the hospital, trying to work and look after the kids. I really thought that I might have slept that night. Instead, I lay there thinking about Ma on her own. Was she all right? Would she pull through? Would she ever know any of us again? I cried so much just thinking about that.

I pottered about the next day, doing a few hours work to keep myself busy, wishing and hoping that the time would come when I could make my way up to Ma, leaving Alan to take care of the kids. I didn't hang about waiting for any of the others. We all said that we'd meet up in the hospital. I got there a bit early and made my way up to the ward.

I was not expecting the sight that awaited me. I thought Ma's head would be covered in bandages. I went into shock when I saw her. She was propped up in the bed. Her eyes were wide open and they were black and blue. Most of her hair had been shaved off and her head was badly swollen. But the part that I couldn't handle was that, from one ear right across to the other, big silver staples were holding her head together. It was like something out of a horror movie. I ran outside and couldn't breathe with the fright I got. I was standing there shaking, I was so upset. Shortly after that I saw Clare walking up the corridor.

'Wha's wrong with yeh, Kathleen? Yeh're green in the face. Don't tell me Ma's dead – Jaysus, don't tell me she's after dyin'!'

'No, no, it's not tha',' I said. 'Oh Clare, yeh'd want to see Ma. It's terrible. Wait until yeh see her. Oh my God, wait 'til yeh see her.'

'Will yeh give it over, Kathleen. It can't be tha' bad.'

The two of us made our way back in and I could see that Clare felt the same as me, but she held it together a bit better.

'Holy Mother of God, this is not righ'. Ma never deserved this.'

I couldn't even answer her, I was crying so much.

As each member of the family arrived, the shock on all their faces said it all. We all stood there, not knowing what to say or do. After a few minutes, Noel spoke up.

'Righ',' he said, 'Ma always did her best for us and now it's our turn to take care of her. We have to make sure there's two of us here at all times every day, keepin' an eye on her.' We all nodded in agreement.

* * *

After a couple of days, the doctor had a talk with us.

'As soon as we take the staples out of your mother's head,' he said, 'which will be after the weekend, we would like her to go home.'

We all started chiming in together, saying the same thing. 'But doctor, Ma's real sick. We can't take her home – not like this.'

'I am sorry, but your mother has to be in her own home, among familiar surroundings. She needs all of you to keep talking to her, over and over again, about the past and the present. That is the only way we will get her brain to start working again. I have done my part now; the rest is up to all of you.'

'We know yeh have, doctor,' said Noel, 'and we all thank yeh for savin' our Ma's life.'

The doctor was well pleased when Noel said that, smiling at each of us before he went about his business.

* * *

And that was it; Ma was back home less than eight days after her operation. It was so hard to watch the mother who was always so strong, who took care of us so well, but who was now like a baby and had to be taught everything all over again. It was very slow and needed so much patience.

Ma didn't come back to her old self the way she had been before, but a little part of her was still there. She still remembered to give you 'the look' if there was something going on around her.

170

I remember the day so well; I was talking away to her, saying my name, going over and over again.

'Ma, it's me, Kathleen. De yeh know who I am? Ma, it's Kathleen.'

I must have said it a dozen times. I was sick listening to myself, when suddenly she turned around, looked me straight in the eye and said, 'Feck off, Kathleen. I know yeh!' She didn't say 'fuck', but feck was good enough for me.

I couldn't believe it; I started screaming. 'Carmel, Carmel, come quick. She knows who I am.' Carmel rushed in and I turned back to Ma. 'Ma, tell me, who's tha' standin' there?' She looked and thought for a minute or two.

'It's Carmel.'

Carmel was delighted when Ma said her name. The two of us started screaming together, jumping up and down, hugging one another. We were over the moon. We knew it would still take time, but it was great to see Ma was on the mend.

19

The Funny Farm

As the weeks and months went by, Ma slowly remembered us all. She was as happy as anything, sitting in her chair every day, looking at the cartoons and all the old films, laughing her head off, with not a care in the world.

But she still needed constant care. I know we all dropped down to see Ma and give a dig out when we were there, but it still wasn't the same. Because Carmel was living there, she had so much more to do than the rest of us. She was worn out from looking after Ma and badly needed a break. So she headed off to Spain for a week's holidays.

We were all down in Crumlin – now, when I say all, I mean me and my sisters; there was no way the fellas could do much for Ma, other than to sit and talk to her, in the hope that she might say something back to them. We were trying to work out what would be the best arrangement for Ma for the week and who would have the most time during the day, with the rest helping out in the evenings.

'I'll take Ma up with me,' said Clare, 'once yiz don't let me down when I'm bringin' the chipper out at five o'clock. Other than tha', it won't be a problem.'

Clare had a mobile chipper van that she would get ready during the day and then tow over to her spot beside one of the local pubs. She had a couple of women working for her, so she had a bit more time on her hands than the rest of us.

I didn't live too far from Clare's house, which was a big bungalow on a half-acre of land. So I made it my business to be there every day. It was like going over to a funny farm. She had two sons, Dominic, who was around thirteen, and Romano, who was going on eight. They were so wild. No, I take that back – they were mad. I never knew what to expect when I went into that house.

I had just arrived one day and Clare was waving to me as she pulled out with the chipper. 'I won't be long, Kathleen,' she said. 'Go on in; the kids are there with Ma.'

I was knocking away on the door for ages, with not a sign of anyone letting me in. They were in there all right; I could hear them screaming and laughing their heads off. I went around to the side window, and I couldn't believe what I saw. They had all the furniture pushed up against the walls. Ma was sitting on a woollen blanket on the floor and there were Romano and Dominic pulling her along, flying up and down the room, twirling her all over the place. Well, you'd want to hear the laughs off Ma, never mind the other two! She looked as if she was having the time of her life.

I nearly lost my breath. All I could think of was Ma's head and what damage would be done if she banged it. The window was only short of shattering all over the place, I knocked on it so hard. Finally I got their attention and they opened the door.

'Ah, there yeh are, Kathleen,' said Dominic. 'We're having great craic here with me Nanny.'

'I know yiz are. Haven' I been watchin' yiz for the past ten minutes? Yeh ravin' lunatics, tha's wha' yiz are. Now, help me get yer Nanny off the floor.'

Ma was still curled over with the laughing. 'Are yeh okay, Ma?' I asked as I got her up and settled in the chair.

Still giggling, she said, 'Funny, great, funny.' Just to hear her say that was worth the fright I got.

'There, we told yeh, Kathleen,' the other two chimed in. 'Nanny does have the best fun ever when she's with us.'

'I can well imagine, after wha' I saw. Now get in there, the pair of yiz and make us a nice a cup of tea while I talk to yer Nanny.'

Clare was back before too long and I told her what had been going on. Now, before I go any further, I have to tell you that Clare is the most easy-going person on this planet. Nothing, and I mean nothing, gets her excited.

'Wha' are yeh gettin' yerself all worked up for, Kathleen?' Clare said. 'I told them before I went out tha' when they got down to the end of the room with Ma to make sure to slow down a bit when they're twirling her around. Just in case one of them would slip, like. But they were grand. She was laughin' her head off.'

'Are yeh for real or wha', Clare? I mean, say she had banged her head . . . wha' would yeh have done then?'

'But she didn't, did she, Kathleen? Now, don't be gettin' yer knickers in a knot there. She's fine.'

'I know, Clare. I'm just afraid somethin' will happen to her, tha's all.'

'Well, the way I see it, Kathleen, we can wrap Ma up in her blanket and have her all nice and cosy and safe there lookin' at the telly. And if the truth be known, she's probably just starin' into space half the time. Believe me, I know them two little fuckers of mine are as mad as hatters, but if they can make Ma laugh the way I just saw, well, tha's good enough for me.'

'I have to say, Clare, even though I nearly had a stroke when I looked in the window, part of me was laughin' along with them. It was great to see her havin' a bit of fun instead of just sittin' in the chair.'

'I know them doctors were real good, Kathleen, with everythin' they did for Ma and, God only knows, she wouldn't be here only for them. But yeh know when they told us not to expect too much? Tha' she'd never come back to anythin' like she was before and tha' we were lucky just to have her alive? Well, I stood there and listened while yeh all asked yer different questions about one thing or the other, and I said to meself, *Yeh're so wrong, doctor, because yeh don't know our Ma and how strong she can be*. She didn't pull through all this just to sit in a chair and be molly-coddled like a baby. It might take a bit of time, but we'll get her back.'

'De yeh know somethin', Clare? Yeh're so righ'. Ma wouldn't want this, and de yeh know wha' else? She's probably fuckin' like mad inside her head, wantin' to give us all a good dig at the same time. Tha's it now, Clare – when I have her on the weekends I'm goin' to back off and start lettin' her do things for herself.'

'Righ' then, tha's enough of all tha' serious talk, Kathleen. Would yeh have a look in at her now.'

There Romano was, breaking his heart laughing, lying on the floor with a feather at Ma's feet, tickling the life out of her; and there she was, fist in the air, trying to swing a dig at him. It was great to see.

* * *

The week was nearly over and Carmel was on her way back from her holiday, so I made my way over early to Clare's to help pack Ma's few bits before bringing her home to Crumlin. When I walked into the kitchen, I thought I was seeing things.

As I said, Clare had a good bit of land around her bungalow and what went with that were a load of chickens and about fourteen dogs at any given time; one cat that looked more like a small lion, mainly because he ate dog food and all the scraps that went with it; 'Goldy' the horse, who was absolutely gorgeous; and a pony called 'One-Eye Jack'. Clare took in every stray from around the area.

When I walked into the kitchen, Ma was sitting there drinking a cup of tea. Dominic and Romano were with her, having their breakfast. But guess who else was there? One-Eye Jack, the pony! And he wasn't a little pony, he was a good size. He was standing beside Ma as she fed him slices of bread and butter.

'Holy Jaysus, Dominic, are yiz gone fuckin' mad altogether? Wha' are yiz doin' bringin' the horse into the house? Where the hell is Clare?'

'She's still in bed,' the two of them chimed in together. 'Nanny was laughin' and wavin' out to Jack to come over to her and it was lashin' rain out. We didn't want to bring her out, in case she'd get wringin' wet, so we brought him in to her! Look, she's havin' great fun with him, Kathleen.'

True enough, when I looked at Ma, she was as happy as Larry, sitting there with nearly half a loaf of bread in front of her as she fed Jack his breakfast.

'Clare will have a blue fit when she sees the state of this kitchen. I'm tellin' yiz, she'll kill the pair of yiz. Yiz better get off side by the time she gets up. Look, there's muck everywhere!'

With that, Jack gave himself a right shaking, drowning the whole lot of us and into the bargain lashing me out of it with his tail. Ma and the other two thought this was so funny. I ran to Clare's room to get away from him.

'Clare,' I roared, 'yeh better get up, it's like a lunatic asylum out there. They have the horse in the house!' Not a blink or a sound came from her. 'Clare, did yeh hear wha' I said – the horse is in the fuckin' house! Will yeh wake up, for Jaysus' sake. I have to get Ma ready for goin' home.'

Still not a sound. I was really getting pissed off at this stage. I had splashes of muck all over me and Dominic and Romano were standing in the hall, laughing their heads off.

'We'll get her up for yeh, Kathleen, but it'll cost yeh!'

'Wha' de yeh mean, it'll cost me? Cost me wha'?'

'Money, of course!' said Dominic. 'Give us a few shillin's and we'll have our Ma out of the bed before yeh know it.'

I stood there and thought for a minute. *The crafty little fuckers.* At the same time, it was like looking at myself and Phil, the way we used to get up to all sorts to make a few shillings.

'Righ' then, anythin' to get out of this madhouse!' I handed over the money.

I thought that they might jump on the bed and maybe shake Clare hard, like most normal kids would do, but I should have known when I looked at the pair of them. You could see the devilment in their eyes.

'Righ',' said Dominic to Romano as they stood at the doorway of Clare's bedroom, 'go down and get Jack and bring him up here to me. I'll get the rope when yeh're doin' tha'.'

While all this was going on, Clare still didn't blink an eye; she was dead to the world. I couldn't believe that she was still asleep with all this commotion going on around her.

'Wha' de yeh mean, Dominic?' I said. 'Why are yeh bringin' the horse down here?'

'Yeh want me Ma to wake up, don't yeh, Kathleen? Now, just stand over there at the window and let us get on with it.'

I stood there with my mouth open as I watched them. I couldn't believe what they were about to do. I have to admit,

177

I was laughing to myself at the same time. While Romano was fixing the rope around the horse's neck, Dominic was tying Clare's two legs together with the other end of the rope. As soon as they were finished, Jack got a right wallop on the arse and he made a charge down the hall, dragging Clare out of the bed along with him! Well, you'd want to have heard the screams of her as she bounced all over the place throughout the house! I swear to God, I wet in my knickers, I was laughing so much. I watched the other two lunatics roll around the floor with laughter.

'In the name of Jaysus,' Clare kept roaring, 'when I get me hands on yiz, yeh're dead – fuckin' dead – de yeh hear me? Dead! Now, get these ropes offa me. Yeh bastards!'

Dominic was trying to keep a straight face as he held Jack and fed him a sweet. In the meantime, Romano was untying Clare's feet. They didn't waste any time in scarpering out the back door, leaving me to face Clare and help her up off the floor.

'Kathleen Doyle, I can't believe yeh helped them two little fucks of mine to do this to me! You of all people! Look at me. I'm in bits. I won't be able to walk righ' for a month.'

'I swear to God, Clare, when I was givin' them the money to wake yeh, I didn't know this is wha' they had in mind.'

'Yeh mean yeh paid them to do this to me? Yeh're fuckin' as bad as they are!'

With all this going on I had completely forgotten about Ma, who was still sitting in the same spot, laughing her head off. She soon stopped us in our tracks when we heard her say, 'Clare, so funny . . . mad . . . Clare.' The two of us screamed together when we heard her speak. She would be quiet for so long and then out of the blue she'd say a few words here and there.

'Oh my God, Clare! Did yeh hear tha'? Ma has said more this week than she has in I don't know how long.'

'Isn't tha' wha' I was only sayin' the other day, Kathleen? I mean, I haven't got time to be pussy-footin' about with Ma every minute of the day. I just have to let her get on with it. When yeh're all asleep in yer beds at night, I'm out until three and four o'clock, towin' tha' chipper home. Then when I have tha' done I start cuttin' me fish up for the next day. And I'm doin' tha' until the early hours of the mornin'. So is it any wonder I'm dead to the world and can't get outta the bed?'

'I'm sorry, Clare. I do forget about tha'. I wasn't thinkin'.'

At that moment the two head-bangers made their way back in to us.

'Are yeh okay, Ma?' asked the pair of them as they stood there with dirty big grins on their faces.

'Yiz are bastards, tha's wha' yiz are!' said Clare.

Romano lay his head on Clare's shoulder and wrapped his two arms around her as he said, 'Ma, tha' was the best fun ever.'

And that was it. Clare melted as usual and they got away with murder once more.

'Anyway, Clare,' I said, 'now tha' all the madness is out of the way, the reason I'm over early is to get Ma ready and bring her back home to Crumlin. Carmel is flyin' in later today. I tell yeh wha', you sit there and I'll pack her few bits. Dominic, make yer Ma a cup of tea and some toast. It's the least yeh can do after wha' yeh just put her through.'

He was up like a light, sucking up to Clare like I don't know what, while I packed up for Ma.

'Are yeh righ', Ma?' I said as soon as I was finished. 'I'll help yeh get dressed now. It's time to bring yeh home.'

She would neither budge nor look at me.

'Come on, Ma, wha's wrong with yeh?'

She looked up at me and then straight at Clare. 'Stayin' here!' she said.

'I'm sorry, Ma, but yeh have to go back home.'

She sat there and didn't say another word, but kept looking into Clare's face.

'She doesn't have to go at the minute, Kathleen. There's no problem if Ma wants to stay on for another week or two with me.'

Well, you'd want to see Ma's face brighten up when she heard Clare say that.

* * *

Those couple of weeks ended up turning into six years for Clare and Ma. There was always hustle and bustle going on in Clare's house. Between the fish man, the chip man and all the other deliveries that went with running her chipper, there was always somebody dropping in or something going on. And that's without mentioning the two head-bangers, Dominic and Romano, who got up to all sorts of mischief along the way.

But between them, they looked after Ma so well. I think in Ma's mind it reminded her so much of all that went on when we were growing up, the bedlam and mayhem that surrounded her throughout her life. Crumlin had gone so quiet, especially since Da's death, with each and every one of us going our own way. Maybe inside her head, she couldn't handle that. We all thought that we were doing the right thing by wrapping her in cotton wool, not realising that we were probably smothering her all the time. So the best thing that could have happened was Ma going to live up in Clare's funny farm. I think that at the end of the day, that's what really helped her come on so well.

Ma still wasn't able to do very much and needed so much care, but as time went on she got a lot better. We signed her up to one of the local clubs, so that she would be mixing with people in and around her age. That helped so much to bring her out of herself. She loved going there. They would have their nights outs and plenty of weekends away. She ended up being the life and soul of the party everywhere she went. Always the first up on the floor and the last one to leave, Ma became more outgoing, in a way that she never was before

The doctors couldn't get over the change. I remember sitting in the hospital on one of the visits with Ma. She was chattering away like I don't know what to the doctor. There was no stopping her. I was well pleased with what he had to say, and very happy with Ma's reply.

'Do you know, Mrs Doyle, you have a great family. The support and hard work you got from them is what has you sitting here today.'

She stopped dead in her tracks and looked me straight in the eye, just like she did so many years ago.

'De yeh think I don't know tha', doctor?'

That's when I knew our Ma was slowly coming back to us.

20

Hospital

I had been attending the Coombe hospital for the past twelve years because of my gynaecological problems, and I have to say the doctors were very good. They kept a close eye on me in that time. I was due back for my yearly visit, which I didn't give much thought to, mainly because I had been told for so long, 'Your smear tests have settled down, Mrs McGrath, but they're still not clear, so we will see you next year.' As usual, I would go off about my business and didn't give it another thought until I was due to go back again.

Now, I was sitting in front of the doctor and I suppose I should have known there was something wrong, because it was the head man himself this time, whom I hadn't seen for years. The difference a few years can make. I had grown up so much and was more confident in myself than I had been the first time I had sat down in front of this doctor in his white coat. I was no longer afraid of him.

There was no beating about the bush; he just came right out and said what he had to say. 'Mrs McGrath, I'm afraid it's time for you to come in and have a hysterectomy. It can't be left any longer.'

I came right out and asked it. 'Doctor, have I got cancer?'

He looked me straight in the eye for a second or two before he spoke. 'Yes, you have, so we can't waste any time. You have to come in straight away or we won't be responsible after that.' Confidence or no confidence, when that word is spoken, no matter how much you think you are prepared, it doesn't half knock you for six. I was really shook up inside and was trying not to let the doctor see it. I could feel myself shaking and my voice trembling as I spoke.

'Can I have a bit of time to sort a few things out at home, doctor?'

'Yes, you can, but I want you back down to the hospital in the next two days. I will schedule your operation straight away.'

I thanked the doctor and left. My head was all over the place as I made my way out of the hospital. *Jaysus Christ*, I thought to myself, *how am I goin' to work around things?* Martina was working away, finishing her apprenticeship, and there was no way she could take time off. Myself and Alan had taken on the role of helping her rear Danielle, who was only around nine months old, and the news I had just been given was not in my plans.

I'm sure anyone who was looking at me while I walked along must have thought I was mad. I was talking way out loud to myself. 'I'll keep Amanda out of school. I know she's only twelve but with the help of Alan they should manage okay. But then again, I swore that, no matter what, I'd never keep any of my kids out of school for anything. But I suppose this is a bit serious and hopefully it'll only be for a few days.'

I was still having a conversation with myself as I got into my car. I sat there for God knows how long, staring out the window before, finally, I broke down and cried. It was only then, when the silence came over me, that I realised what I had been told. Just then I got a flash of Ma. I would have loved nothing better than for her to put her arms around me and say, 'Don't worry, Kathleen, everythin's goin' to be fine.' But that wasn't to be; she was lost in another world and knew very little of what was going on around her.

As soon as I got myself together I decided that I wouldn't tell anyone what the doctor had said, not until it was all over, in the hope that the outcome would be good. I thought there was no point in worrying everybody unless I had to.

I waited until Alan and myself were on our own before I said anything.

'Alan, I was back at the hospital today for me yearly visit.'

'Jaysus, Kathleen, tha' was a quick year all the same. I forgot all about it. Anyway, how did yeh get on? Everythin' okay with yeh?'

'Well, I had a good chat with the doctor and he was sayin' tha', with all the problems I've had over the years with one thing and another, and I'm thirty-eight now, so he said it might not be a bad idea for me to come in and have me few bits out. Well, he said it different, with fancy words and all, but yeh know wha' I mean, Alan. So what de yeh think?'

'Well, Kathleen, I think tha' yeh should listen to wha' the man is sayin', because at the end of the day he's the one tha' knows wha' he's talkin' about.'

'The only thing is, Martina has to go to work. Wha' about Danielle? Will yeh be able to take time off to look after her?'

'Tha' won't be a problem. I'll park the van until Martina comes in from work. And don't be worryin'. I'll still get me night run in. I just had a thought there, Kathleen – wha' about the nappies? I'm no good at changin' them.'

'I'm goin' to keep Amanda off school to help with tha', so yeh don't have to worry there, Alan.'

'Thanks be to Jaysus for tha'! The last time I changed a nappy was when Martina was a baby and I can still remember; the shit was everywhere. And yeh know I never did another nappy change after tha'.'

He just about got a little smile out of me when he said that. I was trying to keep a front up and not fall to pieces, but it was so hard. Alan would usually know straight away when there was something wrong with me. But with Da not too long dead and so much going on with Ma, I wasn't myself anyway. So the fact that I was a bit quiet at that moment wasn't out of the ordinary.

'Anyway, Kathleen,' said Alan, 'when's all this happenin'?'

'I've to be back in the hospital over the next two days. The doctor said tha' he could fit me in straight away, tha' he had an openin', or he could put me on a list. So I thought, best to get it over and done with now.'

I'm not one for telling lies – well, maybe a little white one now and again – but they just seemed to flow out of me that day. I felt that this time it was allowed. I gave the same yarn to the rest of the family, with no-one being the wiser.

* * *

The next two days seemed to go by so slowly. Every time I looked at Alan or the kids, I could feel myself starting to fill up inside, with the tears ready to burst out of me. I would make some lame excuse and head upstairs. I'd sit on the side of the bath thinking, *Wha' if I don't make it? Who'll take care of Alan and the kids? Oh my God, I can't die. I have to be here always to look after my family. Anyway, I've too much to do with me life. I'm only gettin' started. There's no way this is goin' to drag me down – no way!* With that thought in my mind, I'd pull myself together and carry on as best I could.

Alan dropped me down to the hospital and stayed for a while. He knew that I was nervous.

'Don't be worryin', Kathleen,' he said. 'This time tomorrow it'll all be over and yeh'll be grand, so try and get a good night's sleep. Will yeh do tha' for me?' He gave me a big hug and kiss before he left.

There were three other girls in the ward with me, each of them having the same operation as myself. As the nurses moved busily around, getting us all ready for the following morning, we sat there talking away, mostly about our families and life itself. When I think about it now, we all knew why we were there but none of us spoke of it. Maybe they too had been told the same news as myself and none of us wanted to hear the word 'cancer' mentioned. That way, we could pretend it wasn't there, for that moment anyway.

I didn't sleep much at all that night. I lay there thinking about what the future held for me. That's when I decided to have a little chat with the Holy Mother herself.

'Righ',' I said, 'there's no way I'm ready to go anywhere, so please watch over me tomorrow and make this all go away. Please.'

I must have dozed off for a while, because the next thing I remember is someone tapping me and calling out my name.

'Wake up, Kathleen,' said the nurse. 'It's nearly time for us to bring you down to the theatre. I want you to take this tablet to keep you relaxed and I'll leave this gown and hat for you to put on. We'll be back in about ten minutes.'

It all happened so fast that before I knew it, I was on the trolley and on my way. The two nurses were talking away as they wheeled me along, telling me not to worry, that I was in good hands. I smiled and said nothing. I was too busy thinking of Alan and the kids. With that, Da popped into my head. I could see his face as plain as anything and felt that he was really there with me. Maybe the tablet had me feeling like that. I really don't know, but it made me feel a lot better and I wasn't scared anymore. In my mind Da was there watching over me.

As I lay there waiting for the anaesthetic to take effect, counting backwards, the last thing on my mind was Alan and the kids. I just about got a tiny prayer said before I drifted off.

* * *

It took a day or two for me to get back on my feet and I was so sore afterwards, but that didn't bother me. All I cared about were my results, which seemed to be taking forever to come back. I pestered the nurses every time they came into the ward. I'd keep asking, 'Nurse, have yeh heard anythin'? Is there any word back yet?'

'Don't be worrying, Kathleen. As soon as the doctor has your test results back he'll be straight in to see you.'

And so he was, the following day. I remember it so well, as if it was only yesterday. The girl in the bed next to me got her results early that morning, and it wasn't good news. As soon as the nurse pulled the curtain around her bed, I cocked my ears and had a listen as the doctor spoke.

'We're so sorry,' he said, 'but the cancer has spread. It's gone too far, I'm afraid; there is no more we can do.'

I got such a lump in my throat as I lay there listening to her cry. At the same time, I wanted to get sick with the thought of what I might be told myself.

It was well into the day before the doctor arrived to see me. There was a nurse and a lady doctor with him. They both gave me a smile and I thought, *Tha' looks good. They're not all serious, so tha' must mean somethin'*. Either way, I was shitting myself as I waited for the head doctor to speak.

'I have very good news for you, Kathleen,' he said. I couldn't believe it; he was calling me by my first name after all these years. 'The cancer was only in the womb, which we removed, and did not spread to any of your other organs. So you are a very lucky young woman that we have been keeping a check on you over the years.'

The relief I felt when I heard those words! It was like the weight of the world had been lifted off my shoulders.

'Thank you, thank you, thank you so much, doctor. I'm after bein' up the walls with worry, not knowin' wha' yeh were goin' to tell me.'

'You still have to come in to see us for the next two years,' he said, 'because if the cancer was to come back, which I doubt very much, it would be in that timeframe. I will leave instructions with the nurse and your appointment card. You can pick them up when you're leaving. And remember, take it easy for a while. So, best of luck, Kathleen.' He shook my hand and on he moved to the next ward.

I couldn't help but cry, only my tears were out of joy and happiness, unlike the girl who was next to me. She was still sobbing her heart out, trying to come to terms with what she had been told. I thought, *That could so easily have been me.* I couldn't stop thanking the Holy Mother and every angel that I asked to watch over me, but most of all my Da. I really do believe that he was there looking after me.

* * *

I thought Alan would never get up to me so I could tell him my news. Well, he turned green in the face when I told him the truth.

'Holy Jaysus, Kathleen, yeh should've said somethin'. I thought yeh had to get this done because of all the women's problems yeh were havin' over the years. I had no idea it was tha' serious. I can't believe yeh didn't tell me. I mean, keepin' the likes of tha' bottled up inside yeh . . . Don't ever do anythin' like tha' again, no matter wha' it is – de yeh hear me?'

He put his two arms around me and hugged me ever so tight for such a long time afterwards. The kids were none the wiser, but I did tell the family. I especially wanted my sisters to know so that they would go and have regular check-ups. There were loads of snots and tears, with each of them giving out to me for not letting them know. And as for my brothers – well, you know fellas – I got a nod of the head and 'Tha's a grand bit of news yeh got there, Kathleen.'

It wasn't too long before I was home. I was told to stay off work for at least three months and I nearly went mad into the bargain. I had never been out of work before, except to have my babies, and even at that I didn't stay off for long, so I wasn't used to all the sitting around, which was giving me loads of time to think about the fact that I wasn't bringing any money in. I was looking at the few pound that we had stashed away vanishing before my very eyes, having to dip into it for one thing and another.

Even though I made a good living from doing the hairdressing for the locals in my shed, I still had this drive in me and always seemed to want more from life. So that's when I decided to have a chat with Alan about opening my own hairdressing salon. That way I'd have people working for me and I'd always have wages coming into the house. To me that was definitely the way to go forward.

But before I could take that step towards my dream, one more thing was to happen in that horrible year, after Da's death, Ma's operation and then my own scare. We thought the worst was behind us, but how could anyone have foreseen the awful tragedy that lay ahead, which would tear all our hearts apart?

21

Heartache and Joy

So much had happened over the previous few months that I felt my brain couldn't take in much more. I was only starting to get back on my feet after my operation and I was nearly gone mad sitting around the house. Unable to do very much, I would drop over to Clare's to see Ma most days, which helped to kill a few hours for me. Other days I might drop down to Crumlin to see Carmel. There was always somebody dropping in through the day and plenty to talk about.

'Kathleen,' said Noel one day, 'did yeh hear Phil is not feelin' too well over there in Canada? I got a phone call off Joan the other day, tellin' me tha' he's goin' for some serious tests, brain scans and all sorts of things happenin' to him.'

Noel only had the words out of his mouth when I thought to myself, *I wonder did Phil know when he was home tha' there was somethin' wrong with him and never said?* When I look back now, he was so pale and tired-looking. I thought it was because of the grief and sadness he was feeling inside over Da.

As soon as I got home, I phoned Phil up straight away.

'Wha's all this I'm hearin' about yeh not feelin' the best? Why didn't yeh tell me when I was talkin' to yeh last?'

'Now why would I do tha', Kathleen? Yeh know you, I'd only have to listen to yeh whingin' all over the place. If my memory serves me right, as soon as there's anythin' wrong with any of us, yeh get yerself into a state. So I thought it best to wait until the final results come through. Anyway, it's probably nothin'. I think I'm just tired from workin' so hard over the years, Kathleen. I've been holdin' down two jobs for God knows how long. I suppose it's bound to take its toll in the end. Never mind, enough of all tha' shite talk, Kathleen. Fill us in on wha's happenin' with Ma, which is more important. How's she doin'? Give her a big hug and a kiss for me and say tha' as soon as I sort a few things out over here I'll be over to see her.'

The subject was changed so I left well enough alone and didn't keep on at him. I launched into all that was going on with Ma and the others, trying to throw a few laughs in, which was so hard to do at that moment.

* * *

Weeks and weeks went by. When I didn't hear back from Phil, I knew there was something wrong. I checked with the rest of the family; they'd also heard nothing.

Then the phone call came. I knew when I walked into the house in Crumlin that there was something up. They were all there and everybody was too quiet. First of all I thought something had happened to Ma, but when I looked into the kitchen she was sitting there with Clare, not a bother on her, having her lunch.

'There's somethin' wrong,' I said. 'Wha's after happenin'?' The girls all sat there not saying a word and I could see that they had been crying.

'Kathleen,' said Noel, 'Phil's after takin' a stroke. He's paralysed all down one side of his body. They found a brain tumour and they're operating on him as we speak.'

I couldn't believe what I was hearing. I half expected one of the them to jump up and say, 'Got yeh! Only jokin'.' I got such a pain in my chest with the fright that I thought I was going to faint.

'Sit down, Kathleen,' said Clare. 'We're all in just as much shock. None of us can get our heads around this.'

'How can this be happenin' again?' I said. 'I mean, look at Ma – she's only a couple of months over her brain operation. Why, why?' I was starting to scream at this stage. 'Phil's too young, it's not fair, it's not fair!'

I cried and cried for such a long time. I couldn't speak to anyone. I kept thinking about how frightened he must have felt when he went paralysed. Where was he when it happened? Was there anyone with him? And now, having to go through this, and none of us there with him. That's when I snapped out of myself.

'Some of us will have to go over to Phil,' I said.

'It's all arranged, Kathleen,' said Noel. 'Myself and Thomas are goin' to make our way over to him. We're goin' down to book the flights now.'

'And wha' about us? Can we not go with yiz?' I asked.

'I don't think any of yiz are in any fit state to be goin' over to Phil,' said Noel. 'I mean, look at yiz – yeh're all fallin' apart. Anyway, best tha' we go on our own to see wha' way things are and how he is after the operation.'

* * *

Noel and Thomas flew over to Canada within the next couple of days and it seemed to take forever before we heard back from them. When they did finally ring, the news sounded good. They said that they had been hanging around the hospital, waiting to see the doctor, trying to get as much information as they could before passing it on to us.

'Phil is fine,' they said. 'He's sitting up in the bed, talkin' away to us and throwin' the odd joke in here and there.'

I was over the moon when I heard what they had to say – that was, until they came home and told us the real truth.

We all gathered together in Crumlin to meet Noel and Thomas, so as we could find out the details. But I could see straight away how upset they both were. Noel's voice was shaking as he spoke. We listened in shocked silence.

'We didn't want to tell yiz this over the phone, but it's not lookin' too good for Phil. This wasn't his first brain operation. He's already had one previous to this. He didn't want anybody to know because in his mind he's convinced tha' this will pass and everythin' will be okay again. "Wha's the point in worryin' yiz all?" he said. "There's no need for it. This is just a bit of a blip, I'll be fine. Yiz all know me by now, I never let anythin' get the better of me."'

'Maybe Phil is righ',' I said. 'I mean, look at Ma, she's up and walkin' around and gettin' stronger by the day.'

'Kathleen, listen to me,' said Noel. 'Ma's tumour was on the outside of her brain and they were able to get at it easy enough. And another thing, it wasn't cancerous. Phil's is, and it's set down deep in his brain. They've tried to remove it a couple of times but they just can't get to the root of it.'

That's when everyone started chiming in together, all trying to find out what the future held for Phil. Noel wasn't able to hold it together any longer and made his way outside to the back garden, while Thomas carried on filling us in about what we should all do next.

'Phil hasn't worked in nearly nine months and any money tha' he had is gone. Joan has to keep workin' away to keep the house goin' and pay the bills. Now, there was a nurse comin' in every day for a few hours to take care of Phil, but tha's all stopped now because his insurance has run out. So the bottom line is, we'll have to take care of him for as long as we can ourselves.'

I left them all talking and made my way out to Noel.

'Noel, are yeh all righ'?' I asked.

'Well, Kathleen, let's just say I've been better. I can't get Phil's face out of me mind. It was so hard lookin' at him like tha', not bein' able to move. He was such a strong big fella. It's terrible. And de yeh know somethin', after a couple of days he was still tryin' to put a front up. Crackin' a joke here and there – when he wanted one of us to help him sit up or turn him around, he'd come out with the likes of, "Tha' bloody arm of mine is gone asleep again, will yeh give us a lift up there till it comes back?"'

'I know, Noel, tha's Phil, always the joker, and tha's how he always got through everythin' in his life. Maybe tha's wha' will get him through this. I hope.'

'De yeh know wha' else he said to us, Kathleen? And I swear, it nearly killed me. "Don't go," he said. "I do be very lonely here on me own. I miss yiz all so much." Thomas had to leave the room, he got tha' choked up. He couldn't even answer him. I don't know how I held it together.

'"Jaysus, Phil," I said, "yeh know we'd stay if we could, but we have to get back to work."

'"Ah for fuck sake, Noel, if tha's all yeh're worryin' about, sure I'll pay yiz yer wages."

'God love him, Kathleen, and him with not a shillin' left in his pocket. "It's not only the job, Phil, it's Breda," I said. "She's only after havin' a baby a few weeks ago and she's not great in herself since then. I have to get back to give her a hand. Anyway, isn't the rest of them back home only goin' mad to come over to yeh." He just gave me one of his big smiles, showin' his pearly whites, and said no more on the matter. And tha's the way we had to leave him. Still in the hospital, sittin' there, wavin' to us and doin' his best tryin' to smile as we walked away. I swear, Kathleen, to the end of me days I'll never forget the lost look on Phil's face as we left him. Meself and Thomas hardly spoke to one another all the way home, it had tha' much effect on us.'

'Don't be worryin', Noel', I said. 'Phil will pull through this. He's not goin' anywhere. As he said, this is just a blip. Now, come on, let's go back into the house and see wha' plans they're all makin'.' I knew I was trying to convince myself. Noel just stood there and looked me straight in the eye. Before he could say another word, I went on in ahead of him. There was no way I wanted to hear anything more about Phil being sick.

'Righ' then, wha's happenin'?' I asked.

'Well, Kathleen,' said Patricia, 'we were just sayin', if you want to go over first to see Phil, and maybe take Ma with yeh. I'm sure he'd love to see her. Mano said tha' he'll go with yeh and when yiz come back, meself and Jacinta will make our way over next and whoever else can manage to go after us. Then we'll just have to take it from there and see wha' happens along the way.'

'Tha's grand, Patricia. I'm happy enough to go now.'

* * *

I hated leaving Alan and the kids for the next three weeks. We had never been apart this long before, but this was something I needed to do so much and each of them understood that. So I was sent on my way, with loads of hugs and kisses from all.

I thought I'd never get over to Canada to see Phil and take care of him, but part of me was also dreading having to see him so helpless, having to depend on everyone for practically everything. Knowing him, though, he'd gloss things over as always with a laugh and a joke.

The flight wasn't too bad. Mano and Ma slept all the way, while I got lost in my thoughts as usual. I was planning how I would handle things when I got there and at the same time hoping I wouldn't fall to pieces. Before I knew it, the plane was touching the ground and when I looked out I saw that the place was covered in thick snow, which looked really lovely.

Phil's wife Joan was there to meet us. We got plenty of hugs and kisses before we made our way outside to her car. I had never felt such cold in my whole life.

'I know Thomas and Noel told us to wrap up well, but I wasn't expecting anything like this. How in the name of God de yiz stick this weather, Joan?' I said.

'You get used to it and most of the time it doesn't be too bad. Now, having said that, Kathleen, January is one of the worst months for you to be coming out here. But I am so glad that you came because I really do need the help, and Phil is so happy that you're here. He can't wait to see all of you.'

The two of us chatted all the way to the house.

'How is he, Joan?' I asked.

'I won't lie to you, Kathleen, he has been through hell and back. But you know him; he's a fighter all the way. He tells me and everyone around him that he will be back out and about in no time at all. So, just go along with whatever he has to say. It's what keeps him going. Anyway, here we are now. But before we go in, if it's okay with you, Kathleen, I was going to try to work as many extra hours as I can while you're here to look after Phil, which will help out a great deal.'

'Tha' won't be a problem, Joan. You do wha' yeh have to. We'll look after Phil and the kids. Yeh can be sure of tha'. Now, let's go in before we freeze to death out here.'

I'll never forget the look on Phil's face when we walked into the house. He lit the whole room up with the biggest smile ever. I stood back and watched as he gave Ma such a hug with his one good arm. I could see the way he had himself covered up with a blanket, trying to hide how bad he was.

'Jaysus Christ, Phil,' I said, trying to gloss things over, 'how de yeh live in this Godforsaken place? Me face is nearly after fallin' off, it's tha' cold out there.'

'I see yeh're still rammagin' on as always, Kathleen. Now will yeh stop givin' out and give us a big hug.'

We held on so tight to one another and it felt good.

'Now, Mano, come on – yeh're next. Righ' here on the lips – a nice big juicy kiss, come on.'

'Would yeh ever fuck off, Phil,' said Mano. 'Yeh're not gettin' a kiss off me. I don't care wha' yeh have wrong with yeh!'

That was it; the ice was broken and we settled into our first night in Canada.

Phil was really proud showing off his three sons. The eldest, Philip, was a lovely quiet boy of eleven, J.J. was wild as they come, even at nine, and the baby of the family, Andrew, was almost seven. Phil kept talking about the sports they were into and how well they were doing.

Ma sat beside him the whole night, holding his hand. She knew there was something wrong, but never said a word. Every time Phil said something, even if it wasn't funny, Ma would roar laughing. We were all used to her behaviour since the hospital, but Phil couldn't get over it. He thought it was hilarious. He ended up laughing along with her, so much so that the tears rolled down his face.

'Yeh know wha', Kathleen,' he said, 'I haven't laughed this much in I don't know how long, and the thing is I haven't a clue wha's so funny.'

'I know, Phil. When Ma starts tha' at home, and especially if there's a few of us together in Crumlin, she does have us all at it with her. It does be like somethin' out of a funny farm.'

'Ah well, Kathleen, at least she's okay. Tha's the main thing,' said Phil. 'We could easily have lost her back then, but she's as tough as old nails, and tha's who I take after. So, the way I see it, if Ma can beat all them odds tha' was stacked up against her, well then, so can I.'

When Phil said those words, Ma bent over, put her two arms around him and wouldn't let go. I could see Phil was enjoying every minute of it. Talk about me trying to hold myself together – it took me all my energy to hold back the tears, looking at the pair of them like that.

* * *

Joan and the kids were gone from early the following morning. Mano was still asleep and so was Ma, which I was glad of. It gave me some time to spend alone with Phil. I made my way downstairs. As I walked into the room, I nearly died. Phil was crawling along the floor, trying to make his way to the toilet. He stopped dead in his tracks when he saw me standing there. Such a lost look he had on his face as he tried to turn away.

'Now, wha' are yeh doin' down there on the floor, Phil?' I said. 'Actin' the eejit as usual, I suppose.' I bent down on my hunkers. 'Are yeh righ'? Let's get yeh back up onto the chair.'

I needn't tell you, I was strangled, but I managed it in the end.

'Now, yeh know wha' we'll do, Phil? Get yer good arm and put it around me shoulder. I'll hold onto the other one and then we'll just drag yeh along. Wait and see, it'll be a piece of cake. Now, the only thing is, yeh'd better not piss all over me before we get there. I swear to Jaysus, Phil, I'll drop yeh if yeh do.'

'Will yeh stop messin', Kathleen, or I'll start laughin', and then I *will* piss all over yeh.'

It took me every bit of strength I had to walk that short distance. There I was, with my seven and a half stone, trying to carry Phil. Even with all his sickness, he was still one big fella. But I got him there in the end.

'Yeh know somethin', Phil?' I said as I stood outside the door and waited, 'we could kill two birds with one stone here. I'd be able to give yeh a grand wash down while I have yeh sittin' there.'

'No! It's hard enough havin' to let yeh bring me to the toilet, Kathleen, without washin' me as well.'

'Don't start gettin' all shy on me now, Phil. It wouldn't be the first time I saw yer arse. Remember years ago when we were teenagers, all them mooners yeh used to do on me when I would be sittin' on the end of the stairs with Alan? The two of us tryin' to have a wear behind Ma and Da's back. Yeh'd call down to us and all we'd see was this big hairy arse lookin' down at us. I used to get real annoyed, 'cause yeh were makin' a show of me.'

'Tha' was the best part, Kathleen, lookin' at yeh gettin' yerself into a state. And the gas thing was, Alan didn't give two shites wha' any of us did. He just cared about you and nothing was goin' to change tha'.'

'I know, Phil. I was a gobshite back then, tryin' to be Mrs Proper all the time when Alan was around.'

'All the same, Kathleen, we had some great times, the pair of us, when we were kids. We did some mad things together. Wouldn't it be great if yeh could go back in time, even just for a while, and forget about all tha's goin' on at the minute. And yeh know wha'? As poor as we were, I wouldn't change a thing. How about you, Kathleen?'

'Not one single minute, Phil. Anyway, don't be changin' the subject on me. I'm standing out here with a basin full of warm water. Now, hurry up and let me come in and wipe yer arse and I'll have yeh done and dusted before Ma or Mano wake up, and nobody will be wiser.'

I could see he was embarrassed, but he sat there and let me get on with what I had to do.

'Kathleen, did yeh ever think tha' yeh'd be doin' the likes of this for me?'

'Sure, wouldn't yeh do it for me, Phil, if yeh had to?'

I kept rammaging on as I do when I get nervous, and before he knew it I had him back sitting on his chair, as fresh as a daisy.

'Now, tha' wasn't too bad, Phil, was it?'

'Yeh're still a bossy bitch, Kathleen, but thanks, I feel a lot better.'

'I'm goin' to go in now and make yeh a good old Irish breakfast like the way Ma used to.'

'Will yeh stop, Kathleen. I was often sittin' here waterin' from the mouth, just thinkin' about the lovely fry-ups she used to make for us. Remember every Saturday night when she'd put the big pot on and fill it up with pigs' feet and ribs? We'd be sittin' there on the floor, suckin' on the bones for the night while we watched the telly.'

I cooked while Phil continued his trip down memory lane, which seemed to be helping to lift his spirits. I suppose not knowing what the future held for him, he felt it was better not to go there. So I left well enough alone for the moment.

* * *

Joan seemed to be coping well. She never talked about Phil's illness to us; maybe that was her way of handling things. The kids played around as normal, with not a notion of what was happening, and that's the way Phil wanted it; he didn't want them upset in any way. When I think back now, we were all doing the same thing; if you didn't say it out loud then you could pretend it wasn't happening.

I made it my business every day to cook all his favourite dinners. I would get such pleasure looking at him when he'd lick the plate at the end. He would be laughing his head off looking at the antics of Mano, after the kids came in from school. Mano would roll around the floor with them, acting the eejit, bringing himself down to their level – although that didn't take much, as Mano was just a big kid himself.

Mano was arm-wrestling with one of the kids one day when Phil turned around to him and said, 'I bet tha' I could still beat yeh, even with just me one arm.'

'Would yeh get away with yerself,' said Mano. 'I'd have yeh on the floor in seconds.'

Holy Jaysus, I thought I was hearing things. I was going cross-eyed trying to give Mano the look as I stood behind Phil. But as soon as Phil looked the other way, Mano gave me a wink.

He sat down in front of Phil. 'Come on now,' said Mano, 'let's see wha' yeh're made of.'

My heart was bursting, looking at Phil trying to steady himself for the big match.

'Kathleen, hold onto the back of the chair for me, just in case it slips, and I'll show this Mano fella wha' real strength is.'

Mano was great; he started banging the table and making all sorts of mad faces at Phil, like wrestlers do before a fight.

'Tha's not fair, Mano,' said Phil. 'Yeh're makin' me laugh and I can't do it now.'

'Righ' then, roar back at me, Phil. Come on, ROAR,' he shouted, making more crazy faces.

I thought I was going to die with the laughing, looking at the pair of them screaming into each other's face. Ma was clapping her hands and stamping her feet as she called out Phil's name. The kids were like lunatics, trying to make faces along with their Da.

Of course, Mano pretended to be struggling as he went on and let Phil win the match. Such a laugh we had that day.

It cheered Phil up so much that he turned around to me and said, 'Kathleen, I really feel good in meself since yiz all started comin' over to me. I think I'm gettin' stronger as the days go on. I mean, just look at the way I beat Mano, and he's nearly as big as meself. Yeh never know, I might beat this bloody thing yet.'

'Of course yeh will, Phil,' I said. 'This is just a blip, tha's all.' There was no way I would let myself think of anything else, so I changed the subject as fast as I could. 'Now, wha' would yeh like to eat for yer lunch? I have to make sure and keep tha' strength of yers up.'

'Jaysus, I'd love nothin' more than a few beans on toast.'

'I was lookin' for some the other day. I don't think there's any in the press, Phil. But it doesn't matter, I'll go down to the corner shop and get some.' I would have gone to the ends of the earth for any little thing that he wanted.

'Go away, yeh mad thing, Kathleen, there's no such thing as a corner shop here. They're all big malls.'

'Wha' the fuck is a mall, Phil?'

'Shops the size of the whole street out there, tha's wha' they are.'

'It's the same thing, Phil. They're just big corner shops.'

'Anyway, yeh can't go out in tha' weather. Yeh'd freeze.'

'I'll be grand, now will yeh stop fussin'. I'll be there and back before yeh know it. A bit of fresh air won't do me any harm either. I'm not used to being stuck in a house all the time like this. Now, just tell me, do I go righ' or left to find one of these "mall" places?'

'As usual yeh won't take any heed of wha' I'm sayin', Kathleen. So put my big jacket on and when yeh get outside turn righ' and keep walkin' straight ahead.'

I was glad to be getting a bit of break on my own so I could work out in my head how I was going to handle things when it came time for us to leave. It was going to be one of the hardest things I would have to do in my whole life – leaving Phil, knowing that we would never see each other again. I didn't think I'd be strong enough to do it.

I got so lost in my thoughts that I didn't realise how far I had walked or where I was. There wasn't a sign of anyone around – probably because they had more sense than me. It was so cold out and the snow had got really heavy. I could barely see in front of me. I walked and walked until finally I could see bright lights in the distance. There it was, the biggest corner shop you ever saw.

'Thank God,' I said to myself, because at that stage I was starting to panic a bit. I picked up a few tins of beans and made my way back.

Phil nearly fell off the couch from laughing so much when he saw me. I must have looked like a full-size snowman. The snow was actually starting to freeze on me. Mano quickly dried me off, then wrapped me in a blanket and put me lying on the floor beside the fire to thaw me out. All Phil kept saying was, 'I told yeh, Kathleen, but would yeh listen to me? No.'

When I finally stopped shaking and was able to talk again, the first thing I said was, 'Will yeh have them beans on toast now?'

Phil gave me such a smile it made everything worthwhile.

* * *

I started to sleep downstairs on the couch across from Phil. When everyone was gone to bed, the two of us would lie there, talking across to one another, mostly about the past and all the fun and happy times we spent together as a family. We never spoke about the future, not until it was coming to the end of our stay.

'Kathleen, I want to have a talk with yeh,' he said.

I didn't want to hear what he was about to say.

'Now, I'm only sayin', but if this all goes belly-up and goes against me, I want yeh to promise me tha' yeh'll all keep in touch with the kids through the years. Let them know tha' they always have a family there if they need yiz.'

I was in floods of tears and was barely able to answer him.

'The other thing is, I'd like for me ashes to be brought back to Ireland, because tha's where me heart was always. Yiz can put me in the little cabinet beside Da's ashes in Crumlin. Tha' way I'll be back amongst yiz all. So, will yeh make sure and do tha' for me?'

I couldn't speak; I just gave him a nod.

'Come on over here, Kathleen, and lie beside me and we'll pretend tha' there's nothin' wrong.'

He put his good strong arm around me and held me so tight, like he was never going to let go. As I lay there all I could hear was Phil sobbing through the night. It was so hard to take in, to try to understand why, why this was all happening.

* * *

I was up bright and early the next morning and knew I had to keep myself busy; otherwise I would fall to pieces. So I decided that, because it was our last day, I was going to cook a big Christmas dinner with all the trimmings. Joan had all the presses and freezer well stocked up with everything and anything I needed, so as soon as I had Phil and Ma washed and ready, I spent the rest of the day cooking. I have to say, when I finished, it was a spread fit for a king. Phil couldn't believe his eyes when we sat him down at the table.

'Holy Mother of God, Kathleen, de yeh think yeh're feedin' an army or wha'? Now, having said tha', I think meself and Mano will get through a fair share of this.'

'Are yeh on then, Phil?' said Mano. 'Let's see who can eat the most!' As always, Phil loved a challenge. Mano knew he was upset and was doing everything and anything he thought would make him happy. The pair of them stuffed themselves until they couldn't move. The result was a tie.

'Well, little brother,' said Phil, 'yeh're nearly as good as meself now.'

'And me answer to yeh, big brother, is tha's somethin' else comin' from you.'

I thought Mano was going to break down, but he held it together by jumping up and down and chasing the kids around, doing what he does best – acting the eejit, which I suppose is his way of coping with things. Ma sat there for the whole night holding Phil's hand while the rest of us told the kids all sorts of stories about times gone by.

Our flight was early enough the next day, so we had to be up from the crack of dawn. There was no way Phil was letting us go to the airport without him. I was hoping that this wouldn't happen. I felt it might be a bit easier on all of us to say our goodbyes in the privacy of his home. But he was having none of it.

'There's no way I'm sittin' here on me own,' said Phil. 'I want to spend every last minute with yiz before yeh go.'

He was starting to get upset, so I agreed with him. 'Yeh're righ', Phil,' I said. 'Anyway, Jacinta and Patricia's flight will be landin' around the same time tha' we're takin' off, so yeh'll be there to meet them when they come through. They're only dyin' to see yeh.' He seemed happy enough when I said that and calmed himself down.

There was loads of hustle and bustle as we all gathered ourselves into the car to head for the airport. We all sat there in silence as Joan rammaged on about how bad the snow was and hoped that we would get there in time. I wanted to talk but I knew that as soon as I opened my mouth I would break down and cry, and I could see Mano and Phil were feeling the same. As for Ma, well, she was lost in her own little world, and maybe it was better that way for her.

While I was checking us in at the desk and Joan was taking care of Ma, what was Mano doing? Only flying around the airport with Phil in the wheelchair, skidding all over the place. You'd want to see the laughs of the pair of them. Usually I would be giving out like shite and worrying what people might think, but not today. Phil was laughing, and that was all that mattered.

It finally came time for us to board. I was sick to the pits of my stomach and could feel myself start to shake as I watched Phil hug Ma and Mano. He held onto them so tight, as he broke down and cried. Ma touched his face softly, wiping his tears, before Mano took her by the hand and walked away.

I knelt down in front of Phil. He cried so hard as he spoke. 'This is so hard, Kathleen, I'm not ready to die. I don't want to leave everyone.'

'I know, Phil, I know.' I put my arms around him. The two of us held on to one another and neither of us wanted to let go. I could hear Joan's voice calling my name.

'Kathleen,' she said, 'you have to go; your flight's boarding now.'

'Remember wha' we said, Phil,' I whispered in his ear. 'Everythin's fine; there's nothin' wrong; this is just a blip. You just keep thinkin' like tha', de yeh hear me? Now come on and give me one of yer special smiles. Let's see those pearly whites.'

I was sobbing my heart out as I walked away. Just before I went through the gates, I turned around and there he was, waving and smiling as best he could. That was my last memory of Phil. We never saw or spoke to one another ever again.

Myself and Mano sat in silence through the whole flight, while Ma laughed away at the telly. I suppose at the end of the day it was best that she didn't know all that was going on around her. I don't think she would have been able to cope, knowing what was ahead for Phil.

I was so happy to see Alan when we landed. I knew if anybody was going to help me get through this, it would be him.

* * *

I had only been home a day or two after leaving Phil. I tried really hard to keep a front up for the kids' sakes but I found it so hard. I knew deep down in my heart that he wasn't going to make it and when I was leaving we had both pretended that he would.

Alan was so good; he was doing everything for me, but he knew in the end just to leave me and let me try to cope in my own way. For me, that meant keeping busy, busy all the time. That way I didn't have to think or face reality and maybe by some miracle the inevitable might not happen.

I was upstairs tidying around when young Alan, who was sixteen and a half at this time, came into my room and sat on the bed.

'Are yeh okay, Ma? I heard yeh cryin' last night.'

'I'm sorry, pet. I didn't mean for yeh to hear me, but don't be worryin'. I'll be fine.'

'I need to talk to yeh, but yeh're so upset about Phil and no time is goin' to be the righ' time. But I have to tell yeh, Ma, before somebody else does.'

207

'Alan, please don't tell me yeh're in trouble with the police. I haven't got the energy to take anythin' like tha' now.'

'It's nothing like tha', Ma. It's . . . it's . . . it's just . . . just . . . Donna's five months pregnant. There, it's out. I've said it. I'm sorry, Ma.'

I could feel the blood draining from me. I actually went down on my knees with the fright and broke down crying.

'Oh my God! I can't believe this is happenin' again. Wha' the hell is wrong with yiz all? Yeh're too young to be a father,' I screamed. 'Yeh're not capable of lookin' after yerself, never mind a child. I'm not able for all this at the minute, Alan McGrath. Just go. Leave me. I want to be on me own.'

I stared out of the window. My head was all over the place. I couldn't think straight. I didn't want to have to think or worry about anything else. This time in my life was supposed to be for me and Phil. That's all I wanted on my mind right now – nothing else. But, being a parent, that wasn't to be. So I carried on doing what I was supposed to do, which was, like most mothers, trying to fix the problems that are put before us.

When I told Alan, I could see that he wanted to lose the plot, just like I did, but he didn't. He held it together, as always. He was just as upset about Phil as we all were, as he'd been in my family since he was fifteen. They were like brothers.

After a few days, I got young Alan to bring Donna down to see us. The pair of them had been going out since they were both fourteen and I really was very fond of her. She was a lovely little one, which helped so much in this situation. The two of them stood in front of me. What I really wanted to do was to give them both a good box for being so irresponsible and stupid. But I knew that wasn't the way to fix things. So I just put my arms around them and said, 'Don't worry, we'll work things out. All tha' matters now is tha' yeh're okay, Donna, and yeh have a healthy little baby.'

'Thanks so much, Kathleen. I was afraid wha' way yeh were goin' to take things, with Martina only after havin' Danielle not so long ago.'

'Wha' did yer own Ma and Da say when yeh told them yer news?'

'They were in shock at first but, like yerself, they're being very good about it. Once the baby's okay, they'll be happy.'

It was only when she said that to me that I realised this was to be our second grandchild – coming a lot sooner than we thought or expected. It's difficult to take this kind of news in, especially when your own children are only children themselves. But – and I really mean this – after holding my first grandchild in my arms the day she was born, I knew in my heart that when the time came I would be ready to welcome this little baby into our family with open arms.

* * *

The next few weeks seemed to go by so fast and it was nearly time for Jacinta and Patricia to come home from Canada, and time for the next two of us to go over to take care of Phil. Alan was going, with my younger brother Paul.

'Alan, I wish so much tha' I was goin' back over with yeh.'

'I know tha', Kathleen, but yeh know tha' the money is just not there for both of us to go, and I really do want to see Phil meself. Anyway, one of us has to be here to take care of the kids. I promise, I'll phone yeh every day and keep yeh posted about all tha's goin' on. I'll tell yeh wha' – I'll even put Phil on the phone to talk to yeh.'

With that thought in my mind, I felt a bit better and was happy enough to send Alan on his way for the next three weeks. I never did get to talk to Phil again, because by the time Alan and Paul got there, Phil wasn't great. Then he took a turn for the worse and was taken into the hospital. But Alan didn't tell me that at the time. Every time I asked, he would say Phil was in hospital getting a few tests done. He would be telling me everything and anything but the truth so as not to upset me. He knew when the time came the devastating effect Phil's death would have on me.

He was gone less than a week when, early one morning, I woke up to the sound of the phone ringing. When I looked at my watch, it was only seven o'clock. I thought, *Jaysus, who could tha' be at this hour of the mornin'?* To my surprise, it was Alan.

'Howyeh, love,' I said. 'I wasn't expectin' yeh to ring me until later on.'

'Is there anybody there with yeh, Kathleen?' asked Alan.

As soon as he said that, I knew. I didn't give him a chance to say a word; I started rammaging on like I don't know what. I was in complete denial.

'Anyway, fill us in. Wha's happenin', Alan? How's Phil? Is he feelin' any better? When are they lettin' him home? I want yeh to make sure the first thing yeh do is put him on the phone to me. I've loads to tell him. Did yeh tell him I'm goin' to be a granny again? I can just see him now. I bet yeh he was breakin' his heart laughin' . . .'

'Kathleen, stop talkin', please. I've somethin' to tell yeh.'

'No! I won't stop talkin' and don't you dare tell me anythin'. De yeh hear me, Alan McGrath? Don't say it!'

By this stage I could hardly breathe. I was sitting at the end of the stairs with the phone up to my chest, screaming, crying, but I could still hear Alan calling my name. The three kids had made their way down and were sitting beside me with their arms around me.

'Kathleen, come on, love, pick the phone up, please.'

I kept thinking, if I didn't hear it, then it didn't happen. But it did happen and I knew I had to face up to the truth, but it was so, so hard. I slowly put the phone up to my ear and spoke.

'I'm here, Alan.'

'I know yeh are, love . . . I didn't want yeh to hear this over the phone. Thomas was supposed to come down last night and tell yeh. I'm so sorry to have to tell yeh this news. But Phil died last night.'

It was like a knife sticking into my heart, as I sobbed uncontrollably. The kids were getting so upset looking at me that I had to try to pull myself together.

'Please, Alan, tell me, at wha' time did it happen?'

'It was around nine o'clock our time. Why?'

'Because it was me Da's anniversary yesterday. He was a year dead, and it was nine o'clock to the minute when he died.'

At that moment I got a flashback of Phil at Da's bedside, just after he'd passed away, saying, 'Don't be afraid, Da. I'll be with yeh soon'. *Oh my God*, I thought, *I wonder did he know then what lay ahead for him and he never said.*

Just then there was a knock on the door. Martina opened it and let in Thomas.

'Alan, Thomas is here now.'

'Tha's good, Kathleen, because I'll have to go. Joan wants to ring around Phil's friends. Try and hang in there, love, until I get meself home to yeh.'

I was still crying and sobbing as I put the phone down. Thomas put his arm around me and I felt a bit better.

'I was goin' to come down last night, Kathleen,' he said, 'but then I thought I'd be only leavin' yeh on yer own afterwards. I felt it would be better to let yeh get a good night's sleep before breakin' the news to yeh. Meself and Noel

211

phoned around the rest of the family so yeh don't have to do anythin', only get yerself ready. We're all meetin' up in Crumlin.'

The shock on everyone's faces as I walked into the room said it all.

* * *

At the time, none of us could afford to go back over to Canada, so it was left to Alan and Paul to represent the family. We all sent sprays and sprays of flowers, and the biggest bunch of red roses from Ma, making our presence felt.

We decided that it was best not to tell Ma. She had come on so well over the past year, we were afraid that the news of Phil's death would knock her back. Why put her through all that pain if we didn't have to? So, in Ma's eyes, her blue-eyed boy was working away in Canada and she was none the wiser.

It wasn't too long before Alan and Paul were back home and filling us in on all that went on. 'By the time we got there,' said Paul, 'Phil was very weak. Meself and Alan had a few days with him. He was trying to talk and give the odd smile, but you could see he wasn't able. It was so hard, seein' him like tha'. Then he took a turn for the worse and went into a coma. He didn't last long after tha'. I was sittin' there with Joan; both of us were holdin' his hands when he passed away. The doctor told us that he didn't suffer any pain.'

'Thank God for tha', Paul,' I said, 'at least he wasn't on his own and yiz were all there with him.'

'Poor Joan; she fell to pieces. Yeh'd want to hear the cries from her. Tha' was bad enough, but when we went back to the house and told the kids – oh my God, Kathleen, I never want to see the likes of tha' ever again. The cries from the three of them would break yer heart in two. Alan and meself had to get up and leave the room. It was too much. God help them, they were all in bits.'

We all sat there listening, trying to take it all in as Alan and Paul told us about the funeral and how they all tried to cope in the days that followed.

There was nothing but doom and gloom for such a long time afterwards. It was hard enough trying to cope with Da gone, then with so much happening to Ma, and now Phil. All in the space of a year. It was too much to take in.

I felt such a loss and emptiness inside of me, which I kept to myself. I grieved in silence, not wanting to worry Alan or my children. I would keep going over and over again in my head, thinking about the past, all the fun we had when we were growing up, the madness that went on. Not a day would go by without something crazy happening in Crumlin. My God, was it any wonder poor Ma ended up getting a brain tumour, with our carry-on?

* * *

One day in particular stood out. It makes me laugh now when I look back. Who was the culprit? Only Phil as usual, with Noel on the receiving end this time. Da always had half-cans of paint lying around in the back garden and Noel was forever at it. If he wasn't painting planks of wood, bits of bikes or the garden wall, anything he could get his hands on got a lick. He would always end up getting more of the paint on himself than anything else.

I was having a yap with Phil, when he turned around with a dirty big grin on his face. I could see the devilment in him straightaway.

'Phil, wha' are yeh schemin' there in tha' head of yers? I know tha' look. Come on, tell me.'

'Yeh'll know in a minute, Kathleen. Now would yeh have a look at tha' gobshite Noel, tryin' to paint tha' oul bike out there. How many times has Ma told him to keep away from it? But does the little fucker listen? No. So I think I'll teach him a lesson once and for all.'

When I looked out, there was Noel, as happy as anything, painting away, not minding anyone, when Phil went and grabbed him. I couldn't believe what he did next – he actually painted Noel all over, every bit of him. Green, white and orange. He only left his eyes out. Phil was falling around the place laughing while Noel was trying to get away from him. Phil thought this was the funniest thing ever.

'Would yeh have a look, Kathleen?' he said. 'I could hang him out of the line pole there and, yeh know wha'? He'd be like the Irish flag, flyin' in the wind.'

Poor Noel was crying his eyes out, not knowing what Phil would do next.

'For fuck sake, give it over, Phil,' I said. 'Jaysus Christ, yeh've really gone too far this time. How are we goin' to get this paint off him. Ma will be back soon. There'll be blue murder when she sees this.'

Phil wasn't taking any heed of me. 'Yeh'll think the next time, won't yeh, Noel, before yeh go near the paint again.'

'Don't mind him, Noel. Come on into the kitchen with me and let's see if there's any turps there. I'm sure Da would have some for his brushes.' He did, but only a drop. Then I found a bottle of methylated spirits. I was standing there, rubbing Noel's face like mad, when Ma walked in the door. Phil was gone like a light into the back garden, leaving me to face the music. Ma lost the plot altogether, and I mean really lost it. She made a mad run at Noel, who was trying to hide behind my back. She was tearing her hair out when she saw him.

'Yeh little fuck, Noel Doyle,' she screamed, over and over again. 'Wha' did I tell yeh? If yeh went near tha' paint again, didn't I say I'd kill yeh stone dead? Stand aside, Kathleen, and let me at him. I can't take any more of this. Lunatics, I'm after rearin' – fuckin' lunatics!'

'Ma, please calm down. It wasn't all Noel's fault. Phil had a hand in this too.'

I was edging Noel towards the front door, trying to get him off side.

'And wha' reason would Phil have to do such a thing? Don't start telling' fibs to me, Kathleen Doyle, or yeh'll get the back of me hand along with the Noel fella.'

I couldn't believe what I was hearing! To top it all, there was Phil standing at the kitchen window, laughing his head off, taking in all Ma was saying, knowing that he was in the clear. I knew I definitely had to get Noel out of the house, even if it was only for a couple of hours, until I got the paint off him and Ma calmed herself down.

It took her nearly three days to calm her down, with one of the neighbours holding onto Noel in the meantime. His skin was in a right mess for weeks afterwards. It was raw from all the turps we had to use.

Noel never went near the paint ever again. Well, not in the back garden anyway. He knew better. But as soon as he was old enough to work, guess what he became? A painter! And who did he end up working with, only the scourged Phil, who still played many tricks on him and everyone else over the years.

* * *

I think all my happy memories helped me get through those first few months after Phil died. I was trying to live in the past, not wanting to face the present or the future, and I was going around lost in my thoughts, so much so that I was not really looking at what my young son and his girlfriend were trying to cope with.

Here he was, going to be a father very soon. Though it was his own fault, nevertheless, I wasn't there for him. My little grandchild was coming into the world very soon. That thought helped me snap out of the very dark hole I had buried myself in and brought me back to reality.

As soon as Donna went into labour, the word was sent down to us straight away. I was into the hospital with young Alan in no time at all. Donna's Ma was in with her and came out to let Alan go in. We sat there talking for a while.

'Kathleen,' she said, 'would yeh mind if I went home. I'm not feelin' too good. Yeh know I'm a couple of months gone meself with twins.'

'So I believe, Cathy. Tha's no problem, you go ahead and I'll phone yeh as soon as there is any news.'

I have to say, young Alan made me laugh as I sat there for hours on end, with him running in and out of the labour ward, telling me every little thing that was going on – as if I didn't know. At one stage, he came out laughing his head off.

'De yeh know somethin', Ma? I'm after tryin' some of tha' gas – it's deadly!' Before I could say a word, he ran off again.

Then, when it was coming to the end of Donna's labour, he came bursting out the doors.

'Jaysus, Ma, there's really serious stuff goin' on in here now. I'm tellin' yeh, yeh'd want to see it.' I sat there listening to him, thinking there was no way on this earth he was grown up or mature enough for what lay ahead. What seventeen-year-old boy or girl is?

But I wasn't going to worry about that now. All that mattered at that moment was that Donna and the baby were safe, which they were. It wasn't long after that my lovely Jessica was born. My second granddaughter, who melted my heart straight away.

As I sat there holding her in my arms, I thought of Phil. Someone who had been so close and meant so much to me had been taken away so quickly, for whatever reason I'll never really understand. But they say God works in mysterious ways. As one precious life was taken away from me, I was handed another one just as quick, which helped me get through that very hard time in my life. In time, I was eventually able to move on. But never once did I ever forget my brother Phil.

* * *

It was about a year after Phil's death, when Ma was a bit stronger in herself, that we finally felt the time was right to tell her about Da and Phil. She was inconsolable and cried for days after, saying over and over again, 'I want to die, I want to go up to heaven to yer Da and Phil.' It took so much out of her that she didn't talk for weeks. We were all so worried, wondering if we had done the right thing in telling her or if we should have left her in her own little world, happy as Larry. But Ma was a very strong woman and in time she slowly came around, but she was never really the same again.

22

Shops and Robbers

It had been a good two years since I had first spoken about opening up my own salon. But with one thing and another happening within the family, no time ever seemed to be the right time. Then when I did start looking around, the salons were either too expensive or in the wrong location. But that didn't stop me looking. I was back on track now and more determined than ever that this was what I wanted.

Alan was reading the paper while I was pottering about, getting the dinner ready.

'Come over here, Kathleen,' he said, 'and have a look at this.'

'I'm in the middle of peelin' the potatoes, Alan. Just read it out to me.'

'Righ' yeh are then. "Prime hairdressin' salon for sale, leasehold, Rathfarnham area".'

My ears cocked up and I had the newspaper in my hands before Alan could blink an eye.

'I knew tha' would get yer attention fast enough, Kathleen.'

'Tha's not too far from here, Alan. Will yeh come down and have a look with me?'

'Sure don't yeh know I will. Come on, we'll go straight away. Leave wha' yeh're doin' there; yeh can finish tha' when we come back.'

I didn't think twice about it. I had my coat on and we were in the car heading for Rathfarnham in no time at all. As soon as we pulled up outside the salon, which was called Talking Heads, I fell in love with it straight away. It looked quite small from the outside and I couldn't see in because of the white net curtains. There was a chemist's and a post office either side of it, with a newsagent at the end and a garage around the corner. As I looked around, my brain went straight into overdrive.

'This is a great area, Alan. I mean, wha' more could yeh ask for only to be stuck right in the middle of two of the main shops tha' get used all the time, a chemist's and a post office. There'll be people around here all the time.'

'We'll sit here for a while and see how busy it gets. I know yeh're hell-bent on doin' this, but we have to make sure tha' we get it righ', because every penny we have will be goin' into this, or wha'ever shop yeh decide to go for.'

While Alan counted who was out and about, I went into the shop and asked about their prices, so I could have a quick gander around the place. I liked what I saw. It was certainly small, but it had everything you'd need – two dressing out mirrors and chairs, and two sinks. The waiting area had a couch with three hooded hairdryers attached to the back of it, with a glass coffee table to hold magazines and a long standing press against the wall, with a kettle on the top for a cup of tea. Oh yes, and a tiny – and I mean tiny – toilet. I thanked the girl and made my way back out to Alan, filling him in on all that I had seen.

'From wha' yeh're tellin' me, Kathleen, the place tha' I got built out the back garden for yeh is twice the size. To be honest with yeh, I can't get me head around why yeh want to do this.'

'I told yeh why, Alan. Didn't I say after me operation, when I couldn't work for a couple of months and me money stopped comin' in, how hard it was tryin' to get by on yer wages alone? No, I'm sorry, Alan, but I don't want tha' for us, no more than you do, scrimpin' and scrapin' from week to week. Tha's why if I have a shop and there's somebody workin' with me and somethin' happens, at least there'll be a wage there for me. Anyway, I have a plan.'

'Oh, here we go again. Wha' are yeh up to now, Kathleen?'

'I'll tell yeh in a minute, Alan. First of all, was there many people about when I was in?'

'There was. They were comin' and goin' all the time. It's a busy little area all righ'.'

'Good, tha's all I wanted to hear. Now, wha' I have in me mind is this: yeh know Thomas's wife, Trish? Well, with her bein' a hairdresser, I was going to ask if she would like to come in on the shop with me. Yeh know, be partners in business. Tha' way, me back will be covered at all times and we won't have to worry about money ever again.'

'If it's wha' yeh really want to do, Kathleen, I'll back yeh all the way. Yeh know me – anythin' to keep yeh happy.'

* * *

And that was it; I was full speed ahead. I asked Trish straight away.

'The only thing is, Kathleen,' said Trish, 'I only have two more months to go before I have me baby. Yeh'd be on yer own for a while.'

'Tha' won't be a problem, Trish, sure haven't I been workin' on me own for years. I'll look after things while yeh're out. Don't yeh worry about tha'. Come on, I promise yeh won't regret it.'

She said yes and within the month the two of us were standing outside the shop with the keys in our hand and fifty pounds worth of stock to start us off. The first thing we did as soon as we walked in the door was to take the net curtains down and brighten up the shop.

'We might be small,' I said to Trish, 'but from now on everybody will be able to see and know tha' we're here.'

I remember that first day so well; we were so excited. We took the place apart, scrubbing it from top to bottom. There wasn't much we could do in terms of moving things around to change it – even a little bit, just to put our own mark on it. But it looked and felt so fresh, with the kettle full and ready, new magazines on the coffee table and a nice big box of chocolates to make our first clients welcome. The only problem was, there didn't seem to be a sign of any clients around.

'I can't understand this, Trish,' I said as we sat there twirling our thumbs, looking out the window. 'When I was down here with Alan, there was a good few people in the shop.'

'I am a bit surprised, Kathleen, I thought tha' we might have had at least one or two clients in before this. I mean, the day is nearly half over.'

'I know, but we won't panic.'

Having said that, I was doing ninety inside my head, but I didn't let her know that. I had a pain in my face from smiling so much at anyone who passed our door.

All of a sudden, an elderly woman stopped outside the window and stood there for a minute, looking in at us. She looked very annoyed. There we were, smiling and nodding out at her, trying our best to look friendly, when she turned on her heels and came straight in to us. The two of us jumped up together, delighted to see a client at last.

'Are you open today or not?' she asked. 'I'm after coming down here twice today already to get my hair done and all I can see is the two of you sitting there showing your teeth off and doing nothing. Now, I'll ask again, are you open for business or not?'

'Of course we are!' I said. 'We're open since nine o'clock.'

'Well, you have a fine way of showing it, because your closed sign is still up on the door.'

The two of us just looked at one another and all we could do was laugh. We must have looked like two gobshites, smiling out at everyone all day with the sign saying 'closed'.

The woman turned out to be very nice in the end and, being our first and only client of the day, we did her hair for free, which she was well pleased about.

That first day was the joke of the century with everyone inside the family for such a long time afterwards.

* * *

Although I was coming up to my fortieth birthday and Trish was only twenty-four, we got on very well together. It worked out even better with the clients; I looked after most of the older ones and Trish looked after the younger ones. It balanced out very well.

The salon went from strength to strength, so much so that we opened up our second 'Talking Heads' in Walkinstown after about two years. This shop had also originally been a hairdressing salon but was very run down and needed a good overhaul. But that wasn't a problem, because Alan and my brother Thomas got stuck in and did all the work, which saved us a lot of money. It took a few weeks to do but looked very well by the time it was finished.

Martina had just completed her apprenticeship, so she came on board, stepping into my shoes in the Rathfarnham salon and leaving me to get the other salon off the ground. This area was quieter, so it took me a bit longer to get the salon up and running. But I got there, eventually taking on a full-time stylist and a junior apprentice. And that was me on my way once more.

* * *

Everything was going well in Walkinstown until one Friday evening in winter, around half-past-four, just as it was getting dark. The rain was pelting down against the window. I always made it my business to lock the door. As Ma would say, 'better to be safe than sorry'. I was well sorry by the time that day was over.

We were finishing a few clients in the salon when there came a hard knock on the door. I looked over and saw a man standing outside.

'I'm sorry,' I called out, 'we're finished for the night.' He beckoned for me to come over to him, which I did, but I still didn't open the door.

'We're closed. I'll do yer hair tomorrow,' I said again. That's when he held up the umbrella. I noticed that he kept blinking his eyes.

'I just want to give this to me wife.'

What I did next was stupid; I went and opened the door, just enough to slip my hand out to take the umbrella off him. He then pushed the door in on top of me and at the same time dropped his other hand down, slipping an iron bar out of his sleeve. He lashed it on the reception desk, screaming, 'Where's the money? Get me the fuckin' money NOW!' I could feel the blood draining from my face as he screamed at me.

223

The clients all huddled themselves together in the corner while my two staff members dived under the work-top, hugging one another. I was shaking as I spoke.

'Please . . . please, give me a minute. I'll get it for yeh.' I didn't have a till at the time, only a cash box. When I gave him the money, he took one look at it and went crazy.

'Wha' the fuck is this? Where's the rest?' he kept roaring as he banged the bar down on the desk once more.

I was shitting myself at this stage, never mind the clients. 'Tha's all I have; there's no more, I swear.'

He made a swipe at me with the iron bar, missing my head by inches.

'I said, where's the fuckin' money? Where is it?' At this stage he was nearly frothing at the mouth as he made a dash for me. I started running around the reception desk, trying to get away from him, almost pissing in my knickers with the fright. Thank God he didn't catch me.

He gave the desk a few more bangs, taking lumps out of it, while he grabbed the cash box on his way out and ran. He jumped into a car parked outside the salon. I looked out, trying to get a quick glance at the registration, but it was covered over with black plastic. I was trying to calm myself down, as well as the clients and staff, when Alan walked in to collect me.

'Holy Jaysus, Kathleen, wha's after happenin' here?'

'Oh my God, Alan, I'm nearly after gettin' me brains bashed in by robbers. It's only after happenin'. Yeh must have passed them by when yeh were drivin' in.'

He didn't wait for me to say any more. He was on to the police right away and they were up to us in no time at all. They asked the clients and staff a few questions, but they were all too upset to talk and just wanted to go home – which they did, leaving me to fill the gardaí in. The thief's face was right there in front of me when I went to the door, so I had no problem in giving a description of what he looked like to the guards. As soon as I said that he kept blinking, the two guards looked at one another and smiled. They knew who he was, but they weren't telling me.

'You're not the only one who got hit tonight,' said the guard. 'There were two more premises robbed not too far from here, and by the sound of it by the same person.'

They had a quick look around the salon, checking the damage done. Just as they were leaving, they said, 'We will be in touch.' But that was the last I heard on the matter. I checked a few times with the guards to see if they'd been caught, only to be told 'there's still no progress'.

I was very shaken and nervous at work for a good while afterwards, but I soon got my act together. There was no way I would let the likes of your man – a thug – stop me moving forward to follow my dreams.

* * *

Amanda, my younger daughter, who wasn't far off seventeen, had just finished her Leaving Certificate and did very well. She didn't know what line of work she wanted to do, so she settled on a typing course.

I went along with that and didn't say a thing, but when she got six months work experience in the local school, getting paid nothing, I was up the wall. I knew I could give her a full-time job with a good wage to go with it; I kept my mouth shut, which is not an easy thing for me to do. Amanda had always helped me on weekends, just like Martina did, washing hair and tidying around for her pocket money. She was very thorough in everything she did and was great with the clients; I knew she had the makings of a good hairdresser. After a few weeks, I couldn't stand it any longer, so I finally decided to sit her down and have a chat.

'De yeh know wha' I'm goin' to do, Amanda? Now, tha's only if yeh agree; otherwise I'll say no more on the matter.'

'And wha's tha', Ma?'

'I was thinkin' of teachin' yeh how to put colour on and blow-dry hair. Tha' way yeh might be able to judge if yeh would like to go into the hairdressin' or not. Now I'm only sayin', it's up to you at the end of the day, but I think it's worth givin' it a try.'

She thought about it for a while and then came back to me.

'Righ' then, Ma, I'll give it a go. I'm actually lookin' forward to it.'

I was over the moon when I heard that. So over the next couple of months, I taught her every chance I got. I could see she was enjoying the classes more and more as time went on.

In the meantime I got the itch to open up another salon and there just happened to be one not too far from where I lived. It had been a hairdressing salon which had closed down a few years earlier and never reopened. Lately, every time I would go to the shops, I found myself looking at it, and then I'd think *No, no, forget about it, Kathleen. Yeh've enough on yer plate.* So, off I'd go about my business for another while, but it was in the back of my head all the time. I kept thinking it would be a great spot. Everyone in the area knew me from doing hairdressing from my home, so I wasn't worried; I knew I would have plenty of clients.

I spoke to Trish and her very words were, 'Yer instincts are usually very good, Kathleen, so we'll go with them.' And that was it; she was happy enough to go along with the plan, which fell into place straight away.

This salon was very big, but it was just a shell, so we had to start from scratch, which meant borrowing from the bank. We had built up a very good name since we first went into business, so we had a track record and there wasn't any problem getting the loan. It took a few months to get it up and running, but it was worth it in the end. It looked really classy when it was finished and did very well from day one, just like I knew it would.

To put the icing on the cake, Amanda made up her mind and came to work for us. I moved up to the new salon to get it off the ground, taking Amanda along with me, which worked out very well. The younger and older stylists worked side by side, again getting the balance right for the third 'Talking Heads'. We had a very good stylist in Walkinstown who was well able to take over managing that salon.

So I decided to stay working in Tallaght, since I lived just five minutes down the road. I was able to slip down to the house the odd time to do a few bits and bobs, and to pop in to my next-door neighbour, who was now Danielle's child minder.

I couldn't believe it; everything just seemed to have fallen into place for me. I was going around on top of the world.

* * *

One day, after we'd been open about a year, it was coming to the end of the day and we were having a meeting, talking about one thing and another. Thank God there were no clients in the salon. Next thing we knew, two young fellas were in on top of us, screaming and roaring their heads off, 'Give us the money!' I took one look and thought, *Holy Jaysus, here we go again.*

One of them wore a white mask like Hannibal Lecter in *Silence of the Lambs*, and he had a small gun in his hand. The other one had a nylon stocking on his head, covering his face, with a hatchet in his hand. He lashed it down on to the couch, taking lumps out of it, just to let us know the full force of

227

their presence. The girls all started screaming. I wanted to scream with them, but I knew I had to try to keep it together.

'Don't hurt anybody,' I said. 'I'll give yeh the money.'

With that, the one with the mask put the gun up to Amanda's head, saying, 'Get the fuckin' money for me. I said GET IT!'

Amanda was sobbing, saying, 'Please don't hurt me', as she made her way over to the till and handed him the money.

I wanted to jump on top of him and bash his brains out for putting my child through that. But he was the one with the gun so I just bit my lip and said, 'Yeh have the money, now get out.' The other one gave the couch a few more bangs with the hatchet and then both of them ran.

I know I shouldn't have done this but I couldn't help myself. I ran out the door and screamed after them, 'I'll find out who yeh are and we'll see who'll be cryin' then! Yeh won't treat my child like tha' and get away with it – yiz pigs!'

All of this happened in broad daylight and it goes to show you that when these kids – and that's all they were – want money they don't care what they have to do to get it.

Sure enough, as soon as I asked around, within ten or fifteen minutes I was told their names and where they lived by a few of the local kids. When I told young Alan and his Da, they went ballistic and went straight to their houses. Of course, the young lads weren't there, and maybe at the end of the day this was for the best. With the temper everyone was in, God only knows what would have happened. But Alan told their parents what had happened, and let them know that they knew who had done it. There was no way they were going to get away with it.

When Amanda's boyfriend heard, he totally lost the plot, along with a couple of others in the family. That's when the hunt was on. They drove around every inch of the area, asking questions of anyone they could talk to. There wasn't a sighting of the two lads anywhere.

I didn't get much sleep that night. I kept reliving every minute of what had happened. All I could see was the look on Amanda's face and the fear in her eyes when he held the gun to her head. I broke out in a cold sweat just thinking about what could have been if it had all gone wrong.

It was well into the next day as I was tidying around, trying to keep myself busy, when there was a knock on the door. I didn't recognise the man standing on our doorstep.

'Hello,' he said, 'you don't know me but my friend wants to know can he come down with his son and talk to yiz about wha' happened in yer shop yesterday.' My ears cocked up when I heard that.

'Hold on a minute there 'til I get me husband,' I said.

Alan came out and we listened to what he had to say. We agreed to a meeting in our house that evening with both young boys and their fathers.

It turned out that one of them was only fifteen and was shitting himself and too scared to come down, so his father came alone. The other one was nineteen and came down with his father. I don't really know what I wanted or expected from this. The previous night, I wanted to kick the living daylights out of them, but now I think I wanted to see them face to face, with no masks on or gun, and to ask them how they would feel if it was their sister or mother that was put through such an ordeal. I wanted them to understand the trauma and upset that they had caused. I could see how nervous they all were as I brought them into the sitting-room.

We sat there and listened to both fathers talk about their sons' drug habits and how they were trying to get them into rehab and hopefully back on the straight and narrow. They offered to pay for any damage that was done and monies taken.

'Was the gun real?' Alan asked.

'No way, it wasn't a real one,' we were told.

In the middle of all this, Amanda walked into the room. The boy jumped when he saw her.

'Amanda,' I said as I made my way over to her, 'I think it's best tha' yeh not be here.'

'No, Ma, I'm sorry, but I want to see who it is tha' did this to me. I want to tell him how frightened I am now to go to work. All because of him. I need to say this.'

The boy had been sitting there with his head down, not saying a word, from the time he came in, until Amanda stood in front of him. She was in shock when she saw who it was.

'I can't believe it's you,' she said. 'Of all the people, how could yeh do such a thing? We were in school together, in the same class.'

'I'm sorry, Amanda. I'm really sorry. I never would have come into the shop if I'd known yeh were there. But when I saw yeh, it was too late.'

'Yeh shouldn't have come into the shop in the first place – no matter who was there.' She started to cry at this stage.

'I know, I know. I don't know wha' to be sayin' or doin'. I'm sorry. I didn't mean it.'

As I stood there, I could feel myself starting to soften watching my young daughter, so brave and grown-up for her years. Then I looked over at the father of the boy, with his hands up to his face, crying as he listened to his young son. That was hard to watch.

Only then did I realise how lucky we were with our three children, me and the girls working in the salons and our son working with his Da in the ice-cream van, each of them doing well for themselves.

They left a short while later, with the boy promising the sun, moon and stars that he would never bother us again, and no end of apologies from the fathers.

* * *

It took a while for Amanda and myself to settle back down to work without always looking over our shoulders, worrying and wondering if there could be a next time. That thought never really leaves you.

I was to learn in time that the older of the boys carried on in the world of drugs, but eventually over the years sorted himself out. But the younger one stayed in rehab and, when he got older, he became a counsellor himself. If nothing else, at least that bit of good came out of our ordeal. Thank God we never got robbed again.

The three salons did very well over the years and we all earned a very good living along the way.

23

The Hideaway

Alan was dropping me off to work one morning. It had been raining non-stop for the past few days, so the traffic was really heavy. We were just coming up to the lights in Tallaght village and I could see that there had been a bad crash on the opposite side of the road. A young woman was sitting in the crashed car with a baby in her arms. She was covered in glass, with cuts all over her face.

'Oh my God, Alan, de yeh see tha'? The poor girl, she's in an awful state. I hope tha' little baby is okay.'

'I wasn't mindin', Kathleen, I'm too busy tryin' to keep me eyes on the road.'

With that we got an unmerciful bang into the back of our little van. If I hadn't been wearing my seatbelt, I would have gone through the windscreen, the force was so strong. A sharp pain shot into my neck and down into my shoulder.

'Holy Jaysus, wha' was tha'?' said Alan. 'Are yeh okay, Kathleen?'

I didn't get a chance to answer. He jumped out of the van to see what had happened. All I could hear were horns beeping as other cars tried to get around us. As soon as I got myself together after the fright, I went out to Alan. He was talking to a man who looked just as shaken up as we were. He had crashed his truck into the back of us. Because the police were on the scene of the other crash, they were over to us straight away, letting the poor man know that they had seen everything. They left it to Alan to sort things out.

'I'm terribly sorry,' said the man. 'I only took my eyes off the road for a second or two, lookin' at tha' young girl and baby. Jaysus, missus, are yeh all righ'? Yeh're an awful bad colour.'

'Me neck and shoulder got a bit of a jerk, but I think I'm okay.'

I got back into the van and let Alan get on with the paperwork for the insurance, which would be needed badly, looking at the state the back of the van was in.

'Righ' then, Kathleen,' said Alan as he sat in beside me, 'now tha's sorted, I think we'd better go to the hospital and have yeh looked over.'

'Would yeh stop, Alan, I'm fine. I just got a bit of a fright, tha's all. Now, come on, I'm late for work as it is.'

* * *

I didn't feel great over the next few days but didn't say anything to Alan. That was, until I couldn't move my head and was finding it very hard to lift my right arm up. So I eventually had to give in and go to the hospital. They suspected that severe whiplash was probably causing the problem with my arm and told me it would take time to heal.

But it didn't heal. I spent well over a year going back and forth to the hospital, getting all sorts of tests done, before they finally discovered that part of my shoulder bone was stuck through a ligament. I ended up needing some major surgery, where they cut parts of the bone away. This left my right arm very weak. I was out of work once again for months on end, which is not a good thing for me, because that's when I start thinking and planning what I can do next. That's when I came up with the idea of buying a holiday cottage down the country.

'De yeh know wha', Alan, I was just thinkin' . . .'

'Oh, here we go again, Kathleen. I knew it. I said to meself only the other day, with all this time on yer hands, yeh'll end up schemin' somethin' in tha' head of yers.'

'Now, I'm only sayin', Alan, but see wha' yeh think anyway. I'd love to buy a little cottage down the country. Somewhere like Wexford. I always had a bit of a soft spot for the place since our honeymoon, and yeh know wha'? There'd be no problem for us to do it, with me gettin' a few bob from the accident. So wha' de yeh think? Are yeh on for it?'

'Yeh know somethin', Kathleen? Yeh always amaze me with tha' brain of yers. I get tired just listenin' to yeh.'

'Ah, go on Alan, it'll be like a new adventure for the pair of us, and we'll be able to spend a bit more time with one another.'

As soon as I said that, he was hooked.

* * *

We didn't go looking straight away because I still had to go to the hospital every day for a couple of months for physiotherapy, trying to get the strength back into my arm. I never really got the full power back, which limited what I could do at work. But I didn't let it stop me. I still carried on as best I could. Instead, I took on the role of teaching and training all the staff for the three shops, which I really enjoyed doing.

Even though I had to cut back on some of my hairdressing, I was still kept very busy. Over the years since I had started the business, I had taught myself how to do the bookkeeping for the shops. I made plenty of mistakes in the beginning, but as time went on I got so good at it that the accountant said she would give me a job. I was well pleased to hear that.

So between cutting hair, doing the books and training staff, I seemed to be chasing my tail all the time, which made me even more determined to try and get a little hideaway for myself and Alan before we ended up becoming strangers, we spent so little time together.

We must have driven the length and breadth of Wexford before we found what we were looking for. It was a two-up, two-down cottage. I remember when we pulled up outside it with the young girl from the auctioneers. It was lashing rain and the whole place looked so dreary. My first thought was, *No way, this place is in bits*. The cottage looked as if it hadn't been painted in years. The gutters were hanging down the side of the roof; the gate was broken; it was overgrown with weeds. And that was the good part.

When we walked in the front door, there was a tiny hallway with a small room to the right, what we used to call a parlour. It had a small black-iron fireplace. The window was a good size, so plenty of sunlight was shining through, which gave it a warm feeling. On the left-hand side, you stepped straight into the sitting-room, where the first thing that hit you in the face was a huge open fireplace. I could actually stand inside it. Facing that was a press built into the wall. Being nosey, I had a little peep in. There were one or two old black pots and an iron pan to match. It looked like they hadn't been used in a long time. Just to the left was the staircase. An old cap hanging off a nail at the end of the stairs drew my eye.

Looking around, I said to Alan, 'This is like goin' back in time.'

'I know, Kathleen, isn't it great? Now, come upstairs and let's have a look.'

To my surprise, the two bedrooms were a good size but, by God, the cold didn't half hit me in the face as soon as I walked into them.

'Jaysus, Alan, it's freezin' up here. I'm shiverin' with the cold. There must never have been any heat put into these rooms.'

'Tha' wouldn't be a problem, Kathleen. I'd have tha' sorted out in no time at all.'

I looked at him and thought to myself, *Is he for real or wha'?*

As Alan made his way back down I stood there for a minute or two, looking around. There was a really old wardrobe which wasn't too bad, but the bed was riddled with woodworm. I was trying to get a picture in my head of what it could look like freshened up, with a few bits of new furniture about the place. Then I thought, *No, no, I'm not goin' to let meself go there.*

'Are yeh righ', Kathleen? There's more downstairs I want to show yeh. Hurry up, will yeh!'

I made my way down to Alan, who was in the extension at the back of the cottage, which I hadn't even realised was there. I couldn't believe it when I walked in. It was a fine-sized kitchen. Now there was nothing in it but a broken-down sink unit, with a nest of spiders stuck in the corner and a small wooden table. I could see as I looked out the window that there was a large yard out the back with a wire fence around it.

Then I saw the most beautiful sight you could ever see. Just beyond that there was a whole field full of sheep and lots of little baby lambs jumping around.

'Oh my God, Alan, did yeh see wha's out there?'

'I know, I know, Kathleen – and guess wha'? Tha' field, which is a half-acre of land, goes with this cottage. Can yeh believe it?'

'But who owns all them sheep, Alan?'

'The girl was just tellin' me tha' the man tha' lives across from here lets them in there to keep the grass down for the owners of this cottage. Anyway, leave tha' for the minute. Come over and have a look at this.'

Curious, I went and stood beside him.

'Well, wha' de yeh think, Kathleen? There's your shower and toilet.' He gave me a big smile. He pointed into what I can only describe as a disaster area. There was a big hole in the side of the roof. The water was pouring down the walls. The toilet had so many chips out of it that if you sat on it you'd cut the arse off yourself. I didn't get a chance to open my mouth. Alan got in there before me.

'Now, don't say a word, Kathleen, let me get me spoke in first. This is the place I think we should buy. The structure is good, tha's the main thing. Forget wha' the inside looks like now. Think beyond tha'. Yeh know me – once I put me mind to it, I'll have this brand new by the time I'm finished.'

'Okay, Alan, yeh're on.'

'Yeh mean yeh're agreeing with me, Kathleen? Yeh're not goin' to put up a fight?'

'I know the place is in bits, Alan, but I have a good feelin' about it. Anyway, after I saw them baby lambs dancin' out there, I knew this was the one for us.'

The young girl told us that a woman from England had put in an offer the previous week. I got a fright when she said that. We went ahead and put our own offer in. It was accepted straight away and a few weeks later, just before Christmas, we were handed the keys to our very own little cottage.

Alan thought that Christmas would never be over so that he could get working on the cottage.

'Are yeh righ', Kathleen?' he said. 'Throw a few clothes in a bag there and let's head down to Wexford. There's no time like the present. I could get a lot done over the few days.'

'Alan, it's Stephen's Day. Everywhere is closed. It's freezin' down there. We've nothin' to sit on and there's no cooker.'

'Don't be puttin' obstacles in me way, Kathleen. Anyway, I have it all worked out. Yeh see tha' little two-seater couch there in the kitchen. Well, tha's comin' down in the van with us. I have the two-ring cooker tha' we use when we go campin' and I bought two sacks of coal and a couple of bags of logs durin' the week. I'll have the place pipin' hot in no time at all. Grab the two sleepin' bags from under the stairs so we can put them on tha' oul' mattress tha's there. Now, will yeh come on and let's hit the road.'

'Okay, Alan, don't be gettin' yer knickers in a knot! Give me a chance to rustle up a bit of food.'

While I was doing that, Alan loaded the van and soon after we were on our way. He never stopped talking the whole way down, rammaging on about all he was going to do as soon as we got there. The first thing he did was to light the fire. I know the cottage was in a bad way and needed a right going over, but after an hour or two with a bit of heat going through it, things didn't seem to look or feel too bad.

Everything that was moveable was thrown out into the back yard. The pair of us worked non-stop for hours on end, so much so that we actually forgot to eat. It was only when my stomach started grumbling and talking to me that I thought of food.

'Alan, I'm goin' to stop and make us somethin' to eat before we fall out of our standin'.'

'Okay, you go ahead, Kathleen. I'm tryin' to see if I can stop the water pourin' down the walls in the toilet. Otherwise we'll be drowned when we're usin' it.'

I was kneeling down at the fire, cooking away, when suddenly I heard a buzzing noise. I wasn't sure if it was coming from the chimney, but I thought at first it must be the wind. So I carried on with what I was doing, but after a while it got a lot stronger. I went in to Alan.

'Can yeh hear tha' noise in there? I'm not sure if it's up the chimney or up the stairs.'

'Maybe we have a ghost, Kathleen?' he said as he chased me around the kitchen and on up the stairs. I was laughing my head off as I ran into one of the bedrooms.

I ran right into a swarm of monster bees – each of them nearly half the size of your finger. I started screaming.

'Holy fuck! Alan, Alan!' Quick as lightning, he grabbed me by the jumper and pulled me back out, closing the door as tightly as he could behind us. The two of us fell down the stairs with the fright that we got.

'Tha's it, Alan, I'm not stayin' here. This is fuckin' mental. Did yeh see the size of them bees?'

'Will yeh calm down, Kathleen, and let me check to see if yeh got any stings.'

I started jumping up and down, rubbing myself all over in case there were still any of them on me. There weren't and thankfully I had no stings.

'De yeh know wha's after happenin' here, Kathleen? Them bees were hibernating, tha's wha' they were doin'. As soon as we lit the fire and the bit of heat got into the place, they came alive again.'

'Come on, let's go home, Alan. Please. I'll be shittin' meself if we stay here. I won't be able to sleep. Oh my God, can yeh hear them buzzin'? They're goin' mad so they are.'

'Will yeh just sit there and leave this to me, Kathleen.'

With that, he pulled the old lace curtains off the window, covered himself from head to toe with them and ran up into the room, banging the door behind him. I could hear him opening the window and hopefully letting all the bees fly away.

It took a while for every last one to be gone, but that didn't make any difference to me. There was no way I would go up the stairs that first night – no way, despite Alan reassuring me that the coast was clear.

I settled myself back down and made us a bite to eat. That night, we slept on the mattress in front of the blazing fire and I have to say it was nice and cosy. It reminded me so much of when I was a child, how we would all fall asleep every night on the floor in front of the fire before Da would carry us up to bed. With that happy thought in my mind, I fell asleep without a problem.

* * *

I had to laugh the next morning when I went into the toilet. Alan had pulled the gutter that was hanging off the side of the house through the hole in the roof, and had it sitting in a bucket catching the water. I thought to myself, *Isn't he a cute hoor, the things tha' he comes up with*? No matter what happens or goes wrong, Alan always finds a way to fix things.

Later on, both of us were working away. Alan was on the inside, tearing the place apart, while I was outside washing windows and sweeping around, when I heard a man's voice call out to me.

'Hello there,' he said, 'I'm Jim, from just across the road. Them's my sheep on yer land.'

I got a bit of a flutter in my stomach when he said that. *My land*, I thought. *Jaysus, wait till I tell Ma about this; she'll be well pleased.*

'Howyeh,' I said, 'I'm Kathleen. Come on into the garden. Alan, come 'ere,' I roared. 'Come out, will yeh, the man is here about his sheep.'

He was out in a flash, rubbing his hands all over his jumper, trying to get some of the dirt off before shaking hands with Jim.

'I wasn't expectin' yiz down over the Christmas,' said Jim, 'Otherwise, I would have had the sheep out. It's just that the last owner asked me to put them in there to graze and keep the grass down for her. If you like, I'll do the same for yourselves.'

'Tha'll be great, Jim,' said Alan. 'Sure, isn't tha' wha' sold the cottage for Kathleen? She melted as soon as she saw them out there in the field.'

I could see by Jim's face that he was happy with that. By the time we were all finished talking, we were getting on like a house on fire, so much so that we became the best of friends over the years.

It took us a good few days, but by the time we were finished, we had the upstairs ready for the first coat of paint. That was as much as we could get done before heading back to Dublin. Jim told us he'd keep an eye on the place for us. With that in our minds, we drove away happy.

I thought I'd never get home quickly enough to tell Ma and the kids how we had got on, and how I was nearly stung to death by thousands of bees. Well, maybe not thousands, but there really were loads, I swear.

* * *

Ma had come on so well over the previous three years. She was still living with Clare. I was on my way over to her, dying to tell her my news, but at the same time I knew she was going to lash me off for not turning up for the yearly reunion in Crumlin with the whole family on St Stephen's Day. It was a very important occasion for Ma, having us all together under the same roof at the same time. But I had to think about what Alan wanted too. It wasn't very often that he would ask for much and he thought he'd never get started on the cottage.

As soon as I walked in I got the famous look.

'Hmm,' said Ma, 'so yeh've turned up now, have yeh, Kathleen Doyle? Where the hell did yeh get yerself to? The one day of the year tha' I look forward to, when me whole family is all around, yeh went and got yerself missin'.'

'I know, I know, Ma,' I said, putting my arms around her. 'I should've told yeh. I'd no intentions of goin' anywhere. I'm sorry, it's just the way things went.'

I told her about the house, how excited Alan was and all the work we'd got done. She had to give in and laugh when I told her about Alan running around with the lace curtains over his head, chasing the bees.

'Well, I suppose when yeh put it like tha', Kathleen, I can make allowances. But make sure it doesn't happen again, de yeh hear me now?'

I stayed there most of the day with Clare and Ma, the three of us yapping away about everything and anything. Suddenly, Clare's older son Dominic, who was now around sixteen years old, came barging in through the back door, flying past us into the kitchen, nearly knocking me and Clare onto the floor.

'Quick, Ma,' he shouted, 'they're after me.'

Of course, Clare knew what this meant straight away and roared out, 'Quick, Dominic, head for the attic.'

'Holy Jaysus, Clare, wha' the hell is goin' on?'

'Shut the fuck up, Kathleen, and if anybody comes in here, say nothin'. Just zip yer mouth up.'

Ma didn't even blink an eye to what was going on. Then these two fellas came charging into the kitchen, screaming, 'Where is he?' They only had the words out of their mouths when Ma picked up the sweeping brush and lashed one of them across the head with it. He lost his balance and fell against the cooker. The other one grabbed the brush off Ma. My immediate instinct was to stand in front of Ma.

'Don't you dare touch her, de yeh hear me?' I roared.

'Stand aside,' he said.

'No, I won't,' I roared again.

That's when Clare stepped in. 'Kathleen, I told yeh to keep tha' mouth of yers shut. But yeh never listen. Them's the police.'

I stood there and nearly shit a brick with the fright I got. When the policeman Ma had hit got himself off the floor, he said he was going to arrest her for assault.

'Yeh can't do tha',' said Clare. 'Me Ma has brain damage; she doesn' know wha' she's doin' half the time.'

That's when Ma got her spoke in and, like me, should have kept quiet. 'I thought yiz were robbers comin' in to attack us. I was only takin' care of meself and me daughters. Anyway, how was I supposed to know? Yeh should be dressed like proper policemen.'

Now, while this was all going on, from the corner of my eye I could see Dominic jumping through the hole in the ceiling of the sitting room – which had been caused some time before by Romano falling through it. Clare had never got it fixed. Anyway, Dominic slipped out the side door, jumped onto the horse, Goldie, and charged past the kitchen window.

The two policemen fell out of the house, trying to get into their car as quickly as they could. They skidded out, nearly on two wheels, onto the road after him. Just as I was running out to the garden with Clare to see what was happening, Romano was making his way in. He started jumping up and down with excitement.

When I looked, to my amazement I saw Dominic flying through the fields, bareback on Goldie, with his dark brown skin and coal-black hair flying in the wind. He was like a young Indian on the chase. Of course, the police couldn't follow him through the fields in their car. But they weren't long about making their way back to Clare. One of them came in and told her Dominic had been seen joyriding in the area.

'I'm sorry, guard,' said Clare. 'I'll give him a righ' box when I get me hands on him, yeh can be sure of tha'. And don't mind me Ma – yeh'll have to make allowances for her. As I've said, it's her oul' brain.'

'Hmm,' he said, looking over at Ma, who was sitting there smiling and giving him a wink. He just shook his head and made his way over to the door, telling Clare, 'I'll be back up to talk to Dominic. The next time, don't be hiding him on us, because at the end of the day, Clare, you're not doing him any favours.'

'Holy Jaysus, Clare,' I said as soon as they were gone, 'I'll be half afraid to come here in future. I mean, it's bad enough when them lunatic sons of yours are together. I do be lookin' over me shoulder as it is, not knowin' wha' they're goin' to get up to. Now there's the police on top of all tha'.'

'Ah, will yeh ever give it over, Kathleen. I keep sayin' it over and over again, yeh worry too much.'

I got myself all worked up and started giving out like shite. 'Yeh wouldn't be sayin' tha' now, Clare, if Ma had been taken out of here in handcuffs. Wha' would yeh have done then, seein' tha' yeh're all so easy-goin' and worry about nothin'? Go on, tell me – wha' would yeh have done?'

'There's only one thing I could have done, Kathleen, and tha' would be to go down and sit in the cell with her. I mean, yeh couldn't let her go on her own now, could yeh?'

'Ah, for fuck sake, Clare, yeh're really pissin' me off now. I'll burst a blood vessel in me brain in a minute if yeh don't stop.'

'Don't be such a gobshite, Kathleen. There's no way Ma was goin' out of this house – because, in the first place, them policemen shouldn't have set one foot inside my house without a warrant, and they knew tha' as soon as they did it. But they were all fired up and forgot the rules for a minute or two. Just like wha' happened Ma in the heat of the moment. So, if they had pushed it over Ma, then I'd have had them, and they knew tha' at the end of the day. Anyway, they are righ', Kathleen, Dominic is a little fuck; he's gettin' up to all sorts of trouble out there and I don't know how many times I've had the police here. Believe me, it's not easy. Me mind does be in hell at times, but the only way I know how to cope is to keep calm and switch off from all the madness tha's around me. Otherwise, I'd end up being a hyper-hole like you, and I don't think me body or mind would have the energy for all tha'.'

'Yeh can say tha' again, Clare,' I said. 'But seriously, yeh'll have to keep an eye on Ma and make sure she doesn't do anythin' like tha' again. Or they really will lock her up the next time.'

'I will, Kathleen. Now, let's get back to talkin' about yer cottage and them lovely sheep with the baby lambs. I'd say tha' was a sight for sore eyes. Yeh'll have to bring me down with yeh some day.'

'Of course I will, both you and Ma – but yeh can leave yer mad kids behind.'

And that was it; Clare carried on like nothing happened. For her, that would be just another ordinary day. Looking at Ma's face, she was loving every minute of it. She was in her element living with Clare.

* * *

Over the next couple of months, myself and Alan were down in Wexford every chance we got, trying to get as much work done as possible. I grew to love the place and couldn't wait for the weekends to come. After all the hustle and bustle of the week, to get down to the peace and quiet was great.

Alan would be working on the inside of the cottage while I tidied around the garden. I absolutely love flowers and wanted to have every colour of the rainbow planted around me. I seemed to have been raking away for hours and wasn't getting anywhere, when Jim made his way over to me.

'Move over there, Kathleen,' he said, 'and I'll give you a hand, or it will be well into the middle of next year before you get anywhere.'

We had become very good friends with Jim over the months. I always made sure to bring him down a bottle of whiskey for keeping an eye to the place for us, and when I cooked dinner, there was always extra put on for him. He was a very private man who lived alone, but from day one we just seemed to hit it off so well. He was there for every hand's turn when we needed a bit of help.

I remember one day in particular; we had just got a television aerial on the roof a few weeks earlier, but we still couldn't get any of the channels. I wanted to get the man who had put it up to fix it, but Alan wasn't having any of it.

'Will yeh give it over, Kathleen,' he said. 'Wha' de yeh want to be bringin' the man back for when I can fix it meself?'

'Tha' roof is very high, Alan. I don't think yeh should get up on it. I mean, wha' if yeh fall?'

He just laughed and carried on with what he was doing.

'I'm serious, Alan, yeh could fall, and wha' would I do if yeh were lyin' there dead in front of me? Tell me, wha' would I do here on me own?'

'Well, I'd be dead so there wouldn't be much I could do for yeh, so I guess yeh'd have to go over and get Jim.'

'There's no talkin' to yeh, Alan McGrath.' I chased him around, trying to give him a swipe of the teacloth.

'Righ' then, Kathleen, if it keeps yeh happy, I'll go over and get Jim to give me a hand.'

But Jim wasn't there, so Alan went ahead anyway, taking no heed of anything I had to say. I watched him inching his way up along the slates, which he seemed to manage well.

'There yeh are, Kathleen,' he said, 'wha' did I tell yeh? Piece of cake. The only thing is, I still can't reach the aerial. I'll have to get up onto the chimney pot.'

'Holy Jaysus, Alan, are yeh tryin' to kill me with worry? Don't go up any higher. Please.'

But did he listen to me? No. I covered my eyes with my hands and peeped out through my fingers, cringing, looking at him stretching out to turn the aerial. Suddenly a couple of bricks on the chimney broke away, sending Alan flying through the air. Well, you'd want to hear the screams of me as I watched him bounce down onto the roof of the extension and then onto the cobbled stones on the ground. He landed flat down on his face. As I tried to help him up off the ground, all I could see was blood; it was all over his face and down his shirt.

'Oh my God, Alan, where's all this blood comin' from?'

He couldn't even speak and was weak at the knees as I tried to get him into the kitchen. It was only then that I realised there was a piece of an old pen struck through the palate at the top of his mouth. I was screaming inside my head with panic as I watched him pull it out. The blood sprayed out of his mouth, everywhere. I grabbed some cotton wool and tried to plug it as best I could until we got to the hospital.

We were seen to straight away. Alan was given a few stitches to his mouth and told that he had a couple of broken ribs to go along with it. His body was black and blue. His face and hands were cut to bits. He really looked bad.

I wanted to say I told you so, but then I thought better of it, so I zipped my mouth up and we headed back to the cottage. But Jim wasn't long about letting him know the truth.

'I'm surprised at you, Alan, doing something stupid like that. I mean, that's a mighty height to be climbing and with not a bit of help. Maybe you'll think the next time and wait until I am here to give you a hand.'

'Yeh can be sure of tha', Jim,' said Alan, struggling to get the words out.

There wasn't much Alan could do with the state he was in, so we headed back home to Dublin and what he had to listen to from everybody who saw him. The slagging was mighty, with everyone saying I must have given him a few digs. So between the pain that he went through and all he had to listen to, there was no way he ever took a chance like that again. Not unless Jim was around.

* * *

It was a week or two before Alan was feeling okay again. We thought we'd never get back down to the cottage. I was dying to show it off, so I asked Clare and Ma to come with us.

Clare fell in love with it straight away, which I knew she would. As soon as she saw the sheep, she was hooked, and that was before I brought her across to Jim's yard, where he kept his other animals – a couple of pigs, a cock, loads of hens and ducks, and he nearly always had one or two baby lambs that needed a bit of extra care, that he would be feeding from a bottle. Clare thought she was in heaven when Jim handed her one of the baby pigs to hold. I left her there talking away to Jim, while I made my way back over to Ma, who was happy enough sitting beside the blazing fire watching the telly.

'Well, wha' de yeh think, Ma?' I asked her.

'If yeh want me to give yeh the God's honest truth, Kathleen, it looks grand, and if I know Alan, by the time he's finished it'll be massive. But it wouldn't be my cup of tea. No way. Stuck out here in the arsehole of nowhere, with not a shop to be seen anywhere. But if it's wha' yeh want, tha's all tha' matters.'

* * *

That was Ma's one and only visit to the cottage. Clare came down with me a few times and enjoyed every minute. The rest of the family, as well as our own kids, dropped down to see what we were raving about and, just like Ma, for them it was too quiet.

Because we were only able to go down on weekends and the odd holiday, it took us a couple of years to finish the cottage off the way we wanted it. But I have to say, by the time it was done, it was like something out of a picture postcard. It became our very own hideaway – just for us.

We had some great times and many happy years down in the cottage before selling it on. It was much later that we bought the apartment in Portugal. Which brings me back to where I started . . .

Epilogue

'Tha' water was really nice, Kathleen. Yeh should've got in and had a swim with me.'

'I enjoyed lyin' here in the sun, gettin' lost in me thoughts for a while.'

'Jaysus, Kathleen, de yeh ever give tha' brain of yers a rest?'

'Well, I tell yeh one thing for nothin', Alan, the day tha' happens, yeh'll have somethin' to worry about, because tha's when I'm happy plannin' away in me head, thinkin' wha's next out there tha' I can do. Anyway, it's time we started makin' a move.'

As we made our way along the beach up to our apartment, I was bursting inside, thinking about the night I had planned ahead for us. As usual, I couldn't keep my mouth shut.

'Yeh know wha' today is, Alan.'

'Sunday, of course – why?'

'It's our anniversary, we're forty-eight years together and forty-three years married today.'

'Good shite, Kathleen, I forgot all about it.'

'I know yeh did, but never mind. Sure, hasn't it slipped my mind many times over the years. All the same, Alan, the years are really startin' to creep up on us now. Do yeh feel like we're gettin' old?'

'Not at all, Kathleen, yeh're only as old as yeh feel. I certainly don't feel me age and I know tha' you definitely don't, with the carry-on of yeh half the time. If yeh had yer way, yeh'd be out there tryin' to rule the world with the energy tha' yeh still have.'

'I know, Alan, I'm an awful fidget. I can't keep meself easy. But yeh're so right; it's only a number, and I feel great! Now wait till l tell yeh wha' I have planned out for us tonight. We're gonna have the best fun ever. I've booked a table at tha' fancy new restaurant in the old town and then we'll head up to Marco's place for a bit of dancin' afterwards. There's a big '60s night on there later on. We'll be able to have an oul' jive. So are yeh on for it?'

I got the biggest smile off Alan as he put his arm around me.

'Tha's my girl.'

On we went, walking along the beach, with me rammaging on as I do and at the same time thinking to myself:

This is the life!

If you enjoyed *In Ma's Footsteps* by Kathleen Doyle,
why not try her first book,
What Would Ma Say? also published by Poolbeg?
Here's a sneak preview of Chapter One.

WHAT WOULD MA SAY?

KATHLEEN DOYLE

POOLBEG

1

From Jam Jars to China

The phone rang. It was my sister Clare. The call I was expecting but didn't want to hear.

'Kathleen, Ma is gone,' she cried. 'Ma's dead.'

I had only been down with Ma the day before. As soon as I'd walked into the house I could see how weak she looked. She was eighty-four and had been sick a lot over the past two years and her mind was starting to wander. There were days when I would go in to see her and she wouldn't know who I was. I'd get so upset when that happened.

I thought to myself, *This is it. Her time has come.* I could see in her eyes that she was ready to go. The life was gone completely out of her. She was like a little child sitting in her chair, helpless, unable to do anything for herself.

My sister Carmel, who lives in the family home and looked after Ma so well, tapped me on the shoulder.

'You're miles away there, Kathleen. Have you heard anythin' I've said?'

'Sorry, Carmel, I was thinkin'. Wha' did yeh say?'

'You'll have to try and get some food and water into Ma.

She's eaten nothin' for me since yesterday.' Her eyes filled up as she spoke.

'Yeh look tired, Carmel. You go and have a break for a few hours and don't be worryin'. I'll take care of everythin'.'

It wasn't long before the house was empty and I was alone with Ma. I knew in my heart that there wasn't much time left and was grateful for the next few hours we were to spend together. Just the two of us. I sat there holding her hand, trying to get her to sip some water for me. But she wasn't having any of it. As weak as she was, she still put her hand up to stop me, shaking her head from side to side, saying, 'No'. She gestured for me to bend down.

'What is it?' I asked. 'Wha' are yeh tryin' to say, Ma?' It took her a minute or two of struggling in such a low voice to get the words out. But I was so happy when I heard what she had to say. 'Kathleen, make's a cup of tea.' I couldn't believe it. She knew who I was.

They were the last words that Ma spoke to me. I sat there for the next couple of hours, Ma sipping on her tea and me pouring my heart out at last, telling her all the things I had bottled up inside me all these years.

'D'yeh know, Ma, sometimes I used to think as a child growin' up, tha' yeh didn't love me. Yeh never said the words, ever.'

She looked at me the whole time I spoke, listening and giving me the nod every now and then.

'Ah, don't take any notice of me, Ma. I'm just rammagin' on here. They're just thoughts from a child, Ma, tha's all. Thoughts from a child, from long ago.'

She then gave my hand a little squeeze, and with the other hand pointed towards her eye and then to her heart, holding it there for a few seconds longer and then, last but not least, straight at me. Eye for 'I', heart for 'love', and 'you'.

I cried and cried as I spoke the words back. 'And I love yeh too, Ma.' I hugged and kissed her. The words had never been spoken, but they were there all this time, inside her head and mine. That was all that mattered to me.

* * *

The next day, when Clare told me Ma had died, I was sad but didn't cry at first. I knew she couldn't hold on any longer. She had done her time on this earth and what a great job she had done. She was at peace now. All her worrying was over.

In the days leading up to Ma's funeral, the whole family gathered in the house to support one another. There was myself, Carmel, Noel, Clare, Marion, Thomas, Jacinta, Patricia, Mano and Paul, remembering all the funny stories, laughing and crying at the same time. The only one missing was Phil, the oldest of all of us. He had been so young when he died, barely forty; such a character, always full of life. If he'd been here now, God only knows what antics he'd be getting up to. How I wished he could have been there. He'd have helped us get through a very hard time with his funny ways, just like he always did when we were growing up. We all missed him so much.

I could hear Noel and Thomas reminiscing about the day they robbed a dead pig with Phil and how they hid it in the wardrobe so Da wouldn't see it. Then Clare turned around and brought up the day that we all made a swimming pool in the kitchen. The other sisters got their spoke in straight away: 'Wha' are yeh talkin' about, Clare? At least the whole gang of us did tha' together. Remember when yeh went and painted the table and chairs, and every plate and jam jar in the house gold and silver – and yeh did tha' all on yer own!'

'Tha's because I was tryin' to keep meself awake,' said Clare. 'I was afraid to go asleep because of the ghost.'

On went the storytelling while all the grandchildren sat there in amazement listening to all the things that we had got

259

up to! How Ma put up with us I will never know. We went on for hours, all of us going over events from so long ago.

Ma was laid out in the very sitting-room that she had spent most of her life in, where all the bedlam and mayhem went on. Be it good, sad or funny, that's where it all happened. We all felt it was only fitting that she would leave from the home that she and Da had built around us so many years ago.

Down through the years, Ma had always spoken about having a big send-off when she passed away. I would tell her not to be talking about such things, as you never want to think of your parents dying. But no, Ma would never let it go. She made each and every one of us promise to keep her wishes.

'Remember tha' film *Madame X*?' she would say. 'There was these big black stallions and a glass carriage bringin' the woman to her restin' place. Well, tha's wha' I want and if I don't get it I'll come back and haunt every one of yiz. Oh, and another thing, yeh're to make sure the horses trot nice and slow, so as everybody on the road can see me. When me day comes, I want to go out in style. I might not have had much in me life, but by God, when I'm ready to leave this earth, I want everybody to remember the day tha' Lil Doyle died.'

And what a send-off she got. For the outspoken woman that she was, and for all her toughness, she was so well liked that people came from far and near to pay their respects. You couldn't put a price on all the flowers in the house. All Ma's favourites. She loved flowers so much she used to spend half of her pension every week doing the flowers for the church, telling us, 'Now tha' I'm able to, I want to thank the Holy Mother herself for all the years tha' she helped me through all me hard times.'

The day of Ma's funeral was such a lovely November day, the sun splitting the trees. We were all down in the house from early to say our last goodbye. I remember standing back and looking at all the family, from the youngest to the oldest, dressed in black as a mark of respect. I thought Ma would be well pleased with them all.

When the horses and carriage arrived at the house, we were all speechless. I had never seen the likes of it before at any funeral. It was everything Ma had wished for and more. The two black horses were groomed to perfection. They stood tall with their black plumes on the tops of their heads, waiting patiently. The coachmen looked so impressive dressed in traditional uniform – double-breasted coats with big silver buttons, expensive cravats, top hats, snow-white gloves and black leather polished boots. They stood silently on either side of the glass carriage, which was gleaming so beautifully. It was perfect.

It was now my turn to go in to Ma to say my last few words. As I stood there holding Ma's hand, I finally broke down and cried. Such a loss and emptiness came over me as I said goodbye. 'Yeh were a great Ma and will never be forgotten. Yeh'll live on forever in all our hearts. It's time to go now Ma, your carriage awaits yeh.'

My brothers placed the coffin into the glass carriage as Ma left the house for the last time. The horses trotted slowly up the road, while all the neighbours, young and old, stood still, the older men taking off their caps out of respect for Lil Doyle. When we got to the church I couldn't believe the number of people there. It was packed to capacity. We played Ma's favourite songs as the priest said Mass. I sat there listening to all the family as everyone broke down crying. They too were feeling the loss I felt inside.

Her cremation in Mount Jerome was so peaceful. There were no more words spoken. While the song 'In the Arms of an Angel' played, we all sat there in silence. As the curtains slowly closed, I felt Ma was at peace at last. I sat there on my own for a few moments, thinking, 'Well, wha' de yeh say, Ma? Is it everythin' yeh wished for? Did we do yeh proud? I think so, Ma; it was a funeral fit for a queen.'

* * *

The day slowly came to an end. I felt so tired and drained, I thought I would never get home to put my head down. Later, unable to sleep, I made my way downstairs. As I sat there drinking a cup of tea, I thought about the first time Ma sat in this very kitchen with me.

Over the years, Ma had been visiting myself and Alan every Sunday and sometimes used to stay for the weekend. We had bought a new house at the bottom of the mountains in Tallaght. I thought I'd never get her up to see it. We were only in the door and as usual the cup of tea and a smoke had to come first.

'Are yeh right, Ma? Come on and I'll show yeh around while the kettle is boilin'.'

As we went around the house, you could see she was surprised and well pleased, but didn't say it. She had mellowed a lot over the years and only now you could have a bit of crack with her. I laughed as we walked in and out of the rooms.

'Ma, which toilet would yeh like to use today? There's the blue one, the green one and there's the yellow one downstairs. Your choice.'

'Would yeh get away with yerself, Kathleen Doyle, I wouldn't be able for yeh with yer showin' off. There was a time yeh hadn't got a pair of knickers to yer name, and don't yeh ever forget tha', de yeh hear me now?'

In a way I suppose I was showing off. I wanted Ma to be so proud of me for what I had achieved throughout the years. As a child, I craved the slightest bit of attention. Even the tiniest bit of praise meant so much to me. But I rarely got it.

'All the same, Kathleen, did yeh ever think tha' yeh'd see the likes of it? Three toilets and all in yer own house, for only yiz to use and nobody else. Isn't it a far cry from the tenements and the shite bucket, and you know tha' more than the rest of the kids – helpin' me carry it down all them stairs to tha' filthy toilet in the yard. We've come a long way since then, so we have.'

'Yeh should be very proud, Ma. Yeh built a lovely home around yerself and Da over the years and look at the way all the kids turned out. Yeh did well.'

'I have to say – and I'll say it straight to yer face, Kathleen – it was a long, hard road, but yiz didn't turn out too bad for a shower of ticks.'

And by that she meant we had done well for ourselves, which we all did. Believe it or not, that was a big compliment coming from Ma.

'Kathleen, me mouth's waterin' here. Are yeh makin' me tha' cup of tea or wha'?'

I took out my special set of china cups and saucers as Ma sat there puffing away. 'Wha' de yeh say, Ma? Will we go all posh for the day to celebrate the new house or would yeh prefer a jam jar?'

The look on her face was priceless. I was still showing off and I didn't care.

'God be with the days, Kathleen, when we had nothin' else only jam jars to drink our cup of tea out of. Such poverty, how did we ever get through it all?'

I sat there listening to Ma while she reminisced about the past. I let my own mind slowly fade back to a time gone by so long ago.

If you enjoyed this chapter from

What Would Ma Say? why not order the full

book online @ www.poolbeg.com

See last page for details.